6 \80

DATE DUE

AP 23 '08			
AP 17 '02			
JY 1 4 10			

Demco, Inc. 38-293

Costume for Births, Marriages & Deaths

"Wedding Day" *c* 1824. Bridegroom in green tail-coat, frilled shirt, a muslin cravat, the ends floating, a white waistcoat and white breeches. He carries a top hat. Bride in white dress and long white gloves, a wedding veil decked with flowers on her head and flowing down her back to the hem of her skirt.
Hand coloured lithograph.

Phillis Cunnington & Catherine Lucas

Costume for Births, Marriages & Deaths

ADAM & CHARLES BLACK
LONDON

FIRST PUBLISHED 1972
BY A & C BLACK LIMITED
4, 5 AND 6 SOHO SQUARE LONDON WIV 6AD

© 1972
PHILLIS CUNNINGTON
& CATHERINE LUCAS

ISBN 0 7136 1192 8

PRINTED IN GREAT BRITAIN
BY W & J MACKAY LIMITED, CHATHAM

CONTENTS

Appendices

THE PLATES

The sources of all illustrations are given with their captions.

"Wedding Day" *c.* 1824 *frontispiece*

ACKNOWLEDGEMENTS

We should like to thank the following for expert help: Dr E. J. Dingwall, Miss Christina Hole, Major Alan Mansfield, Mr John Morley, and the staffs of the following institutions: *Bedford*, the Higgins Museum; *London*, British Museum (departments of Printed Books, MSS., and Prints and Drawings), Library of the College of Arms, Courtauld Institute of Art, Guildhall Library, especially Mr J. L. Howgego, London Museum, especially Miss Zilla Halls, National Monuments Record, University of London Library (general, and photographic services), the Wellcome Historical Medical Library; *Manchester*, Gallery of English Costume, especially Miss Anne Buck; *York*, Castle Howard Costume Galleries, especially Miss Cecile Hummel.

We are particularly grateful to Mr B. E. Freeman, photographer, for skilful services, to Mrs R. Luckham for untiring help throughout and finally to Dr Alexander Walk for reading the MS. and giving much valuable advice.

NOTES

Notes indicated in the text by *numerals* refer to *sources* and will be found at the end of the book (pp. 292–301).

Notes otherwise indicated (e.g. by asterisks) are explanatory *footnotes*.

INTRODUCTION

The present book treats of English costume connected with births, marriages and deaths from medieval times to 1900. Costume has always played an impressive part at these three turning-points in human existence, particularly because of its symbolism in the ceremonies that have grown up around them.

The public announcements of these events, when they concerned either royalty or the local aristocracy was at first by church-bell ringing. Bells for a birth were as customary as wedding bells and funeral tolls. The Parish records for St Lawrence Church, Reading, contain this entry:

> 1533 For ryngyng at the birth of Princess Elizabeth . . . ivd.

This was for the future queen.

Early eighteenth-century periodicals contained announcements of the deaths of eminent people, for example the *Gentleman's Magazine* published these from its inception in 1730. Marriages trickled in later and births had the last and the least attention. Provincial newspapers began local announcements near the end of the century.

> Thursday fortnight, the lady of Major Morgan of a daughter.
> *Chester Chronicle*, 5th Feb. 1779

It was not until April 1854 that *The Times* opened its famous columns for the national announcement of private people's Births, Marriages and Deaths.

CHAPTER I

BIRTHS —THE MOTHER and ATTENDANTS

(a) Lucky Charms for the Mother

The high mortality rate of both mother and baby at childbirth, before science came to the rescue, explains why reliance on charms during pregnancy was so widespread. The superstitious belief in the magical properties of the eaglestone for inducing easy labour and a safe delivery is the most ancient. Pliny the elder wrote learnedly on the subject in A.D. 79, and specimens have even been found in a Bronze Age barrow. The eaglestone was a hollow stone with loose fragments inside that would rattle.

> To these hollow nodules the Greeks gave the name of eaglestone, from a notion that the eagle transplanted them to her nest to facilitate the laying of her eggs. Also called *aetates*.
>
> *The Century Dictionary*

This stone was worn during pregnancy as jewellery by those women who believed in it. It is said that Henry VIII obtained one for Anne Boleyn's confinement. In a treatise of 1658 we are informed also that

> it maketh women able to conceive, being bound to the wrist of the left arm, and if all this time the woman is great with child, this jewel be worn, it strengthens the child and there is no fear of miscarrying.

Sir Thomas Browne in 1688 had some misgivings:

> Whether the aetates or *eaglestone* hath that eminent property to promote delivery or restrain abortion respectively, applied to lower or upward parts of the body, we shall not discourage by our quotation.
>
> *Enquiries into Vulgar and Common Errors*, ii.5

Dr John Bargrave D.D. (Canon of Canterbury 1662–1680) appears to have had complete faith in the magical properties of the eaglestone, for he wrote in 1662:

> Item aetatis Lapis Aquilaris or the eagle stone which I bought of an Armenian at Rome. They differ sometimes in colour. This is a kind of rough, dark, sandy colour and about the bigness of [a] good walnut. It is rare and of good

value, because of its excellent qualities and use, which is, by applying it to childbearing women, and to keep them from miscarriage . . . It is so useful that my wife can seldom keep it at home, and therefore she hath sewed the strings to the knitt purse in which the stone is, for the convenience of the tying of it to the patient on occasion; and hath a box she hath to put the purse and stone in.

It were fit that either the dean's or the vice-dean's wife (if they be marryed men) should have this stone in their custody, for the public good as to neighbourhood; but still, that they have a great care into whose hand it be committed, and that the midwives have a care of it, so that it still be the Cathedral Church's stone.

> Catalogue of Dr. Bargrave's Museum,
> ed. James Craigie Robertson, 1867

Even as late as the eighteenth century, faith in this jewel continued. We find it listed in Sir Walter Calverley's Memorandum in January 1706.

> Schedule of things the Lady Blacket left Lady
> Calverley . . . 1 eagle stone in a box.
> *Yorkshire Diaries* . . . (Surtees Soc., 1886)

Here is another source of help: in the *Creed of Piers Plowman* it was said of the monks that they

> . . . maken wymmen to wenen [believe]
> That the lace [girdle] of our Lady smok
> Lighteth hem of children [eases the birth].

The eighteenth century tried other magical remedies, such as leaves of various kinds; but these were not usually worn as decoration. "Win", the maid in Smollett's *Humphrey Clinker*, wrote:

> As for me, I put my trust in the Lord and I have got a slice of witch-elm sewed in the gathers of my under-petticoat. 1771

(b) Dress during Pregnancy

As for clothes worn during pregnancy, these were usually adaptations of the fashions of the time, perhaps simplified. However, as suggested by John Page-Phillips,[1] the brass shown in Fig. 7(a) may illustrate a type of medieval pregnancy gown.

Pepys wrote in 1669:

Thence by and by to White Hall, and there I waited upon the King and Queen . . . in the Queen's lodgings; she being in her white pinner* and apron, like a woman with child.

In 1735 Sarah, Duchess of Marlborough, in a letter to her granddaughter wrote:

> I wonder you should be so very uneasy after dinner if your stays are not made too long waisted. Though I remember when I was within three months of my reckoning, I could never endure to wear any bodice at all; but wore a warm waistcoat wrapped about me like a man's and tied my petticoats on the top of it. And from that time never went abroad but with a long black scarf to hide me I was so prodigeous big.
>
> *Letters of a Grandmother* ed. Gladys Scott Thomson 1943

In 1803, when dresses were high-waisted and stays less evident, Dr William Buchan wrote in his book *Advice to Mothers*:

> Among many improvements in the modern fashions of female dress . . . is the discontinuance of stays . . . It is indeed impossible to think of the old straight waistcoat of whalebone and of tight lacing, without astonishment and some degree of horror . . . I need not point out the aggravated mischief of such a pressure on the breasts and womb in a state of pregnancy. . . .
>
> Let me also very earnestly forbid the use of tight necklaces, tight garters, or any ligatures which may refrain the easy motions of the limbs, or obstruct the free circulation of the blood . . . I should further observe, that it is not enough to have discontinued the high-heeled shoe, unless the shape of the foot and toes is a little attended to.

Dr Thomas Bull, on the other hand, somewhat later, allowed corsets, if constructed according to his advice.

> . . . the corsets worn during pregnancy should have lacings over each bosom so that they may be loosened, or otherwise, at pleasure . . . They should also have lacings on each side for the same purpose: and as gestation advances, the unyielding steel blades so commonly used, should be removed, and thin whale-bone substituted.
>
> Thomas Bull M.D. *Hints to Mothers* 4th End. 1844

(c) Dress for Confinement and Nursing
Garments worn by women in labour are not often described. There is an

* A lady's white head-dress.

interesting picture in Thomas Raynolde's *The Byrth of Mankinde*, 1545, where the mother is giving birth, fully clothed. This, however, is not English, the book being a translation from the German of Eucharius Rosslin, the first printed work on midwifery, in 1513. The lady in this picture is leaning back in a "birth chair".

In Fig. 1, "The Birth of Twins to Rebecca", the mother is naked. (See also Fig. 4.)

In the Middle Ages, a woman in childbirth was said to be "in the straw" since this was the type of mattress used. The phrase lingered on long after its origin had been forgotten.

1. Birth of Twins to Rebecca. She is naked in bed but wears the "veil" head-dress, usual at this date. 1320.
Detail after Queen Mary's Psalter *B.M. MS. Roy. 2 B VII f. 12v.*

The fairies steal away the good women that are in the straw if so be as how there an't a horse shoe nailed to the door . . .
                              T. Smollett, *Humphry Clinker*, 1771

And *The Times* of 1st July 1799 had this announcement:

The Lady Mayoress is in the straw, and the bambino according to the costom of the City, is to be rocked in a cradle of solid silver.

For Royalty great preparations were made for the adornment of the lying-in chamber. Thus when Elizabeth, Henry VII's queen, in 1486, was about to give birth to Prince Arthur we are told that her chamber was hung with rich tapestry, but this must not have "imagery", which was considered unsuitable for women in childbirth.[2]

Whether she wore the following garments during, before or after confinement is uncertain.

> For the Queen . . . . 1 round Mantle, Velvette playne, forryd [furred] throught with fyne Armyns [ermine] . . . for the Queene to weare about her in her covits [closet] and all other things necessary for the same.
>
> *Leland's Collectanea*, Vol. 4, 301

Of the lying-in of Queen Jane Seymour, who died in 1537, a fortnight after giving birth to Edward VI, we read:

> She reclined, propped up with fair cushions of crimson damask with gold, and was wrapped about with a round mantle of crimson velvet furred with ermine.
>
> Quoted in Richard Davey, *Furs & Fur Garments*, 1895

Dr Thomas Bull in his *Hints to Mothers*, 1841, mentioned above, gives advice as to the best garments to wear during labour.

> A loose dressing-gown is best in the earlier part of the labour. This must be exchanged when the patient lies down for good, for a chemise and bed-gown folded up smoothly to the waist, and a flannel petticoat, without shoulder straps, that it may afterwards be readily removed.
>
> A broad bandage, too, must be passed loosely round the abdomen as the labour advances to its close; and its application must not be left until after the delivery, for it then would be attended with some difficulty and some risk . . . The breadth will depend upon the individual size of the female; but it should be wide enough to extend from the chest to the lowest part of the stomach. The best thing is a new and sufficiently large towel . . .
>
> Some persons suppose that wearing their stays during labour assists them, affording support, but they are improper, being rather in the way than useful . . .
>
> The belt must be worn so long as the abdominal muscles appear to require support, which in some cases will be a few weeks only; in others (in very fat and stout persons, for instance) it can never in future be dispensed with.

The warning against tight lacing is again given, by Pye Henry Chavasse

> A pregnant female should wear her stays very slack . . . Tight lacing frequently causes women to miscarry . . . and in numerous instances it has so

> pressed in the nipples that . . . females . . . have been unable to suckle
> their children.
>> *Advice to a Wife on the Management of herself during the Periods*
>> *of Menstruation, Pregnancy, Labour and Suckling, 1842*

Henry Davies in *The Young Wife's Guide* in 1854 gives similar advice regarding the clothes worn during labour.

A strange notion, as to the ideal garment for a woman in labour, was voiced in a letter to the Princess Royal ("Vicky") by Queen Victoria, about her second daughter's first confinement in 1863.

> Of course I shall take great interest in our dear little grand-daughter, born . . .
> in the very bed in which you were born, and poor dear Alice had the same
> night shift on, which I had on, when you all were born! I wish you could
> have worn it too.
>> *Dearest Mama: Letters between Queen Victoria*
>> *and the Crown Princess of Prussia 1861–1864*, ed. R. Fulford, 1968

After recovery from her confinement the mother, at her churching, was enjoined in a rubric of the first Prayer Book to be "decently apparelled". Percy Dearmer[3] explains that these words were inserted again in the 1661 Prayer Book to ensure the woman's wearing the customary white veil which the Puritans had tried to give up. Herrick in *Hesperides* (1648) suggests that it had persisted.

> Put on thy Holy Filletings and so
> To the Temple with the sober midwife go.

Incidentally, Dearmer tells us that "a candid [white] stole" would be "thrown o'er the Priest" for the service.

A wealthy lady would wear a dress specially made for the occasion. In 1316 at the birth of John de Eltham, the King's second son, the Wardrobe Accounts of Edward II tell us

> . . . to Stephen Faloyce, the Queen's tailor, five pieces of white velvet for
> the making thereof a certain robe against the churching of the Queen after
> the birth of her said son.
>> *Archaeologia*, Vol. 26

At the Churching of the Queen, after the birth of Prince Arthur in 1486, we are told:

> . . . and when the Queen shall be purified she must be richly beseene in

tyers and rich laces about her neck . . . and lynyn cloth upon the bed of estate and there shal be a Dutches or Countes to take her down of ye bed and lede her to her chamber dore . . . a Duke shall lead her to the Church.

B.M. MS. Add. 6113

2. Nursing dress of 1796. Mother in the height of fashion with slits in gown for suckling infant. The nurse in homely garments, wearing apron and mob cap.
After an engraving by James Gillray.

In the seventeenth and eighteenth centuries in many country parishes it was customary for the woman at her churching to make an offering of a white handkerchief to the parish priest, for her a symbol of purity, for him a perquisite. In the Register book of Wickenby, Lincolnshire, of the early seventeenth century we find

> The chrysom and a grace penny is always to be given at ye woman's church-ing. The chrysom must be a yard of fine linnen long and a full yard in width.
>
> J. C. Cox, *Parish Registers of England*, 1910

The white handkerchief evidently represented the chrisom cloth in which the mother's baby had been wrapped after christening in earlier times (see Ch. 3).

Nursing gowns for convenience in suckling were often necessitated by the fashions of the day. They were made to open at the breasts (see Pl. 1) so that the dress need not be pulled off the shoulder as in Fig. 5.

In an Inventory belonging to Skipton Castle, taken in 1572, transcribed from an original roll among papers at Bolton Abbey, we find "Item one black damask nurcis [nursing] gowne, with iiii burgullion gardes, trimmings xxs", among women's clothing in a chest in the great Chamber.[4] There is little doubt that they were the wardrobe of Lady Eleanor Brandon, being far too rich and elegant to belong to a nurse in the modern sense.

See Fig. 2 for an eighteenth-century nursing dress.

Pye Henry Chavass in 1842 (op. cit.) again condemns the wearing of stays:

> A mother who is suckling should have her dress made loose, more especially the stays.

He advises removing all the bones from the stays and the wearing of a flannel waistcoat.

The Gallery of English Costume in Manchester has a number of nursing dresses, with various arrangements for openings at breast level, dating from the 1820s to the 1850s (see Pl. 2(a)).

(d) The Attendants during and after Childbirth

The usual attendants were, of course, the *midwives*. Right up until the nine-teenth century their clothes were simply those of their own day with nothing that was adaptive, except possibly an apron.

In an illustration of the birth of twins in the eleventh century two mid-wives are depicted, each holding a naked infant. They wear simply the long coloured kirtle and veil head-dress of their times. (See Fig. 3.) In Fig. 4 they do likewise, but their attire is noticeably more work-a-day than that of the lady friend.

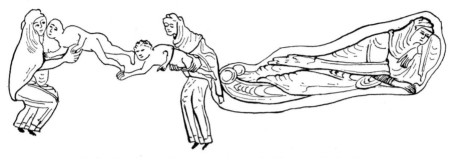

3. Birth of twins, 11th century. (Jacob holding Esau's heel.) Two midwives attending. See text.
B.M. MS. Cot. Claudius B IV f. 40v.

Not until the eighteenth century were men as doctors or midwives allowed to attend at a confinement.

Preparations for the confinement in 1442 of Henry VI's Queen, Margaret of Anjou, show that men attendants were strictly forbidden:

> . . . in the second chamber, (a secret oratory for dyverse matters) must be a travers★ which shall never be but drawen untill she be purified . . . After that traverse there may not openlye no man officer or other come there nerer than the utter chamber . . . In stede of men officers must be gentle-women . . .

> B.M. MS. Add. 6113, f. 122.

With the entrance into the profession of the "man midwife", a keen rivalry was set up between him and the woman midwife. The famous accoucheur Dr William Smellie, about the middle of the eighteenth century, was attending the "best people" and, recognizing perhaps that the presence at a lying-in of a person too obviously masculine in appearance might offend feminine delicacy, recommended that

> men midwives should adopt an effeminate but commodious dress, namely a loose washing night-gown.†

> *Treatise on Midwifery, 1745*

★ Movable screen or low curtain (Halliwell).
† Informal day wear.

4. Birth of Earl of Warwick depicted *c.* 1485. The mother naked in
bed using a sheet as a forehead cloth. Attendants wear typical kirtles of
the period with tight sleeves extending over the hands. Lady "gossip"
holding the swaddled baby wears a butterfly head-dress.
After a drawing B.M. MS. Cot. Julius E IV art. 6.

The objection to the presence of a male in the lying-in chamber is amus-
ingly stated by William Hutton in his autobiography.[5]

A few weeks after, I saw my mother in the pangs of labour . . . the midwife
and assistants about her. I, being the only male in the room, was ordered out.
(1726)

The "only male" was but a child of three years old, which seems to be sufficient reason for ordering him out!

Dr Smellie (loc. cit.) gives a remarkable description of a male midwife's attire.

> In the year 1748, I received a message from a lady to go to one who had been her servant . . .
>
> On my arrival I found another practitioner there . . . His dress was as forbidding as his countenance, consisting of an old greasy matted wrapper or nightgown, a buff broad sword belt of the same complexion round his middle; napkins wrapped round his arms and a woman's apron before him, to keep his dress from being bedaubed. At the same time to make him appear of consequence, he had on his head a large tie periwig.

A satirical notice in the *Morning Post* of 19th November 1788, shows that unqualified male midwives were still in practice well after Dr Smellie's time.

In addition to the midwives, "gossips" were usually present at a confinement, even as late as the early nineteenth century. The gossips were originally the sponsors selected to be the child's godparents (Anglo-Saxon God-sib, i.e. God-relative). As they sat round the patient waiting for the birth, no doubt they chattered to pass the time and so presumably gave us our verb "to gossip". At the confinement of the Queen in 1486 this order was given:

> . . . the Gossippes must be lodged nighe the Queenes Deliveraunce, that they . . . may be ready to attend upon the Yonge Prince or Princesse to the Christeninge.

Leland, Collectanea, Vol. 4, 181

In 1666 Pepys wrote:

> After dinner my wife and Mercer [her woman] by coach to Greenwich, to be gossip to Mrs Daniel's child.

It was their duty to see that all essential preparations were made for the "good hour", that is the safe delivery. The gossips would also see that the patient was wearing some garment of her husband's, whereby a portion of her sufferings would be transferred to him. They themselves wore the clothes fashionable for their day, without any thought of spreading infection.

In 1803 Dr Buchan (op. cit.), believing that science was more trustworthy than tradition, suggested that mother and child would benefit if the gossips were removed from the lying-in chamber.

Rockers were the women employed to rock the cradle containing the newly born baby (Pl. 3(a)).

CHAPTER 2

THE BABY

(a) Layettes

Among prenatal duties of the midwife and mother was the preparation of items that might be required for the infant. An interesting list of a midwife's needs is given in Thomas Delaney's book *The Gentle Craft* (1597–1600):

> Sope and candles, beds, shirts, biggins, wastcoats, headbands, swaddlebands, crossclothes, bibs, tailclouts, mantles, hose, shooes, coats, petticoats, cradle and crickets.

The crossclothes were probably ready for the mother. The crosscloth was a piece of material worn across the forehead and tied behind. It was often worn in bed and was supposed to prevent wrinkles. The tailclout was a delightful name for a baby's nappy. The cricket was a low stool for the attending midwife. Bibs were already in use in the early fourteenth century.

> To protect his clothes from slobber you will say to his nurse "Make the child a bib."
>
> *Treatise of Walter de Biblesworth*[1]

The biggin was a baby's bonnet (Pl. 3(b)). A doctor writing in the *Lady's Magazine* of 1785 explains:

> As to the head, it is covered with two or three small biggins, the first of which is of linen, and the others woollen, and these are tied behind the neck. In many places they add a stayband [headband] or a kind of headdress with two ends which hang down on the side of the head and are fastened on the breast with pins in order to make the infant hold its head straight.

In 1879 the anonymous writer, in *Babies and how to take care of them*, mentions a popular addition to the layette consisting of an ornamental pincushion (see Pl. 2(b) and (c)) which was not to be kept in the basket.

Part of an interesting list of requirements for a layette follows. These garments were all a gift to the expectant mother from a member of the Cunnington family who wrote in 1843:*

* The original list and the covering letter are in the possession of Mrs Elizabeth Attrill *née* Cunnington.

My dear Jane,

As I went to Miss Cook's this morning and paid for the robe we selected from her stock last week, I now write to beg your acceptance of it as a token of my esteem and sincerely hoping you may be spared to become the happy mother of a living, well formed child.

I remain my dear Jane with kindest love,

Yours most affectionately, Eliz. Cunnington

Enclosed is the list of necessaries (to the best of my recollection) against the important anticipated event.

> 4 night gowns
> 4 first sized day caps
> 5 long robes
> 4 day gowns for first month
> 8 pinafores
> 2 doz. napkins
> 3 flannel barrows [see footnote p. 26]
> 9 back wrappers
> 4 flannel belts or soft calico binders
> 3 whittles [large white shawls]
> 6 first sized shirts
> 2 flannel caps
> 2 short chemises
> Baby linen, basket and cover
> Powder box, pincushion
> Feather for bed* and blanket
> Soft sponge and soft brush for the hair.

For the nurse, presumably, there was to be a "flannel apron" and another of "India rubber". It is interesting that in this, the year of Charles Mackintosh's death, his invention should have already been exploited in the nursery.

A writer in *Babyhood* gives in great detail an account of what was required for a layette in 1891. Fresh points of interest are as follows. For bands or binders the article recommends "Jaeger stockinet . . . in white or natural wool shades", instead of flannel. As for shirts:

> For "*first shirts*" the finest and lightest weight stockinet should be chosen, white, of course . . .

* "3 Day blankets, called by some 'beds' " are included in a very similar list given in *Babies and how to take care of them*, 1879.

Since some infants with sensitive skins are irritated by wool, under the wool shirt "little shirts of silk or cotton mull" are recommended.

For socks of wool:

> As a rule pink dyes in wool wash far better than blues and this should be borne in mind in buying socks or any knitted goods for a baby.

> *The skirts*
> Two skirts are considered necessary to the baby's toilet, one of flannel, the other of nansook or cambric, and the old-fashioned method of making them was to attach them to wide bands, which were lapped and pinned around the baby's waist, tightly enough to keep the skirt in place.

The writer disapproves of this method and advises the wearing of a low-necked bodice on to which the skirts can be buttoned. On the subject of the *barrow*★ "the time honoured garment" the writer deplores the number of pins used to keep this garment in place "round the waist and down the front" and the way the baby still managed to stick his feet out through the unpinned spaces.

In the nineteenth century nearly everything connected with the layette tended to become an object of display and in 1889 we are told that

> Mr Peter Robinson provides for the glory of King Baby, the dainty ber-ceaunette, the ribbon-bedizened basket, the satin hood in which he takes his walks abroad and the smart pinafore which he wears when he is brought down into the drawing room to see visitors.
> *Baby: The Mother's Magazine*

In contrast to the "dainty" layettes so popular in earlier times, we read in *Our Baby*, 1897, of something quite new:

> The very mention of the word "wool" dispels the idea of muslins and laces, which seem naturally to connect itself with a baby's outfit.
> The Jaeger Company sells a baby's outfit or "layette" as it is called composed throughout of wool, or one can be made at home.

(b) *Wear for the New-born*

Directly after birth the baby, before being dressed, was wrapped in a cloth called a "receiver", in the seventeenth century, the term surviving into the nineteenth century.

★ A long flannel wrapped round under the arms and pinned up over the feet.

After the birth of Prince James, later the "Old Pretender", in 1688, depositions were made at a Council meeting held because the child's identity had been questioned. These were reported as follows. The dry nurse stated that:

> The Midwife parted the Child [severed the umbilical cord] and put it [the child] into the Receiver . . . and then delivered the Child to the Deponent [dry nurse] and bid her go and carry it to the Fire . . .

The Earl of Middleton said that the midwife

> fetched a child out of the [Queen's] Bed into that Cloth . . . the King said "Let me see it", thereupon she laid open the Cloth and showed all the child.

In a chapter on the "Management after the birth of the Infant" in *The Good Nurse* by Mrs Hanbury, 1828, the term "receiver" is again used.

> When the nurse has finished washing the baby it should be wrapped in a blanket . . . called a *receiver* . . . leaving an aperture to admit the air. [!!]

Advice follows for treatment of the cord:

> The management of the cord . . . In the course of a week, it generally separates from the child. A split raisin under a piece of singed rag accelerates this process. A bandage of fine flannel to wear over it till it is perfectly healed and detached is better than cloth.

Dr Buchan, again in *Advice to Mothers* in 1803, spoke of a blanket, to be used directly after the first bath

> . . . the nurse to have a soft warm blanket in readiness to wrap up the infant on being taken out of the bath. In that wrapping the child should be kept for at least ten minutes, in gentle motion, and then dressed.
> A piece of fine flannel round the navel, a linen or cotton shirt, a flannel petticoat and a linen or cotton robe, are soon put on.

(c) Swaddling

> When the child is born
> He must be swaddled.
> *Treatise of Walter de Biblesworth*[2] (Early fourteenth century)

Swaddling was the rule from early Middle Ages to early nineteenth century, but it was under severe criticism by some of the medical profession

5. Suckling of Samson. Swaddled baby fed by mother wearing a long-sleeved kirtle slipped off one shoulder. On her head the usual veil head-dress. The baby's swaddling bands are mauve over white. 1320.
Queen Mary's Psalter (*B.M. MS. Roy 2 B VII*) *f. 43.*

in the eighteenth century when its use began to decline among the upper classes.

Swaddling consisted of bandaging the baby's body over a cloth, a shirt or small garment, at first in such a way as to include the arms and feet. This made the infant a bundle easy to carry and was, moreover, thought to protect its fragile limbs from harm. Figs. 6 and 7 illustrate methods of swaddling, the criss-cross arrangement being the earlier one. Peter Erondell's Dialogue 5 "In the Nursery", which is reproduced in M. St Clare Byrne's delightful book *The Elizabethan Home*, shows how garments were worn over the swaddling bands. (See also the layette for 1597 listed at the beginning of this chapter.)

The Lady to the Nurse

How now, how doth the childe? . . . Unswaddle him, undoe his swadling bands . . . wash him, before me . . . Pull off his shirt, thou art pretty and fat my little darling . . .

Now swadle him againe, But first put on his biggin and his little band

6. *"La Visite à la Nourrice"* showing the child being swaddled. (Although French, the picture shows the usual way of swaddling the infant in England.)

Engraving by Abraham Bosse at the Wellcome Institute. By courtesy of the Trustees.

7. Two ladies who died in giving birth to twins. (*a*) Mother in gown laced across, widely open in front, suggesting a pregnancy gown. (Her rosary has been omitted for clarity.) Babies swaddled with criss-cross bands. 1512. (*b*) Babies each swaddled with a single spiral band. They wear bibs, biggins, and ruffs like their mother's. 1592. *Both from brass rubbings reproduced in John Page-Phillips* Children on Brasses, *1970.* (a) *from Blickling, Norfolk* (b) *from Houghton-le-Skerne, Durham.*

[collar] with an edge, where is his little petticoat? Give him his coate of changeable [shot] taffeta and his sattin sleeves.

Where is **his** bibbe? Let him have his gathered aprone with stringes, and hang a Muckinder [handkerchief] to it.

You need not yet to give him his corall★ with the small golden chayne, for I believe it is better to let him sleepe until the afternoon.

(*c. 1568*)

Jane Sharp, herself a midwife, wrote *The Midwives' Book or the whole Art of Midwifery* in 1671. The following extract is some of the advice she gives concerning the new-born infant.

. . . roul it up with soft cloths and lay it in the cradle: but in the swaddling of it be sure that all parts be bound up in their due place and order gently without any crookedness or rugged foldings; for infants are tender twigs and as you use them, so they will grow straight or crooked . . . lay the arms right down by the sides, that they may grow right. When the Navel-string is cut off, . . . bind a piece of Cotton or Wool over it, . . . and if the child be weak after this, anoint the child's body over with oil of acorns, for that will comfort and strengthen it and keep away the cold . . . Carry it often in the arms, and dance it, to keep it from the rickets and other diseases.

After four months let loose the arms [Pl. 4] but still roul the breast and belly and feet to keep out cold air for a year, till the child have gained more strength. Shift the child's clouts often, for the Piss and Dung . . .

When the child is seven months old you may (if you please) wash the body of it twice a week with warm water till it be weaned . . .

As already stated, the eighteenth century was beginning to protest against the ancient custom of swaddling. In Richardson's novel (1740) *Pamela*, having studied John Locke's *Treatise on Education*, the heroine says:

Next he forbids too *warm* and too *straight clothing*. This is just as I wish it. How often has my heart ached, when I have seen poor babies rolled and swathed, ten or a dozen times round; then blanket upon blanket, mantle upon that; its little neck pinned down to one posture: its head more than it frequently needs, triple-crowned like a young pope, with covering upon covering; its legs and arms, as if to prevent that kindly stretching which we rather ought to promote, when it is in health, and which is only aiming at growth and en-largement, the former bundled up, the latter pinned down; and how the poor thing lies on the nurse's lap, a miserable little pinioned captive, goggling and staring with its eyes, the only organ it has at liberty . . .

★ Coral was a symbol of good luck.

8. Older baby, the arms set free, but the rest of the body firmly bound
up. 1741. Compare the advice given in 1671 (p. 31).
Engraving by E. Stalker after Hogarth's "The Enraged Musician" (detail).

In 1748 Dr William Cadogan fulminated against the practice of swaddling.
He directed the following to one of the Governors of the Foundling Hospital.

You perceive, Sir, by the Hints I have already dropp'd, what I am going to
complain of . . .

The first great Mistake is, that they think a new-born Infant cannot be
kept too warm; from this Prejudice they load and bind it with Flannels,
Wrappers, Swaths, Stays etc. commonly called Cloaths; which all together

are almost equal to its own Weight; but which means a healthy Child in a Month's Time is made so tender and chilly, it cannot bear the external Air . . . The Truth is, a new-born Child cannot well be too cool and loose in its Dress . . .

Moreover . . .

> . . . . these Swaddling-cloaths, . . . are put on so tight, and the Child is so cramp'd by them, that its Bowels have not Room, nor the Limbs any Liberty, to Act and exert themselves in the free easy manner they ought . . .
> I would recommend the following Dress: A little Flannel Waistcoat without Sleeves, made to fit the Body, and tie loosely behind; to which there should be a Petticoat sew'd, and over this a kind of Gown of the same Material, or any other, that is light thin and flimsy. The Petticoat should not be quite so long as the child, the gown a few inches longer; with one Cap only on the Head, which may be made double, if it be thought not warm enough . . .
> Shoes and stockings are very needless Incumbrances . . . there should be a thin Flannel Shirt for the Night.
>
> *Essay on Nursing*

Dr Smellie (1745) agrees with Dr Cadogan in wanting to abolish swaddling. He recommends much the same baby clothes except for allowing "head band" passing over the head to be sewn to the "waistcoat".

Dr Buchan, a later physician to the Foundling Hospital, had sharp comments to make, in 1769, about the constricting and even deforming effect of "rollers and wrappers, applied to the baby's body as if every bone had been fractured at birth" (*Domestic Medicine*).[3] Though he adds:

> In most parts of Britain, the practice of rolling children with so many bandages is now in some measure laid aside.

Yet he repeats the strictures in his edition of 1803.

In 1826 W. Dewees, M.D.,[4] still had to protest against swaddling. He suggested that the reason for its practice probably arose

> from the inroads made by rickets.
> Analogous is the common practice of even the present day, of pinning the ends of its garments close up to the feet of the child, thus preventing all movements of its limbs . . . In the same way all motion is prevented by the arms being confined in a napkin when the child is laid down.

(d) Danger of Pins

Apart from the danger to life and limb from swaddling, another hazard was often present in the use of pins. Pin cushions were frequently added to the layette basket in the nineteenth century.

In 1709 Steele, in the *Tatler*, put into words the thoughts of a new-born baby on the subject of pins.

> The Girl was very proud of the womanly employment of a nurse and took upon her to strip and dress me anew, because I made a noise, to see what ailed me; she did so and stuck a pin in every joint about me. I still cried: upon which she lays me on my face in her lap, and, to quiet me, fell a-nailing in all the pins, by clapping me on the back.

Again, Dr Buchan wrote, in *Domestic Medicine* (edn 1803):

> It would be safer to fasten the clothes of an infant with strings than pins . . . Pins have been found sticking above half an inch into the body of a child, after it had died of convulsion fits, which in all probability proceeded from that cause.

And Dr Dewees agreed with him (loc. cit.):

> In general, nurses are in the habit of using from 8 to 12 pins for the dressing of the child . . . the same ends can be completely answered by two . . . Strings, and tapes must be used . . .
>
> The diaper requires one [pin] made to serve the double purpose of holding the folds of this article as well as keeping the belly band in its proper place: the latter having a small tag of double linen depending from the lower margin by which it is secured to the diaper by the same pin.
>
> [For] a display of 'best bib and tucker' a 3rd pin may be admitted to ensure the well-sitting of the 'frock' waist.

Happily, by the end of the nineteenth century, the pin problem was solved by the invention, in 1878, of the "Danish Safety Pin", so that an anonymous writer in 1879[5] was able to give the following advice:

> In dressing a child, no matter what age, use as few pins as possible and then only those called "Safety".
> . . . . . .
> Very young children often have their under-garments sewn on them by their nurses.

The safety pin was again recommended in 1891 by a writer in *Babyhood, the Mother's Nursery Guide*.

> A word on the subject of safety pins . . . Select a pin that fastens easily *from both sides* and is durable and well plated. The "Clinton" safety pin is very satisfactory in all of these respects.

Even safety pins might be a danger however:

> I have many times recalled the story once told me by a mother . . . of the hours of agonised suspense which she had passed in watching her baby who had swallowed his bib pin, which a careless nurse had allowed him to play with.
>
> (Ibid.)

Fortunately the pin was clasped and the baby survived.

A superior kind of safety pin was advertised in 1893.

> *Why make Baby cry* by using "Safety" Pins badly made of common wire, when for 6d. per box or 1s. per card, you can buy GOODMAN's royal silver SAFETY PINS which are made entirely of Nickel Silver which cannot ironmould . . . and cannot bend or come unfastened.
>
> *Nursing Notes*, Vol. 6, p. 54, advert.

A writer in 1879 was anxious to point out how sensitive an infant's skin might be.

> . . . even a little corner of lace turned in will irritate the skin. There should not be a wrinkle nor a crease left large enough to do this . . . A head flannel should be discontinued as soon as possible.
>
> *Babies and how to take care of them*

Mrs Ada Ballin in *Baby, the Mother's Magazine*, 1889 was anxious about dyes for infants.

> From time immemorial white has been chosen, and wisely so, for the best outer garments of the little ones.
>
> Dyes bring new dangers as poisonous matters are often employed in the process of dyeing.

She goes on to deplore red, despite the superstition that red flannel

> has some mysterious curative property. I have noticed that among the poorer classes, red is decidedly the favourite colour for children's clothes.

Then she explains that many aniline dyes are powerful irritants to the child's skin.

(e) Long Clothes

The long or medium long garments seen in aristocratic portraits of the sixteenth and seventeenth centuries were mantles worn over the swaddling and apart from providing extra warmth were also ornamental (Pl. 5, 6 and 7). In the same way when swaddling was gradually given up in the eighteenth century, this was mainly done among upper ranks of society, for it gave an opportunity for displaying costly lace. Babies arms were now free, but it was still thought necessary to support the fragile spine. In the domestic accounts of a clergyman's wife in 1851 we find a reference, "baby's stays 3/-", a garment in common use in spite of many warnings. As early as 1769 Dr Buchan, who, as we have seen, frowned upon stays, had written in *Domestic Medicine*:

> Stays are the very bane of infants. It is to be hoped that the world will in time become wise enough to know that the human shape does not solely depend upon whalebone and bend-leather.*

Yet again as late as 1887, Mrs Ada Ballin, in *Baby, the Mother's Magazine*, was having to warn:

> I have now to plead against the use of those baby stays with which so many little ones are provided. Here mothers will exclaim "But what harm can they do? They are not at all stiff. Why they are only made of corded jean, or something of that sort." The answer is: They can do harm in many ways.
>
> In the first place, if they are not stiff they are unyielding and thus not adaptable to the changing proportions of the little body . . . if the stays are loose they slip down and press on the pelvis . . . if shoulder straps are added . . . these give rise to stooping . . .

Here is a description from *Our Baby* in 1897 of modified stays used merely to support the petticoat:

> The little flannel stays are made from layers of health flannel, with arm holes bound with flannel binding and quilted by the machine. On these it is convenient to sew the knitted petticoat which is put into a flannel band.

True "long clothes" consisted of a long robe and under petticoat worn over the stays, etc. (Pl. 8). Though not so restrictive as swaddling bands, long

---

* Leather from the back and flanks of an animal.

clothes were far from ideal and these too were much criticized, as also was the display of finery which they encouraged. In 1803 Dr Buchan laid down this rule in *Advice to Mothers*:

> No part of an infant's dress should hang down above two or three inches lower than the feet. Long robes and long petticoats serve only to conceal the nurse's inattention to cleanliness . . .

In 1828 an article in *The Good Nurse* gave the following opinion of long clothes and lace trimmings:

> The robe, from an idea of being graceful, is of an inconvenient length, and the petticoat and cloak being of a corresponding size, the dress is thereby rendered far too heavy and fatiguing. The fashion of fastening the sleeve of the robe up to the shoulder-strap with a ribbon is very objectionable, more particularly in cold weather.
>
> The cap, from being loaded with lace, and this lace so stiffened that the points in the edge are almost as sharp as thorns, of course must be exceedingly teasing: . . . this full-trimmed cap, now so universally worn, is also a cause of preventing the face from being defended from the glare of the sun . . . as the hat can only be placed on the back part of the head.
> . . . . . .
> The bunch of lace to distinguish the male infant is ridiculous in the extreme and must injure the baby by heating the head which part should always be kept cool.

Susan Sibbald in her *Memoirs*[6] was already complaining, in 1811, at the sight of

> the little infant [two months old] which I thought from its being so young would have looked better in its nursery attire of bedgown and nightcap, instead of robe and sash and tied up sleeves, a bare neck and a cap like a sunflower, with scarlet cockade to match the ribbons of the robe.

Although from earliest times it was considered necessary for a baby's head to be covered, by night and day, Dr H. Davies in 1854 had the courage to say "No".

> The head is the only part which need not be covered, except by thin muslin for the sake of appearance; there is often a tendency to over excitement in the brain which may be checked by keeping the head cool.
>
> *Young Wife's Guide*

Dr Walsh in his *Manual of Domestic Economy* in 1856 states exactly how an infant should be dressed. His list begins with "an outer garment, variously ornamented, and named a night-gown, day-gown or robe"; and includes "a swathe for effecting a certain amount of pressure at the navel". The swathe was later usually known as the binder. As regards this Mrs Ballin in *Baby* in 1887 recommended in place of the "tight calico bandage":

> a carefully shaped flannel binder . . . It has the front made of silk elastic, shaped to the abdomen, so that there is just enough pressure to prevent protrusion of the bowels, but not enough to be injurious.

Finally, here is a list from *Our Baby* of long clothes required for any baby in 1897.

> 2 or 4 Muslin Shirts
> 2 or 4 Flannel Binders
> 3 or 4 Flannel Petticoats or Barrow coats
> 3 or 4 Flannel Nightdresses
> 3 or 4 Flannel Dresses
> 6 Flannel Squares or Pilches
> 36 Fine Cotton Linen or Turkish Towelling Diapers
> 2 Head Flannels
> 1 Knitted Shawl or Cloak
> 1 Woollen Hood
> 4 Pairs of Knitted Shoes
> 1 Veil.
> Mackintosh pilches should never be used. Let the outdoor cloak be a wrap not a trimmed ornament for the nurse's arm, and the bonnet a soft woolly one . . .
>
> A veil is required when it is windy or very cold and a sunshade in hot weather.

(f) Lucky Charms for the Baby
As with the mothers, belief in charms that would bring good luck to the new-born infant not only for survival, but for its well being, was wide spread.

The most important "charm" appears to have been coral which continued as a child's speciality long after belief in its magical property had ceased. Disbelief was actually shown in the sixteenth century by Reginald Scot in his *Discoverie of Witchcraft*, 1584, when he wrote:

The coral preserveth such as bear it from fascination or bewitching and in this respect they are hanged about children's necks. But from whence this superstition is derived, or who invented the lye, I know not, but I see how ready the people are to give credit thereunto, by the multitude of corals that ware emploied.

Jane Sharp in her *Midwive's Book*, 1671, states:

Some children grow lean and pine away and the cause is not known; if it be from Witchcraft good prayers to God are the best remedy, yet some hang Amber and Coral about the child's neck as a sovereign remedy.

William Cole in 1657 suggested a practical use for coral:

It helpeth children to breed their teath, their gums being rubbed therewith and to that purpose they have it fastened at the ends of their mantles.

Adam in Eden

From Sir Walter Calverley's Memorandum[7] we read:

June 1707. My Lady Blackett [his mother-in-law] was pleased to give my son Watty [aged 6 months] . . . a corell and correll necklaces; which she wore herself when a child, and all her children after her.

Coral is even included among the "needs of a new baby".

Your silver will be ever flying
Something or other always buying
Clouts, Blankets, Barrows, Hippins,* Swaddles
Fine painted gew-gaws, corals, rattles
Caps, aprons, Bibs, White frocks, Mantling
To Cloath the little sh . . . n Bantling.
"An Epistle to my Friend J.B. having got a girl with child" in
R. Dodsley, *A Muse in Livery or
The Footman's Miscellany*, 1732

Rattles at this time frequently had coral handles.

Another lucky symbol is probably very ancient. The anticipation of favours to come was marked by a curious custom that the new born baby's first garment should be its mother's smock, wrapped round it. This, it was believed, would ensure that the child would grow up richly endowed with sex appeal.

* Hippins was a general term for infants' clothes.

Indeed, Miss, I believe you were wrapt in your mother's smock, you are so well-beloved.

J. Marston, *What You Will*, 1607

A lackey in the same play (Act V, Sc. i) derides a fellow saying:

You were not lapt in your Mother's smock,
you ha' not a good cheeke, an inticing
eye, a smooth skinne, a well-shapt leg, a
faire hand, you cannot bring a wench into
a fooles parradize for you?

An article in *Nursing Notes* (Vol. 6, p. 53 (1893)) entitled "Folklore Jottings" tells us of two other superstitions:

In Northern Ireland it is considered right for the new born baby to be laid on his *father's* shirt and in Scotland he will have luck . . . if a small bag of salt be hung round his neck.

. . . An Irish nurse . . . recommended that any child who was "wished" by the fairies should never be left alone unless his father's coat protected his cradle . . .

In the Isle of Wight Nurses warn the expectant mothers not to put any pins in the pin cushion when they prepare the dainty basket for the new comer. "More pins, more pain" is the proverb . . . they often inist on every pin being taken out however pretty and fanciful the pattern.

CHAPTER 3

THE CHRISTENING

In the early days of baptism, the candidate, more or less unclothed, was immersed in a bath of flowing water, a fount. Hence the name "font" for the basin used when infant baptism (with which alone we are concerned) became established. The infant still had to be immersed—dipped naked in the water, as is shown in Pl. 9(a) and (b). This must have been inconvenient in more ways than one. William of Malmsbury[1] records that poor little King Ethelred as an infant (c. 968) when held naked over the font ready for baptism "did in the water what he ought not to have done".

Immersion was gradually given up in both the Anglican and Roman Catholic churches, during the seventeenth century, in favour of pouring on or sprinkling the water. Even the first English Prayer Book allowed this "if the child was weak". With the new method the child could be at least partially clad during the ceremony.

Some early customs connected with baptism must be mentioned to explain, for example, the various meanings of the words *chrism* or *chrisom* and *chrisom-cloth*.

In the Roman Catholic rite and in the Baptismal service in the first Prayer Book (but not later versions) the child was "confirmed" (Pl. 10(a)), being anointed with "chrism" oil as a mark of this, directly after baptism. He was then wrapped in a special cloth, the chrisom-cloth, often called simply a chrisom.* The Prayer Book's rubric enjoins that the minister is to put this on the child with the words: "Take this white vesture for a token of innocensie." It was customary for the infant to wear the cloth for a month afterwards. Hence:

> Chrisms in the bills of mortality are such children as die within the month of birth, because during that time they used to wear the chrisom-cloth . . .
>
> J. O. Halliwell, Dictionary of Archaic Words

---

* In the very early church, confirmation had likewise followed immediately upon baptism, at Easter and by a bishop. After confirmation the candidates, adults, put on white garments (which they wore for the Octave). Hence the chrisom-cloth, in later times. (P. Dearmer, *Everyman's History of the Prayer Book*, 1912.)

The chrisom-cloth, at first plain and white, turned into an ornate affair, at least for royal christenings (Fig. 14). Some Roman Catholic customs connected with the chrisom, and also with the dress of the officiating priest, were described in the early eighteenth century as follows:

> When a child is brought to be baptised, the Priest meets him at the church door . . .

9. A Roman Catholic christening in 1723. Godmother supports baby, whose swaddling bands have been removed to free the shoulders for anointing (note box for the oil). Lady on extreme right (probably the mother) holds chrisom-cloth; lady on extreme left holds baby's mantle. *Engr. in* Histoire Générale des cérémonies . . . religeuses *Edn. 1741 Vol. 2 p. 74 (first pubd. 1723). Photo. by courtesy of The Wellcome Trustees.*

The priest himself has to wear a surplice and a purple stole (Fig. 9):

> . . . the Priest lays the end of the stole upon the child, and taking hold of his swaddling clothes by one corner, he brings it into the church . . . towards the font . . . the Assistants pull off the swaddling clothes, or at least strip it below the shoulders . . .
>
> The Priest anoints the child between the shoulders in the form of a Cross and after that lays aside the Purple Stole and puts on a white one . . . takes some of the Baptismal water which he pours thrice on the Child's Head . . . anoints the top of the Child's Head with the Chrisma [chrism oil] in the Form of a Cross, lays a Piece of white Linen [the chrisom-cloth] upon his head to represent the white garment mentioned in Scripture and puts into the Child's Hand or rather into that of the Godfather, a lighted taper.
>
> Bernard Picart (*et al.*), *Ceremonies & Religious Customs* (French edn. 1723), English translation, 1733–7

The medieval use of the child's lighted taper (still part of the ceremony today in the Catholic church) is shown in Fig. 10.

One curious medieval custom which survived into the eighteenth century may be mentioned. This was in regard to the baptism of an illegitimate child. Penance in a white sheet was general for offences against chastity and before a bastard could be "christianized" the parents, or at least the mother, had to appear in church or in the market place clad in a white sheet.

An example appears, as an item of news, in the *Gentleman's Magazine* for 1731:

> Sunday Sept. 5th. A man of sixty years of age stood in a white sheet at the Cathedral church at *Norwich*, for getting his own Daughter with child.

The Baby's Clothes

Whether it was to be wholly or only partly undressed for the actual ceremony, the baby in a well-to-do family was generally taken to church in rather elaborate robes. Apparently one of these used to be the *christening shirt* described by Howe in his addition to Stow's *Chronicle*.[2] He states, writing of the beginning of Queen Elizabeth's reign:

> At this time, and for many yeares before, it was not the use and custome (as now it is) for godfathers and godmothers generally to give plate at the baptism of children (as spoons, cupps, and such like) but onely to give *christening shirts*, with little bands [collars] and cuffs wrought either with silke or blew thread,

10. Priest in surplice and stole. Infant naked, holding a lighted taper in
his supported hand. 1506.
Thordynary of Cryste Men (*Anon.*) *edn. 1506 pubd. by Wynkyn de
Worde. British Museum.*

the best of them, for chiefe persons weare, edged with a small lace of blacke
silke and gold, the highest price of which for great men's children was seldom
above a noble, and the common sort two, three or foure and five shillings
a piece.

The most conspicuous garments of the infant were the mantle and bearing
cloth. For royalty the *mantle* was highly ornate with a very long train. Ordinances for the "Christening of a Queen's child" written probably in the late
fifteenth century lay down that:

Yf it be a prynce, A Erle to bear his trayne and yf it be a prynces[s],a Countesse to bear yt.

B.M. MS. Add. 6113, f. 122v.

Actually, for Prince Arthur, Henry VII's son, a lady bore the train (see below).

Another Ordinance of the same period prescribes:

A riche Mantell of cloth of Golde [the one used for Prince Arthur was crimson] with a longe Traine furred throughe out with Ermyn.

B.M. MS. Harl. 6079.

Everything was done to make so small a creature as a new-born baby look important.

The *bearing-cloth* or "palm"* was a wrap in which the baby was carried, and this again could be distinctive. (See Appendix 1.)

Thy scarlet robes, as a child's bearing cloth.

Shakespeare, *Henry VI*, I, iii (1590).

In Lord William Howard's accounts[3] in 1623 we have:

For 5 yard of damaske to make a bearing cloth £3. 6. 6.
For Taffetie to lyne it 32s.
For lace, eleven onceies to it 57s.

Even for humbler folk the bearing cloth was usually valuable, and in 1649 Mary Chapman, widow, wrote this in her will:

My bearing cloth should be for the use of my sister and daughters, each to have it when they have occasion to use it and she that last bear children to have it for ever.

Wills and Inventories of Bury St. Edmunds (Camden Soc.), 1850

Historical Examples

Most of the contemporary accounts of christenings that have come down to us from Tudor times relate to those of royalty or the aristocracy. Some further particulars of Prince Arthur's christening as described in B.M. MS. Add. 6113, Art. 41† will be given here, complemented by some Ordinances laid

* Still called christening palm in Dorsetshire.
† A less exact copy, B.M. MS. Julius B.XII, is transcribed in Leland's *Collectanea*, Vol. 4, pp. 205–7.

down in advance of it (B.M. MS. Harl. 6076, ff. 26–9). This example and some later ones will be illustrated by a series of sixteenth-century drawings of a royal christening.*

> The Fonte must be set of a great Height, that the People may see the Christen-inge withoute pressinge too nighe the Fonte, and the same must be hanged all aboute with Clothe of Golde.

Details are given regarding costume and properties.

> When the childre goeth to the Churche to be christened, a Dutchesse must beare the Childe and a Dutchesse must beare the Crisom before upon her shoulder,† on a Kerchewe of smalle Raines.‡
> Also there must be provided a little Taper for the Childe to carye in his Hande up to the highe auterafter his Christendome. [cf. Figs. 10 and 12]

Four men "of worshippe" (of distinction) were to carry a canopy over the child (Fig. 11).

Since at this period the infant had to be baptized in the nude, special arrangements were made for this. An area near the font was screened off by curtains, the "travers" where he was disrobed; this was furnished:

> with carpets and Quishins [cushions] to the same, a faire Panne of Coles welle burnte before they come there for smellinge, and sweete Perfumes to caste therein, chafrons of Water, with Basons of Silver and gilt, to washe the childe if neede be . . . The Prince or Princess being broughte into the Churche, it shal be forthwith borne into the Travess . . . ready for the changinge of the Childe out of the clothes and making it ready unto Christon-dome.

The train of the Prince's mantle (Fig. 11) was so heavy that not only did "my Lady the Marquesse of Dorset" bear it, but Sir John Cheyney supported "the Midell of the same".

---

* The originals of these drawings are in the College of Arms MS.6 and are produced by kind permission of the Chapter of the College. Copies exist, e.g. B.M. MS. Stowe 583 ff. 11v–16v (reproduced by crude engravings in *Antiquarian Repertory*, Vol. 1, opp. p. 353). The drawings have been variously described as showing Prince Arthur's and Edward VI's chris-tenings, but do not, in details, correspond with contemporary accounts of either. The fashions depicted, e.g. style of trunk-hose, dresses, etc., indicate a date of *c.* 1565–75.

† In Fig. 14 the lady carries the chrisom over her folded hands. Prince Arthur's chrisom was carried by his Aunt Anne, "pynned to the right brest . . . hangynge over the left arme".

‡ Fine linen from Rennes.

11. A royal christening depicted c. 1565–75. Infant in fringed mantle, its long train supported by two noblemen. All attending are in elegant costume of the period—men in gowns and trunk hose; feathered hats (except canopy- and torch-bearers). Women in Spanish farthingale gowns with embroidered fore-parts. *College of Arms MS. 6 f. 78. (Photo.) By courtesy of the Chapter of the College.*

After being baptized "the prince was led to the Traves, and above him his crysom; [he was then] clothed as befor" and was thus carried with his now lighted taper of virgin wax (cf. Fig. 12) up to the altar to be confirmed. Finally: "The Bishop of Saresbury knytt the lynen cloth about his Nek."

A drawing (see Fig. 13) made in about 1485 shows the christening of Richard Beauchamp, Earl of Warwick.* All the participants (except the infant) are interestingly dressed for the occasion. The officiating bishop is vested in a magnificent cope with jewelled border (orphrey) and wears his mitre. The others are thus described by Dillon and Hope.[4]

12. Nobleman carrying christening taper "garnished with iiii wrythen bughts" (twisted candlestick); towel round his neck (see p. 51). *As for Fig. 11.*

On the other side of the font stand the sponsers: King Richard . . . in his crown and parliament robes with his right hand on the infant's head; Bishop of Lichfield, mitred . . . and a lady of quality, the godmother probably, with butterfly headdress and long gown trimmed with ermine. Behind the King stand the sword bearer and a nobleman and . . . on the bishop's right a canon in cassock, surplice and grey amess† bears the open chrismatory [a

* This baptism occurred in 1389, but is represented in late fifteenth-century guise.

† The ecclesiastical *almuce* or *amess*, a hood with an ample cape, was, when furred with grey squirrel, a mark of special dignity. Thus a "grey amess" came to mean a canon. (Not to be confused with *amice*, a garment worn at the neck.) See also Fig. 16 (a).

13. Christening of Richard Beauchamp, Earl of Warwick, depicted in
c. 1485. (See text.)
B.M. MS. Julius E IV art. 6 f. 1 v.

receptacle for the chrism or holy oil] . . . Behind the bishop stand two other canons, one of whom holds the bishop's gloves and a crozier.

Henry VII's daughter, Margaret, had, in 1489, an imposing christening. Her train was supported by a Lady and a Lord and we are also told:

14. Lady carrying ornamental chrisom-cloth. (A fashionable pomander hangs from her waist.) A nobleman escorts her.
As for Fig. 11.

My Lady Anne, the Quene's Sister bere next before her the crysome with a mervelous riche Cross Lace . . .

Immediately following the christening (as at Prince Arthur's) hundreds of torches were lit, also the baby's taper, and "the Officers of Armes put on ther Cotys of Armes", i.e. the attending heralds donned their tabards which bore the royal arms (Fig. 15). Then

the Lord . . . Archbishop of Yorke being in Pontificalibus confirmed her.

Leland, *Collectanea*, Vol. IV, 253

An account of the christening in 1533 of Princess Elizabeth, later Queen Elizabeth I, is given in *Hall's Chronicle*. The proceedings follow the same pattern, but we are also told about the dresses of civil dignitaries and clergy.

The maior and his brethren, and fortie of the chiefe cittizens, were commanded to be at the christening the Wednesdaie following [the birth]. Upon which daie the maior Sir Stephen Peacocke, in gowne of crimosin Velvet, with his collar of esses* and all the Aldermen in scarlet, with collars and

* Lancastrian SS collar.

15. Heralds in procession carrying their tabards, embroidered with the royal arms, to don them at the actual moment of the christening of a prince. *c.* 1565–75.

Detail of engraving, Antiquarian Repertory *Vol. 1, p. 353 (1782) after* B.M. MS. Stowe 583 *ff. 11v–16v.*

chaines, and all the councell of the cittie with them, tooke their barge . . . and the citizens had another barge, and rowed to Greenwich . . .

The font was of silver, and . . . was covered with a fine cloth; and divers gentlemen, with aprones and towels about their neckes, gave attendance about it, that no filth shoulde come to the fonte: . . .

When all these thinges were ordered, the Childe was brought to the hall.

Then a procession of grandees followed, including

the Kinges chappel in coaps, [the staff of his Chapel, in copes] then barons, bishops, earles . . . the lady Mary of Norfolke bearing the crisome which was very rich of pearle and stone. The old dutches of Norfolke bare the Childe in a mantle of purple velvet, with a long traine furred with ermine . . . [which took three people to carry it] . . .

The christening of Henry VIII's son, later Edward VI, in 1537, was in the same grandiose style. Of special interest is the mention of the baby's sisters,

16. (*a*) Tonsured priests in fur almuces
(amesses) with pendant tails.
(*b*) Priests each in cope and square cap (pileus quadratus). *c.* 1565–75.
After B.M. MS. Stowe 583 f. 15v (detail).

both afterwards Queens of England. Lady Mary was godmother and the
Lady Elizabeth had a part to play, though only four years old at the time:

> Then the Crysome richly garneshed [was] borne by the Lady Elizabeth the
> King's Daughter, the same Lady, for her tender Age, was borne by the Vis-
> count Beauchamp with the assistance of Lord Morley.
>
> B.M. MS. Add. 6113, Art. 42.

17. Godmother in procession, her train-bearer and lady with posy.
As for Fig. 11.

18. Nobleman with towel, carrying basin for the ritual hand-washing
following the christening—as at Prince Henry's, 1594 (see text).
As for Fig. 11.

It was not only royal babies that were elaborately dressed for their christenings. In 1575 a little granddaughter of the Earl of Bedford appeared:

> in a mantell of crimson velvet garded* with two wrought laces; having also
> over the face a lawne, striped, with bone lace of gold, overthwart and powdred
> with gold flowers and white, wrought thereon; borne by the midwife.
>
> College of Arms MS. M6, f. 152.

Prince Henry, the eldest son of King James VI of Scotland (later James I of
England), was christened in the Chapel Royal of Holyrood Palace, Edinburgh, in 1594.

> . . . the Prince's robe-royall, being of purple velvote, very richly set with
> pearle was delivered to the Duke of Lennox, who put the same about the
> Prince . . .

Various noblemen followed, carrying the "Prince's honours" which included
"a laver of water, a towel, and . . . a low crowne . . . richly set with
diamonds, saphires, rubies, and emeralds . . . Lastly, the pale [canopy held

* Garded = edged. For clarity, in this quotation punctuation has been added.

over the infant] was carried in before the pulpit", and the poor baby changed hands four times, finally ending up in the arms of "the Mistresse Nurse". The Bishop of Aberdeen, with Protestant zeal:

> stood up in his seate and taught upon Sacrament of Baptisme, first in the vulgar tongue, and next in the Latine, to the end all men might generally understand.
>
> . . . . . .
>
> Then they proceeded to the action.
>
> J. Nichols, *Progresses of Queen Elizabeth*, Vol. 3.

In the account of this christening no chrism cloth is mentioned. Anointing with chrism oil was not part of the ceremony in the Protestant church, but the traditional cloth was in fact often used long after the Reformation.

The following is a record of the baptism of King James's second son, afterwards Charles I, written by J. Blinsele, Hay Herald, who was present at the time. (He uses the language of a Scotsman.)

> Upon Tuesday the 23rd December 1600 the King's Majesty came from his Chamber to the Chapel Royal . . . And there was a Pall [canopy] of gold, Silver and Silk, very magnificent, wrought (as it was spoken) by His Majesty's Ump* Mother† of good Memory, . . . Lord Livingstone . . . bare up the Bairn's Robe Royal of purple Velvet lined with Damask. The Bairn was covered with Cloth of Gold and Lawn. And before the Pall was the Bairn's Honours borne. . . . the two Frenchmen . . . were his Majesty's Gossips . . .
>
> B.M. MS. Add. 6340.

The Countess of Derby, Charlotte de la Trémoille, French by birth, wrote this interesting letter in 1628 about the christening of her nephew.

> I have informed Madame of the baptism of your nephew . . . He was carried by my sister-in-law, and attended by the ladies of four gentlemen of rank of the country. I had him dressed in white, after the French fashion, for here they dress them in colours, which I do not like. The Bishop of Chester baptised him in our private chapel and as you know, by the King's name only . . . The King has presented him with two gold mugs, which is his custom with those upon whom he bestows the honour of his christian name.
>
> Mary Rowsell, *The Life Story of Charlotte de la Trémoille,*
> *Countess of Derby*, 1905.

---

* Umquihill, the Scottish form of umwhile = late or one time.
† The reference is, of course, to Mary Queen of Scots.

When James II's son, James Francis Edward, received a Roman Catholic christening in 1688, we learn from the *Verney Memoirs* that

> Abbot Barberini is to bring the consecrated clouts to England; they are 3 suits richly embroidered with gold, the Pope and the Qu. Dow. Catherine of Braganza being gossips.

A humble christening is described by Ned Ward in 1703 when he had stood as Godfather himself to the new born child.

> . . . I put on a clean band [collar] . . . I sneak'd up to the Parson's elbow . . . whilst old Mother Grope stood rocking the Bantling in her arms, wrap'd up in so rich a Mantle as if both *Indias* had club'd their utmost riches to furnish out a noble covering for my little kinsman who came as callow into the world as a bird out of an eggshell.
>
> *The London Spy*

The costliness of royal christenings is again shown in this eighteenth-century account of the baptism of George III's third daughter, which was not even solemnized in church.

> . . . The Mantle which the young Princess wore . . . was white satin, lined with pink, edged with ermine, and adorned with precious stones; the principal of which is said to be worth 1000 l., the whole mantle is valued at 2800 l.
>
> *The Ipswich Journal*, 19th June 1770.

Non-royal christenings could be dressy too, as shown by Hogarth's picture (Pl. 11). The baby wears a long robe, trimmed with gold, and a white frilled cap.

With the decline in the use of swaddling there evolved, for wear under the mantle or wrap, a white "christening robe" with sleeves, of the type familiar today. Such a garment, dating as early as the eighteenth century, can be seen at the Gallery of English Costume, Manchester. It is made of white linen, embroidered all over, and shows a typical little yoke with V shaped trimming in front and a gathered skirt more than a yard long—all features which persisted. A rather similar robe is seen in Pl. 12 and one of a different design in Pl. 13. For royalty, as we shall see, the robe was often overlaid with Honiton lace.

The baby's headgear, usually a close-fitting white cap, is rarely described, however magnificent the christening outfit, before the eighteenth century. Nevertheless it gradually became an important feature.

In December 1734

> Mrs Harris, a Quaker, well known for her great skill in Needlework, was introduced to her Majesty, and presented her with two caps of uncommon fineness, designed for the Princess of Orange [Anne, daughter of George II] as part of her childbed linen.

Mrs Harris wrote in her loyal address:

> I have O Queen with my own Hands (tho' I am more than 64 years of Age) wrought this Linnen which I have taken the Liberty to present to thy Royal Hand. I beseach thee suffer thy Grandchild to wear it.
>
> *Gentleman's Magazine*, Vol. 4, p. 702

Since the child was as yet unborn, Mrs Harris had embroidered one of the caps with a verse to welcome a prince, the other a princess.

Maria Lady Stanley, referring to the christening of her own baby in 1797, wrote:

> Mrs Biggs has gone to town and is so good as to promise to get me some caps, the only part of the young animal's apparel in which I feel a wish to be smart and coxcombical.[5]

Susan Sibbald, recalling her sister's christening in 1792, describes a startling alternative (or addition?) to the caps.

> Grace had laid out for the occasion a . . . blue hat and feathers, presents from Lady Paines, one of her Godmothers.

In the nineteenth century we find that the mantle was important even in middle-class christenings.

> Out went the servant, and in came the nurse with a remarkably small parcel in her arms packed up in a blue mantle trimmed with white fur. This was the baby.
>
> "Now, Uncle," said Mr Kitterbell, lifting up that part of the mantle which covered the infant's face . . . "Who do you think he is like?"
>
> The Bloomsbury Christening in Charles Dickens's
> *Sketches by Boz*, 1834

Nineteenth-century royal christenings are described in the greatest detail as regards costume. This account of the christening of the Prince of Wales in 1842 is worth giving in full. Lady Lyttleton wrote:

When the Duchess of Buccleuch set off to do her arduous part, taking the Prince of Wales and giving him up to, and then taking him back from the Archbishop, she made a little room, and I forced my way into it, so as to see the child perfectly, and also how well she did it, and how neatly she picked His Royal Highness, mantle and lace and all, out of the voluminous folds of the Primate's lawn sleeves and the dangers of his wig* which it was feared the Prince might have laid hold of and brought away at least on quitting his arms. I did not even see what I heard admired—the Queen's very devout and affecting manner of kneeling quite down, in spite of her cumbrous robes of the Garter, on first entering the Chapel.

Correspondence of Sarah Spencer Lady Lyttleton 1787–1870

A year later Princess Alice was christened, wearing the now conventional long white dress or robe, described as being of Honiton lace over white Spitalfields silk.[6]

At the christening in 1850 of Prince Arthur, Queen Victoria's third son, in Buckingham Palace, the Queen, four princesses and various duchesses all wore white.

The Duke of Wellington who attended

> wore a Field-Marshal's uniform, with the collar of the Order of the Garter and ensigns of the Golden Fleece.
>
> *Illustrated London News*, Vol. 16

The christening of a grandchild of Queen Victoria in 1874 (Fig. 19) was described in the *Illustrated London News* on 5th December:

> The infant having been placed in the arms of the Queen and the Archbishop calling upon the sponsors to name the child, the Queen answered "Alfred, Alexander, William, Ernest, Albert," and his Grace baptised the child in those names. The infant was attired in a mantle, gown and cap of Honiton lace—being the same dress in which all the Queen's children and those of the Prince and Princess of Wales were christened.

Then follows a description of the costumes of the most important people present. All the royal ladies wore the order of Victoria and Albert.

> Her Majesty wore a black satin dress, two rows of large pearls with a diamond cross attached to them . . .

---

* Archbishop Howley (1766–1848). He was the last Archbishop to wear a wig. The sleeves were those of his rochet.

19. Christening in 1874 of a grandchild of Queen Victoria (first child of her son Alfred Duke of Edinburgh). Adults, L to R: Archbishop (note "bishop" sleeves), a clergyman, the head-nurse in customary cap with streamers, Queen Victoria in widow's weeds, Prince of Wales (later Edward VII) with order of the Garter. For further details see text.
Illustrated London News 5 Dec. 1874.

The Princess of Wales wore a dress of crimson satin, with polonaise* of crimson relief trimmed with fur . . .

The Duchess of Edinburgh wore a petticoat† of rich pale pink corded silk, trimmed with plaitings of the same, and a tunic of pale pink crepe de chine, with rich lace and feather trimmings; ruby earrings and necklace, with pearl and diamond pendant brooch . . .

Morning dress was worn by the ladies present. Evening coat with morning trousers, and orders and decorations by the gentlemen.

Much curtailed as was the ceremony itself, there is no denying that royal christenings were still very formal and dressy affairs.

* A dress with an overskirt bunched up behind and open in front, very fashionable at the time.

† A skirt.

MARRIAGES—INTRODUCTION AND BRIDAL ATTIRE

Wedding garments were generally of rich material. As regards their cut and style, these nearly always conformed to the fashions of the day and tended to be very elaborate. Details of bride's wedding dresses will be given later in the descriptions of weddings.

As regards the colour of her dress it is only in fairly recent times that white "the symbol of virginity" has become the general rule. The custom was beginning in the mid-eighteenth century.

> I wish you could take the white and silver to be married in; its the worst luck in the world in anything but white.
>
> O. Goldsmith, *The Good-natured Man*, 1768

Again (in 1769)

> . . . who by her dress was a bride . . . in white and silver.
>
> *Letters and Journals of Lady Mary Coke*, ed. J. A. Home, 1889–96

Earlier, colours were common. The Parish Clerk of Knaresborough, Yorkshire, recalling in 1472 the marriage of Sir William Plumpton in *c.* 1451 stated (in his evidence to its having taken place) that:

> Sir William was clad in a garment of green checkery [a checkered cloth] and Joan [his bride] in one of a red colour.

Sir William was Master Forester and Constable of the Castle of Knaresborough. The marriage was performed in secret, but with all due custom, by the vicar "in his vestments" in Knaresborough Church "very early in the morning" (Plumpton Correspondence, edited by G. T. Stapleton).

Lady Anne, daughter of the Earl of Bedford, was married in 1565:

> . . . the sayd Bryde was apparelled in a kirtle of cloath of silver mixed with blew, a Gowne of purple Velvett embroydered about with Silver, a call of gold on her Head, her trayne borne by Katherine Knoles Daughter of Sir Francis Knowles Vice Chamberlayne.

An interesting description of coloured wedding dresses is given in Thomas Baker's play *The Fine Lady's Airs*, 1709.

Lady Rodomont [to the Mercer who supplies her]
> Mr Farendene, this silk has so glaring a mixture of preposterous colours, I shall be taken for a North Country Bride . . . Have you sold any Wedding suits lately?

Mercer
> Yes, Madam, I sold a yellow and white Damask, lin'd with a Cherry and blew satin, and a Goslin Green Petticoat [skirt] to Mrs Winifred Widgeon i' the Peak . . . 'twas her Grandmother Trott's Fancy.

Lady Rodomont
> Nay, those old Governants that were Dames of Honour to Queen Bess make their Daughters appear as monstrous in this Age, as they themselves did in that.

The wedding dress of a bride in 1714 is described as a

> blue satten manteau and petticoat [skirt] trimmed with silver, a rose-coloured lustring—Pair of earrings cost £70.
> Letter from a Miss Twisden. *Archaeologia Cantiania*, Vol. 5 (1862–3)

In Mrs Cowley's play *The Belle's Stratagem* (1780), the bride expressed uncertainty:

> Whether I should be married in white or lilac, gave the most cruel anxiety.

An actual preference for a coloured wedding dress is shown by this bride in 1762.

> The bride, instead of being disguised in tawdry stuffs of gold and silver, and sweating under a harness of diamonds, according to the elegant taste of the times, appeared in a negligée of plain blue satin without any other jewels than her eyes which far outshone all that ever was produced by the mines of Golconda. Her hair had no other extraneous ornament than a small sprig of artificial roses . . .

The Bridegroom

> made his appearance on this occasion in a white coat and blue satin vest, both embroidered with silver.
> Tobias Smollett, *The Adventures of Sir Lancelot Greaves*

Generally speaking in the nineteenth century, coloured bridal gowns never became popular, but a number have survived and can be seen in museums. The London Museum, the Bethnal Green Museum, the Gallery of English Costume, Platt Hall, Manchester, have interesting specimens (Pl. 14). Castle

Howard Costume Galleries have (among others) a cook's wedding dress of the 1880s in two shades of russet brown.

Perhaps the strangest "colour" ever worn by any bride is dead black. This, however, did occur once in 1874, when the bride, whose father had died a month previously, was married in a wedding dress with a long train, made of black satin throughout. This appears to be unique. The original still exists in very good condition and belongs to the Whitby Literary and Philosophical Society.

Bridal veils were always white and the lace used was very special. Brussels and Honiton were popular in the nineteenth century. The veil was sometimes worn by brides as early as the seventeenth century:

> The Mrs Mas[ter] made the rarest bride veil that ever was seen. (1667)
> *The Oxinden and Peyton Letters, 1642–70*

But very few examples occur, even in the eighteenth century. Here is one:

> The bride was dressed in a white sarcenet and a white silk bonnet with a very long veil to it. (1785)
> *Retrospections of Dorothea Herbert 1770–89*

It was the nineteenth century that started the real fashion for wedding veils when brides were bedecked in special costume for the occasion (Pl. 15). The veil was attached to the top of the head and hung down the back almost to the ground (cf. frontispiece).

> I cannot better conclude this epistle than with the description of the wedding dress of Lady H. Villiers; for a bridal costume possesses considerable interest for us young girls who one day hope to be ranked amidst the votaries of Hymen.
> From the crown of her head flowed a Brussels lace veil of the most transparent fabric . . .
> Letter in *La Belle Assemblée*, Feb. 1807

In the *Wynne Diaries*, Eugenia writes in 1806:

> I was obliged to dress in a hurry to attend my little Catholic Priest who received my confession . . . We were instantly married by the Catholic Priest . . . We had just time to breakfast, and then I had to dress for the second marriage [Church of England]. My bridal array consisted of a white satin underdress and a patent net over it, with a long veil.
> *The Wynne Diaries*, ed. by Anne Freemantle, Vol. 3

At the wedding of the Marquis of Kildare with Lady Caroline Leveson-Gower the bride's head-dress:

> was composed of a guipure lace veil with a wreath of convolvulus and orange blossom.
>
> *Illustrated London News,* 1847

The marriage of Emmeline Benson in 1828, which took place at her father's house by special licence, is described in *A Marriage in High Life* by the Hon. Caroline Lucy, Lady Scott.

> The ceremony was like most others of its kind; the drawing room was crowded with relations and friends . . . dressed in congratulatory smiles, and new bridal finery . . .
>
> Mrs Benson betrayed her anxious agitation by the nervous twitching of the gold chain round her neck, to which was suspended her daughter's portrait, and the constant rearranging of her lace shawl . . .
>
> Emmeline was nineteen . . . crimson in her cheeks was very apparent, even through the folds of the beautiful lace veil that hung all over her.

In *Armstrong's Norfolk Diary* (selection edited by the son and introduced by Owen Chadwicks) we find this statement:

> 1854 Feb: 7th. A day of excitement in the parish in consequence of Miss Dingle's wedding and her wearing a *veil* supposed to be the first ever seen in Dereham.

A nuptial veil was spread over both the heads of the married couple at their nuptial mass in early Christian and medieval times. Whether this had any connection with the bridal veil is doubtful. Certainly its use died out long before the bridal veil came into vogue. An example is referred to in the Wardrobe Accounts of Edward II (*Archaeologia,* Vol. 26, 338) with regard to the marriage of the King's niece Isabella, to a son of the Earl of Arundel in 1321.

> Delivered for a veil to be spread over the heads of Richard . . . and Isabella . . . at their nuptial mass . . . one piece of Lucca cloth.

CHAPTER 5

TRADITIONAL WEDDING CUSTOMS

Before describing wedding garments in detail through the past centuries, a few words on the curious bridal customs of our ancestors will be given.

(a) *Wedding Favours*

Wedding favours were gifts to relations, friends and others connected with the wedding ceremony. The favours varied considerably, but gloves, scarves and garters were always on the list till the nineteenth century, and ribbon decorations were also included.

The *bride's garters*, worn during the wedding ceremony, were of great importance in the seventeenth and all through the eighteenth century. They were very elegant silk sashes tied below the knee and arranged there for a special purpose, so carefully described by Henri Misson in *c.* 1698 (*Memoirs & Observations in his Travels over England*, translated by J. Ozell, 1719):

> When bed-time is come, the bride-men pull off the bride's garters, which she had before unty'd that they might hang down and so prevent a curious hand from coming too near her knee. This done, and the garters being fasten'd to the Hats of the gallants, the bridesmaids carry the Bride into the bride-chamber, where they undress her and lay her in the bed.

In William Barnaby's play *The Reform'd Wife*, 1700, a lady dressing for her wedding says:

> This new Tower does not please me [a tall head-dress] . . . I forgot my Bridall Garters . . . O, no, They're on, what striving there'll be about 'em and pinching one's legs.

Herrick in his *Hesperides* (1648) says:

> Let the young Men and Bride-Maids share
> Your garters; and their joynts
> Encircle with the Bridegroom's points.

The "points" were decorative ties which were often worn in the young men's hats, as also were the garters themselves.

Which all the saints, and some since martyrs
Wore in their hats like wedding garters.

> Samuel Butler *Hudibras*, 1663

Garters were also worn by men officiating at a wedding.

> The bride had three very good great cakes . . .
> One Dosin of Gloves was disposed of to relations . . . .
> Her two bride men that led her to church have white garters a quarter of a
> yard deep with siller lace at ends. The favours were topenny, broade pinke
> colour satten ribbon eyed with narrow blake. (1667)
>
> *The Oxinden and Peyton Letters, 1642–70*

The myths connected with garters appear to have survived, in remote
districts, even into the twentieth century. In *Folk-Lore*, v. 19 (1908), we read:

> A trained nurse, a Scotswoman, born about five miles from Balmoral, tells
> me that in part of the country when a younger sister marries before the elder,
> the latter is forcibly made to wear green garters at the wedding, and any
> young man who takes them off is destined to be her future husband.

The bride's garters were generally blue, the colour associated with the
Virgin Mary, but they were sometimes red or white.

Ribbons generally known as bride laces and ribbon bows known as "knots"
were distributed as favours, royal specimens being greatly prized.

> . . . upon the 21st of May [1662] the King [Charles II] married the Queen
> [Catherine of Braganza] at Portsmouth in the presence Chamber of his
> Majesty's house . . . the Bishop of London declared them married . . .
> and then they caused the ribbons her Majesty wore to be cut in little pieces,
> and as far as it would go, everybody had some.
>
> *The Memoirs of Ann, Lady Fanshawe*

Henri Misson in his *Travels over England* (1698) describes them thus:

> T'other Day, when the eldest Son of M. de Overkerque marry'd the Duke of
> Ormond's sister, they dispers'd a whole inundation of these little Favours.

These consisted of bride laces in different colours, gold, silver, carnation and
white. They were worn on the hats for several weeks.

> Nothing else was here to be met with from the Hat of the King down to that
> of the meanest servant.
>
> (Ibid.)

In a letter from Mrs Pendarves to Mrs Granville she describes the wedding in 1724 of Margaret Rolle to Sir Robert Walpole, afterwards Earl of Orford.

> Dear Sister,
>   Yesterday I was to see the bride my Lady Walpole who was married the day before. She was excessively fine, in the handsomest and richest gold and white stuff that ever I saw, a fine point [lace] head and very fine brilliant earings and cross . . .
>   Everybody had favours that went, men and women—they are silver gauze six bows, and eight of gold narrow ribbon in the middle; they cost a guinea a piece: eight hundred has already been disposed of. Those the King, Prince, Princess and the young Princesses had were gold ribbon embroidered; they were six guines a piece.

In a letter in 1796 about the marriage of her son, Lady Stanley writes:

> Do ask . . . whether we may go colours flying tomorrow—that is to say, whether any objection lies to our bedecking our folks with favours, namely, cockades of white riband in their hats, for we think it would look mighty pretty along the High Road and announce to the people that we are a joyful train, and make them stare and say "Who's that?"
>   *The Early Married Life of Maria Josepha Lady Stanley,*
>   ed. by Jane H. Adeane

At Queen Victoria's wedding in 1840

> Every lady exhibited a white favour, some of which were admirable specimens of refined taste. They were of all sizes, many of white satin riband, tied up into bows and mixed with layers of rich silver lace. Others merely of riband intermixed with sprigs of orange flower blossom . . . here and there were seen bouquets of huge dimensions of riband and massive silver bullion having in their centre what might almost be termed a branch of orange blossoms. Large as they were, however, they were not more so than the apparent devotion to their owners . . . "Favours" didn't form a very general appendage with the male branch of the spectators [but many had them].
>   *The Times,* Feb. 11, 1840

Gloves too were important favours presented to the wedding guests. Even at the wedding of a Merchant's daughter in 1560

> . . . they gave a C [100] payre of glovys.
>   *Diary of Henry Machyn*

Not surprisingly they often did not fit.

Five or six pair of white innocent wedding gloves did in my sight choose
rather to be torne in pieces than drawne on.

> T. Dekker, *Satiromastix*, Act 1 (1602)

In 1611 the mother of a bridegroom writes:

I believe stockings and slippers is usual for lovers to give before the wedding
. . . I could not get so many woman's Jessamy gloves [gloves perfumed with
jasmine] as [she] wrote for: and at the last was fained to pick upon cordinent
[leather] for men and perfumed kid for women. I had them perfumed better
than ordinary that they might give content.

> *The Gurdon Papers*, 1611

Ben Jonson remarks in *The Silent Woman*, 1609:

We see no ensign of a wedding here, no character of a brideale—Where be
our scarves and our gloves?

Again:

My wooing's ended: now my wedding's neere
When gloves are giving . . .

> Robert Herrick, *Hesperides*, 1648

In the eighteenth century, on the matter of glove-giving, Sir Walter Calverley
records:

1700, 12 June. Was at the wedding of Mr William Calverley (a younger son
of Mr Calverley of Leeds) . . . and I led the bride to the church, had pair of
gloves and a favour [given me].
1706, 7 January. I was marryed to Miss Julia Blackett (eldest daughter of Sir
Wm. Blackett) . . . and my Lady was at cost of entertaining all friends and
relations upon this occasion. But I gave them gloves . . . a bill for gloves
bought at London . . . also for more gloves at Esholt and it cost me for my
own weding clothes, and a long wigg and liverys etc. near 300 l.

> *Yorkshire Diaries*, Vol. 1, 2

(b) Evergreens, Flowers, Orange Blossom

Evergreens and flowers were important wedding accessories in later times
and were given to and carried or worn by bridesmaids and guests. Gilded
rosemary and bay were particularly fashionable in the seventeenth century.

Nosegays and bride laces in their hats.

> Thomas Heywood, *A Woman Kilde with Kindnesse*, 1607

Come sit we under yonder Tree . . .
And talk of Brides; and who shall make
That wedding-smock, this Bridal cake:
That Dress, this Sprig, that Leaf, this Vine,
That smooth and silken Colombine.
This done, we'l draw lots, who shall buy
And gild the Bais and Rosemary.
What posies for our Wedding Rings:
What gloves we'd give and Ribaning.

       Robert Herrick, *Hesperides*, 1648

The symbolic significance of rosemary was very widespread in the seventeenth century. Rosemary used at weddings was often previously dipped in scented water. In his *Wonderful Year* (1603) speaking of a bride who died on her wedding day, T. Dekker says:

> Here's a strange alteration for the rosemary that was washed in sweet water to set out the bridall, is now wet in teares to furnish her buriall.

The strewing of rushes, herbs and flowers along the bridal path was a seventeenth-century custom.

> Enter Adriana and another strawing hearbes;
> *Adr.* Come straw a pace, Lord shall I never live
>   To walke to Church on flowers, O tis fine
>   To see a bride trip it to Church so lightly,
>   As if her new choppines would scorne to bruze
>   A silly flower?
>   Lodowicke Barry, *Ram-Alley or Merrie Tricks*, 1611

A protection to footwear, a chopine was an over-shoe consisting of a toe-cap fixed to a high stump-like sole of wood or cork.*

The wearing of flowers began in the eighteenth century and for country folk wild flowers were used.

In a letter from Pope to Lady Mary Montagu in 1718, there occurs this charming description† of a farm hand "John" and his milk-maid sweetheart.

---

* "Your ladyship is nearer heaven than when I was you last, by the altitude of a chopine." (1603) Shakespeare, *Hamlet*, II, ii.

† Taken from a letter of John Gay's, according to Thackeray in *The English Humourists of the 18th Century*, 1853.

20. Bridal pair coming out of church, with flowers strewn before
them by village maidens, *c.* 1860.
Mary Evans Picture Library (*contemporary print*).

. . . in the intervals of their work, they were talking of their wedding
clothes; and John was now matching several kinds of poppies and field
flowers to her complexion to make her a present of knots for the day.

Flowers strewn before the bride and bouquets carried by bridesmaids added
to wedding festivities also in the nineteenth century (see Fig. 20). Men, too,
usually wore a flower in the buttonhole. For example, the bride's brother,
in a fictional wedding of 1815:

Jos Sedley was splendid . . . in his light green coat there bloomed a fine
wedding favour, like a great white spreading magnolia.

Thackeray, *Vanity Fair,* 1847–8

21. "Things one would rather have left unsaid. Jones, 'I will'."
Bridegroom wearing a white button-hole favour.
Punch, *October 1881.*

An extra hole made for holding a flower in the top of the left lapel began to be tailored in the 1840s though it was then more usual to use the uppermost buttonhole for this purpose. By 1865 the "flower-hole" had gained the day and it sometimes had "a piece of broad ribbon put under the turn to hold a glass flower bottle" (*West End Gazette*, 1865). In Plate 16 rosettes representing flowers are seen pinned, for lack of buttonholes, to the sailor's blouse and the father's smock. White button-hole favours were usual in the nineteenth century.

Orange Blossom
The all-important question as to when *orange blossom* became the wedding flower *par excellence* is difficult to decide exactly, but it certainly began to be the fashion in the 1830s.

In America the bride in a white dress and veil was occasionally seen, but as often, she simply wore a wreath of white roses on her head.

American girls followed the *English* bridal custom of roses in the hair, and June, the month of roses, as the time to marry.

Orange blossoms, so definitely associated with the bride in our day, was a French fashion. To America, in 1838, from the South of France, came a goodwill shipment of the delicate blossoms, from which time our brides have worn orange blossoms on their wedding day.

Ruth T. Wilcox, *The Mode in Hats and Headdresses*, 1959

Empress Eugenie, at her marriage to Napoleon [III] in 1853 . . . wore . . . a small wreath of orange blossom [with her veil] and a coronet of sapphires.

(Ibid.)

By the 1840s it was well established and a number of orange blossom wreaths and bonnets trimmed with orange blossoms survive in Museums.

The bride was elegantly attired in a rich white gros de Naples, handsomely trimmed with Honiton lace, a beautiful veil of the same costly material and a chaplet of orange flowers.

The Stockport Advertiser, 1847

Like the Empress Eugenie, English princesses sometimes combined the blossom with a jewelled tiara. Princess Augusta, at her marriage in 1843, "wore on her head a wreath composed of orange flowers and myrtle and a tiara of sapphires and diamonds and was covered with a very large and most beautiful veil of point lace" (*Illustrated London News*, Vol. 3, 1843).

Orange blossom might even continue to decorate the head-dress of the bride's "going away costume".

. . . he found Rosa—we beg pardon, Mrs Jasper Goldspink, getting admired in her white Maltese lace bonnet with small white roses and orange flower buds, and her well set out light lavender coloured silk dress, surmounted by a large black Maltese lace mantle.

R. S. Surtees, *Plain or Ringlets*, 1860

(c) *Wedding Knives*

In the sixteenth and seventeenth centuries a curious symbol of the bride's married status, in addition to the wedding ring, was a pair of knives contained in one sheath.

> Here by my side do hang my wedding knives.
>> *King Edward III*, Act II, sc. ii (Author unknown, 1596)

The words are spoken by the Countess of Salisbury as she shows the King her two daggers.
Again:

> See at my girdle hang my wedding knives.
>> T. Dekker, *Match me in London*, 1631

In Samuel Rowland's play *Well Met Gossip*, 1619, a wife says she was wooed with gifts.

> In conscience I had twenty pair of gloves,
> When I was maid, given to that effect;
> Garters, knives, purses, girdles, store of rings
> And many a thousand dainty pretty things.

Presumably the knives were sharp, but sharp pins had to be avoided at all costs. There was a curious superstition about pins, mentioned by that careful observer of English customs, H. Misson, in 1698. The bridesmaids during the undressing or dressing of the bride

> must throw away and lose all the pins. Woe be to the bride if a single one is left about her; nothing will go right. Woe also to the Bridesmaids if they keep one of them, for they will not be marry'd before *Whitsuntide*.

(d) Stocking Throwing, Shoe Throwing

Two traditional practices connected with weddings must be mentioned as each involves a garment. The one is stocking throwing, the other, shoe throwing, and both were symbolic of good luck. The former came to an end in the eighteenth century, but the latter is of course practised to this day.

Stocking throwing is again ably described by Henri Misson (ibid.).

> The Bridegroom, who by the help of his Friends is undress'd in some other Room, comes in his Night-gown, as soon as possible to his Spouse who is surrounded by Mother, Aunt, Sister and Friends, and without further cere-mony gets into Bed. The Bride-men take the Bride's stockings, and the Bride-maids the Bridegroom's. Both sit down at the Bed's Feet, and fling the Stockings over their Heads, endeavouring to direct them so as they may fall upon the marry'd Couple. If the Man's stockings thrown by the Maids fall upon the Bridegroom's Head, it is a sign she will quickly be marry'd herself;

and the same Prognostick holds good for the Woman's stockings thrown by the Man.

Stocking throwing is mentioned in a letter to Edmund Verney, in 1675.

> We saw Sir Richard and his fine lady wedded . . . and flung the stocking and then left them to themselves and so in this manner ended the celebration of this Marriage à la Mode.
>
> *The Verney Memoirs*

The British Apollo of 1708 has this rhyme on the subject of stocking throwing.

> Q. *Apollo* say
>   Whence 'tis I pray,
> The Ancient Custom came;
>   Stockins to throw
>   (I'm sure you know)
> At Bridegroom and his Dame?

> A. When Britons Bold
>   Bedded of old
> Sandals were backward thrown;
>   The pair to tell
>   That ill, or well
> The Act was all their own.

As late as 1771 the practice is recorded by Smollett in *The Expedition of Humphry Clinker.*

> . . . Humphrey and his spouse, who were bedded in an upper room, with the usual ceremony of throwing the stocking.

Various explanations have been given as to the origin of shoe throwing, but all imply that it brought good luck.

According to a Sumptuary Law of 1291 in Hamburg, the bridegroom had to present his bride with a pair of shoes. Ancient tradition advised the girl to treasure these shoes if she wished to be kindly treated by her husband, for he would not beat her until they were worn out.

English folk-lore suggested that the shoe was a symbol of renunciation of authority over the bride by her father, and this was transferred to the bridegroom on receipt of the shoe. The luck here seems rather one-sided.

Shoe throwing was considered a lucky omen for travellers. The married couple, departing after the wedding ceremony, would need good luck on their journey, an undertaking usually involving some risk.

> And home again, hitherward
> > quick as a bee,
> Now for good lucke, cast
> > an old shoe after me.
> > > John Heywood, *Proverbs*, Pt. 1, Ch. 9 (1546)

> And whereso'er thou move, good luck
> Shall throw her old shoe after.
> > Tennyson, *Will Waterproof's Lyrical Monologue* (v. 27)

The left shoe was always to be preferred.

(e) Fertility Symbols

Wheat, later rice, and finally the mere symbol, confetti, were thrown over the couple after the ceremony, to promote their fruitfulness.

> As the bride enters the house, wheat is thrown upon her head.
> > Polydore Vergil, 1499

This and another fertility rite are described in the pleasing picture of a simple country wedding in 1796, given by the Rev. Henry Rowe (Rector of Rengshall, Suffolk) in his poem *The Happy Village*.

> The vestal zone which bound her slender waist,
> With valley's lilies fair Aminta grac'd.
> The wedding cake now thro' the ring was led, [cf. p. 101]
> The stocking thrown across the nuptial bed.
> The wheaten ear was scatter'd, near the porch,
> The green broom blossom'd strew'd the way to church.
> Now Sunday come, at stated hour of prayer,
> Or rain or shine, the happy couple there.
> Where nymphs and swains in various colours dight
> Gave pleasing contrast to the modest white
> . . . the plainer garb became the damsel best,
> Peerless in native innocence array'd
> The Bridegroom led the newly-brided Maid.

Passing portions of the wedding cake through the wedding ring was an eighteenth-century custom. It implied that bachelors and spinsters who partook of this cake would soon be married themselves. (See Jacob Houblon's wedding in 1761, p. 101.)

One constant feature of all weddings dating back to early Middle Ages is the wedding ring, the "tool of matrimony" as Butler called it (*Hudibras*). It is the golden link in the chain which connects wedding ceremonies of long ago with those of today and will therefore be described in the last chapter on wedding costume (ch. 9).

(*f*) Some Legal Curiosities

Of the many customs connected with dress that have grown up around the ceremony of marriage, some have even had a legal connotation.

A very curious Act passed in 1770 was aimed (without success) at abolishing cosmetics, lest the overscented belle might ensnare the innocent male by this means into matrimony.

> That all women of whatever age, rank, profession or degree, whether virgins, maids or widows that shall from and after such Act impose upon, seduce, and betray into matrimony any of his Majesty's subjects, by scents, paints, cosmetic washes, artificial teeth, false hair, Spanish wool★ . . . shall incur the penalty of the Law now in force against witchcraft and like misdeameanours, and that marriage, upon conviction shall stand null and void.

There were, however, husbands who approved of make-up.

> As soon as we are married I will make her put on rouge.
> Isaac Bickerstaffe, *Lionel and Clarissa*, 1768

There was a vulgar error lasting for several centuries to the effect that a man was not responsible for his wife's debts if she appeared, by being married in her smock or shift, to have no possessions. The Parish Register of Much Wenlock records in 1547

> Here was wedded Thomas M. Smith and Alice Nycols, which wedded to him in her Smock and bareheaded. ·
> J. C. Cox, *The Parish Registers of England*

Then in the eighteenth century we find in the Chilterne (Wilts) Register:

> John Bridmore and Anne Sellwood . . . were married Oct. 17, 1714. The aforesaid Anne Sellwood was married in her smock without any clothes or head gier on.

★ Wool impregnated with carmine and used as rouge.

Again, J. C. Cox (ibid.) quotes an entry in Prescott's *Journal*:

> (Feb. 12, 1774) . . . was married at Saddleworth . . . a Widower of about 30 years of age to Mary Bradley, a Widow near 70, but as the Bride was a little in Debt, the Bridegroom obliged her to be married in her shift, and the weather being very severe, threw her into such a violent fit of shaking as induced the compassionate Minister to cover her with his coat.

A bride in these circumstances, if she wore a shift, was said to be married "*en chemisette*". It was not unknown for her to be married actually naked (*Chambers' Book of Days* Vol. I p. 259).

An Act of Parliament in 1823, preceding the institution of marriages before Registrars, has some interest. It provided that church marriages lacking many of the usual formalities should yet be valid. Hence such a simple wedding as that shown in Plate 17.

CHAPTER 6

WEDDINGS OF ORDINARY PEOPLE

Since marriage was not only a solemn ceremony but also a joyful occasion, festivity and feastings were always associated with weddings and this implied appropriate garments not only for the bride and bridegroom but also for the wedding guests—in fact costume for the occasion was essential even for humble weddings. This is very aptly demonstrated in St Matthew's Gospel in the parable of the unworthy guest who was turned away from the wedding feast because he was shabbily dressed. Although this was an Eastern wedding, the source from which our picture (Pl. 18(*a*)) comes is English and the illustrator has depicted the guests and the host in garments that were worn in England in the early twelfth century. In episode (i) the host, who is turning away the unworthy guest, wears a blue tunic, red mantle, green hose, black boots and a "Phrygian Cap". The respectable guests, seated at the table, wear red or green mantles and have tidy hair. The imposter wears a green cloak over his nearly naked body showing his navel. In episode (ii) where he is seized by his untidy hair, his braies (pants) are seen to be long, an unfashionable peasant style, and he is bare-footed.

> The wedding feast is ready . . . When the king came in to see the company at table, he observed one man who was not dressed for a wedding. "My friend" said the king, "how do you come to be here without your wedding clothes?" He had nothing to say.
> *New English Bible*, St Matthew 22, vv 8, 11 and 12

The importance of wedding garments for all concerned is again shown in the following:

> . . . is supper ready, the house trimmed, rushes strewed, cobwebs swept; the serving-men in their new fustian, their white stockings and every officer his wedding garments on?
> Shakespeare, *The Taming of the Shrew*, IV, i, 47

Compared with aristocratic and royal weddings, illustrations of simple weddings are rare in medieval illuminated MSS. The example we give is from Hereford Cathedral Library, late thirteenth century (Pl. 18(b)).

Both bride and bridegroom are dressed in the usual fashions of their day. The bridegroom wears a supertunic known as a herigaut or garde-corps. It is hooded and has hanging sleeves with an opening through which the tight tunic sleeve passes. He is bare-headed. The bride wears a fur-lined mantle over her kirtle and on her head she has the usual barbette (linen chin strap) and fillet (linen crown) over a fret (hair net). The bishop in canonical dress helps the bridegroom to place a large gold wedding ring on the bride's finger.

The wedding festivities of a peasant in the reign of Queen Elizabeth I took the form of a martial sport in a Tilting Yard.

> . . . and after divine servis in the parish church . . . a solemn Brydeale of a proper coopl waz appointed; set in order in the Tylt-yard . . .
> And thus they were marshalld. Fyrst all the lustie lads and bolld bachelarz of the Parish, sutablie every wight with hiz blu buckeram bridelace upon a braunch of green broom (cause rozemary iz skant thear) tyed on his right hand, . . . too and too in rank: Sum with a hat, sum in a cap, sum in a cote, sum a jerkin, sum for lightness in hiz dooblet and his hoze, clean trust [trussed] with a point [lace] afore: Sum botes and no spurz, he spurs and no boots, and he neyther nother: . . . And these to the number of a sixteen wight riding men and well beseen.
>
> But the bridegroom formost, in his fartherz tawny worsted jacket (for his freends wear fayn that he shoold be a brydegroom before the Queen), a fayr strawn hat with a capitall crooun, steept wyze on hiz hed: a payr of harvest glovez on his hands, az a sign of good husbandry; a pen and inkhorn at his bak; for he woold be known as bookish: lame of a leg, that in his yooth was broken at football: well beloved yet of his mother, that lent him a nu mufflar for★ a napkin that was tyed too hiz girdl for lozyng.

After them, the cupbearer

> in his nu cut canvas dooblet.
> Then folloed the worshipful bride.

She, alas, is described as old and ugly and her apparel is not mentioned. She was followed by

> a dozen damsels for bride-maides.

The bridegroom's horse was too lively, but he kept his seat, though he

---

★ A square of material, like a handkerchief, folded diagonally and worn over the mouth and chin.

lost his pen and inkhorn that he waz redy to wep for; but his handkercher, az good hap waz, found hee safe at his gyrdl; that cheerd him sumwhat, and had good regard it should not be fyeld* . . . yet durst he be bollder too blo hiz noze and wype his face with the flapet of his fatherz jacket, then with his mother's mufflar 'tis goodly matter, when youth is manerly brought up, in fatherlie loove and motherly aw.

> John Nichols, *Progresses & Processions of Queen Elizabeth*, Edn. 1823,
> Vol. 1, The Queen at Kenilworth Castle 1575. Extract from a letter
> by R. Laneham, Merchant, written at the time

The wedding of a bride of "middle rank" is described in the *History of Jack Newbury* by Thomas Deloney, in 1597.

The bride, being attired in a gown of sheep's russet and a kirtle of fine worsted, attired with abillement [head ornament] of gold and her hair as yellow as gold hanging down behind her, which was curiously combed and plaited, she was led to church between two sweet boys with bride laces and rosemary tied about their silken sleeves. There was fair bride-cup of silver gilt carried before her, wherein was a goodly branch of rosemary, gilded very fair, hung about with silken ribands of all colours.

Musicians came next, then a groupe of maidens, some bearing great bride-cakes, others garlands of wheat finely gilded; and thus they passed into the church; and the bridegroom finely apparelled, with the young men followed close behind.

A countryman's dislike of costume for the occasion is described by himself in a letter to a friend, Mr Ironside, in 1713.

I have lately married a very pretty Body, who being something younger and richer than myself, I was advised to go'a wooing to her in a finer suit of cloathes than I ever wore in my Life, for I love to Dress plain, and suitable to a Man of my rank. However I gained her Heart by it. Upon the Wedding-day I put my self according to Custom, in another suit Fire-new, with silver Buttons to it. I am so out of Countenance among my Neighbours upon being so fine, that I heartily wish my Cloathes well worn out. I fancy every Body observes me as I walk the Street, and long to be in my old plain Geer again. Besides, forsooth, they have put me in a Silk Night-gown and a gaudy Fool's Cap and make me now and then stand in the Window with it. I am asham'd to be dandled thus, and cant look in the Glass without blushing to see myself turned into such a pretty little Master. They tell me I must appear in my

---

* Soiled (Fylyng = defiling).

22. (*a*) Ordinary marriage, early 17th century. Fashions of the day,
rather than distinctive wedding attire, but note bridelace tied round
attendant girl's sleeve. Bride's hair no longer worn loose. Parson in
gown without surplice (Puritan style).
Woodcut to Ballad "Easter Wedding" reproduced in John Ashton
A Century of Ballads.

Wedding Suit for the first Month at least; after which I am resolved to come
again to my every Day's Cloaths, for at present every day is *Sunday* with
me . . . As bad as I hate my Silver-button'd coat, and silk Night-Gown, I
am afraid of leaving them off, not knowing whether my Wife wont repent
of her Marriage when she sees what a plain Man she has to her Husband. Pray
Mr Ironside, write something to prepare her for it, and let me know whether
you think she can ever love me in a Hair Button.
P.S. I forgot to tell you of my white Gloves, which they say too, I must wear
all the first Month.

                                  The Guardian (1713), Vol. 2, p. 115

In the next account, given by Sarah, Duchess of Marlborough, of a
humble wedding in 1733, the bride's dress is unfortunately omitted.

22. (b) Ordinary marriage, 1794. Again no distinctive attire. The bride's dress is blue, not white; her head-dress and low-necked jacket-bodice (grey) were fashionable day wear at this date. Bridegroom's "square cut" waistcoat came into vogue in 1790s.

Coloured print "The Wedding", dated 1794. (Author's collection.)

I have a mind to give you an account of a very fine ceremony performed this morning at Windsor Church, a marriage between my maid in the kitchen and one of the carters . . . The man is more than 60, the woman 30 . . . The procession to church was very fine . . . His hair was powdered, a flourished [trimmed with lace] cravat, a very good suit of clothes with brass buttons and in short he was better dressed than ever I saw the Right Honourable Horatio Walpole . . .* There were bride-maids and bride-men . . . As soon as the ceremony was performed, the bridegroom with a very white pair of gloves would lead his lady himself to lodge where they are to have dinner in plenty and state.

Letters of a Grandmother 1732–1735. Being the correspondence of Sarah Duchess of Marlborough with her granddaughter Diana Duchess of Bedford

In Hogarth's painting of "The Marriage", 1735, from "The Rake's Progress", the couple are wearing dress clothes of the period (Pl. 19).† The bridegroom is preparing to put the wedding ring on the bride's finger. She is a lame but well endowed old widow. Her dress is being adjusted at the back by a maid.

In "The Wedding" of 1794 the young couple are in ordinary day clothes (Fig. 22 (b)).

The humble maid Pamela, about to be married to a man far above her station in life (see Pl. 20), describes her wedding dress thus:

I was dressed in the suit of white, flowered with silver, a rich head-dress, and the diamond necklace, ear-rings etc. I mentioned before: and my dear Sir in a fine laced silk waistcoat, of blue Paduasoy,‡ and his coat a pearl-coloured fine cloth with gold buttons and button-holes, and lined with white silk. I said, I was too fine, and would have laid aside some of the jewels; but he said it would be thought a slight to me from him, as his wife.

S. Richardson, *Pamela,* 1740

A dislike of finery is shown in Fielding's description of the wedding of Joseph Andrews, whose bride was married in the informal dress known as a nightgown (see Fig. 23).

At length the happy day arrived which was to put Joseph in the possession of all his wishes. He arose and dressed himself in a neat but plain suit of Mr.

* Uncle of Horace Walpole.

† Since this is an engraving after the painting, the picture is in reverse and the bride's hand for the ring appears to be her right hand, which is incorrect.

‡ A strong corded silk.

23. Wedding of Joseph Andrews (Fielding). The procession to church
is led by the parson in gown and "tricorne" hat.
From an illustration by J. Hulet dated 1742/3.

Booby's which exactly fitted him, for he refused all finery; as did Fanny likewise who could be prevailed on by Pamela to attire herself in nothing richer
than a white dimity night-gown. Her shift indeed which Pamela presented
her was of the finest kind and had an edging of lace round the bosom; she
likewise equipped her with a pair of fine white thread stockings which were
all she would accept: for she wore one of her own short round-eared caps and
over it a little straw hat lined with cherry-coloured silk and tied with a cherry-
coloured ribbon. In this dress she came forth from her chamber, blushing and
breathing sweets . . . and was by Joseph . . . led to the church . . .

The History of Joseph Andrews, 1742

The wedding clothes of Joseph Nollekens the sculptor and his bride in 1772 are very fully described in *Nollekens and his Times* by John Thomas Smith.

The lady's interesting figure, on her wedding day was attired in a sacque and petticoat [i.e. skirt] of the most expensive brocaded white silk, resembling net-work, enriched with small flowers, which displayed in the variation of the folds a most delicate shade of pink, the uncommon beauty of which was greatly admired. The deep and pointed stomacher was exquisitely gimped and pinked, and at the lower part was a large pin consisting of several diamonds, confining an elegant point-laced apron; certainly at that period rather un-fashionable, but, on this happy event, affectionately worn by the lady in memory of her dear mother, who had presented it to her . . . The sleeves of this dress closely fitted the arm to a little below the elbow, from which hung three point-lace ruffles of great depth. A handkerchief of the same costly texture partly concealed the beauty of her bosom; wherein, confined by a large bow, was a bouquet of rose-buds, the delicate tints of which were imperceptibly blended with the transparency of her complexion, and not a little increased the beauty of a triple row of pearls, tied behind with a narrow white satin ribbon.

Her beautiful auburn hair, which she never disguised by the use of powder, according to the fashion of the day, was, upon this occasion arranged over a cushion made to fit the head to a considerable height, with large round curls on either side; the whole being surmounted by a small cap of point-lace, with plaited flaps to correspond with the apron and ruffles.

Her shoes were composed of the same material as her dress, ornamented with silver spangles and square Bristol buckles,★ with heels three inches and a half in height; as if she meant to exult in out-topping her little husband, whose head, even when he had his hat on, reached no higher than her shoulder.

. . . . . .

The bridegroom's dress was a suit of Pourpre du Pape [purple velvet], silk stockings with broad blue and white stripes and lace ruffles and frill, the whole of which articles he had bought from Rome. His hair was dressed in curls on either side with an immense toupee and finished with a small bag† tied as closely as possible to his neck.

★ These buckles were large and set with Bristol stones which were rock crystals.

† The bag-wig of the eighteenth century, and often simply called "a bag", had the queue of the wig enclosed in a square black silk bag, drawn in at the nape of the neck with a running string concealed by a stiff black bow. This was a wig worn with "dress" or "full dress" suits.

With cynical smile at the efforts to bedeck a blushing bride, a contributor to the *Universal Magazine* of 1776 wrote this rhyme.

> Give Chloe a bushel of horse-hair and wool
> Of paste and pomatum a pound,
> Ten yards of gay ribbon to deck her sweet skull,
> And gauze to encompass it round.
> Let her flaps fly behind for a yard at the least,
> Let her curls meet just under her chin;
> Let these curls be supported to keep up the jest
> With a hundred instead of one pin.
> Let her gown be tucked up to the hip on each side,
> Shoes too high for to walk or to jump,
> And to deck the sweet creature complete for a bride
> Let the cork-cutter make her a rump.

At this date the fashionable coiffure reached fantastic heights and the first two lines of this verse refer to some of the methods used to raise the structure.

In a less humble marriage, the nightgown again appears as the wedding dress of a bride in 1786.

> Her dress was a silver muslin night-gown trimmed with white satin, a very fine sprigged muslin apron,* and handkerchief trimmed with beautiful lace, and white and silver shoes . . .

The bridegroom

> was in a dark green coat, with a very pretty waistcoat.
> *The Autobiography and Correspondence of Mary Granville*, 2nd Series,
> 1862 (Letter of Miss Clayton about her sister's wedding)

In "A Marriage Procession to Church" in *c.* 1765 (Pl. 21(a)) all are dressed in the fashion of the day, without anything suggestive of a wedding. "The Wedding" of 1832 is a simple country affair (Pl. 21(b)).

The wedding of a middle-aged Major to a girl of rather inferior middle-class status is described by Susan Ferrier in her novel *The Inheritance*, 1824. For the dinner the night before:

> Uncle Adam (a dour Scot) was the first to arrive wearing in his button hole a very fine Camellia Japonica, together with a piece of southernwood but he protested that the camellia was a senseless thing without any smell and gave it to a lady guest who adjusted the japonica in her dress.

* The apron at this date was often an elegant accessory.

On the wedding morning:

> The family [were] all in full dress. The Major looked the gay bridegroom
> from top to toe. The beauteous bride [was] decked in India muslin—a full
> dressed head, done up with a profusion of beads and braids, and bands and
> bows—a pocket handkerchief at her face . . . [She] sobbed and had even
> the vulgarity to blow her nose.

The bride's going away "travelling habit" consisted of

> . . . a navy blue riding habit (the Major's favourite colour) allowed to sit
> uncommonly well—a black beaver hat and feathers—yellow boots—gold
> watch and brooch containing the Major's hair, set round with pearls.

A humble wedding, as taking place in 1815, is described by Thackeray in
Vanity Fair.

> The bride was dressed in a brown silk pelisse (as Captain Dobbin has since
> informed me) and wore a straw bonnet with a pink ribbon: over the bonnet
> she had a veil of white Chantilly lace . . . Captain Dobbin himself had
> asked leave to present her with a gold chain and watch, which she sported
> on this occasion; and her mother gave her her diamond brooch.

In 1873 we have the description of a housemaid's sister who was married
to a blacksmith in a village church in Norfolk.

> . . . the bride who wore a grey silk gown, a white cape and white tulle
> bonnet with orange blossom, in which she looked very nice . . . one brides-
> maid who wore a green silk gown striped with yellow, a white cape and
> bonnet.

Rice and old slippers were thrown at the couple afterwards. (*Life among the
Troubridges.*)

The wedding clothes of a coster and his bride in 1894 are described by
George Newnes in an article in the *Strand Magazine*, Vol. 8 (See Fig. 24):

> Bridegroom and bride have spared no resource of alleydom to insure the
> most presentable appearance possible. His billycock hat is turned well down
> at the ends of the brim and well up at the sides; he wears a velveteen coat
> with numerous pearl buttons, flannel shirt and gorgeous necktie, and
> trousers which fit closely about the thighs and from the knee downwards are
> suggestive of a giant candle-extinguisher. She wears a large hat with a feather
> or combination of feathers . . . a long black jacket, a bright red dress and a
> white kerchief round her neck.

Next we come to clandestine marriages, for example those at the Fleet Prison, and subsequently to the run-away marriages at Gretna Green.★ The Fleet had a chapel of its own and a chaplain so that marriages might be celebrated there.

Towards the mid-seventeenth century, owing to the cost of public weddings, clandestine marriages became very prevalent, and Fleet parsons

24. "A Coster Bride", 1894. See text p. 86.
John Gülich in The Strand Magazine *Vol. 8,
July–December.*

did a roaring trade in irregular marriages, not only in the chapel, but in neighbouring taverns and elsewhere. Any misgivings that the candidates for marriage might have were dispelled by the appearance of the parson, who was attired in orthodox canonicals—though often rather old and dirty. He kept his marriage registers in pocket notebooks, some of which have survived. Hence the following extracts quoted in the *Cornhill Magazine* 1867

(1) John & Elisabeth, Aug: 30th 1737 at Mr Sandey's, the Fleet. He said he belonged to the sea and had his own hair [not the usual wig].
(2) Dec: 12th 1739. About ye Hour of 10 in ye Evening there came 2 men and one woman . . . the man yt [that] was married appear'd by Dress as

★ The Act providing for civil marriages before Registrars was not passed till 1836.

a gentleman of fortune and ye woman yt was married like a Lady of Quality . . . pd a g [guinea] in all and went away without telling their names.

Ye Gentlewoman when married had on a floured [*sic*] Silk Round Gown and after she was married she pulls off her flower'd Gown and underneath she had a Large full Black Silk Gown on and went away in ye same.

(3) Oct. 1741. Robt . . . married. Poold of [pulled off] his coat because it was black.

The wedding ring was often loaned for the occasion, and in one instance in 1742 the married couple

Behaved very Vilely, and attempted to Run away with Mrs Crooks Gold Ring.

Article "*The Fleet Parsons and Fleet Marriages*" in *Cornhill Magazine*, 1867

It was at the Mayfair Chapel★ that the beautiful Miss Gunning was hastily married to the 4th Duke of Hamilton at half-past twelve at night in 1752 with, according to Horace Walpole, "a ring of the bed-curtain" (*The Letters of Horace Walpole, Earl of Oxford*, ed. Peter Cunningham 1857).

An amusing description of the Fleet district is given by Thomas Pennant in his *Account of London*, 1790.

In walking along the Street in my youth on the side next to the prison, I have often been tempted by the question, *Sir will you be pleased to walk in and be married?* Along this most lawless space was hung up the frequent sign of a male and female hand conjoined, with *Marriages performed within*, written beneath.

A dirty fellow invited you in. The parson was seen walking before his shop, a squalid profligate figure clad in a tattered plaid night gown, with a fiery face and ready to couple you for a dram of gin or roll of tobacco.

Fleet marriages were said to be abolished by Act of Parliament in 1753.

Last of all in this series of humble weddings we come to the Gretna Green marriages.

This village became notorious from the 1770s for the celebration of irregular marriages contracted by runaway couples from England. (These marriages were rendered invalid, unless one of the parties had resided for some weeks in Scotland, by an Act passed in 1856.)

★ Used by Fleet parsons.

The weddings were conducted by the ferryman, the toll-keeper, or the blacksmith on his premises, and the ring apparently proved the validity of the marriage. A labourer performing this ceremony is quoted as having said:

Put on the ring . . . the thing is done, the marriage is complete.

No wedding clothes were worn; the couple always appeared in travelling dress.

A hand-coloured print of 1792 entitled *Gretna Green, a Red Hot Marriage*, has this caption:

O Mr Blacksmith ease our Pains
And tie us fast in Wedlock Chains.

25. "The Marriage [by a blacksmith] Gretna Green" *c.* 1834. Bride in white dress, red cloak with fur cape and feather trimmed bonnet. Bridegroom in long blue cloak, top hat, brown coat and white trousers.
After a contemporary coloured print.

GRETNA.

26. "Gretna". The bride in the fashion of the day, the bridegroom in
uniform. 1834.
Contemporary print.

The bridegroom is wearing a grand naval uniform. He places a ring on the
fourth finger of the bride's left hand. The bride has a ground-length overcoat
with a cape which, being open in front, shows a dark green skirt with a pink
sash. She wears a tall straw hat trimmed and tied on with pink ribbon. This is
worn over a white undercap and her hair flows loose to the shoulders.

One of the registers of Gretna Green has this announcement:

William—and Sarah—; he dressed in a gold waistcoat like an officer; she a beautiful young lady, with two fine diamond rings and a black high-crowned hat and very well dressed—at Boyce's.

Mr Knight's *Old England*

Two illustrations are given for 1834, one marriage taking place in a blacksmith's forge, the other in his sitting-room (Figs. 25 and 26).

CHAPTER 7

GRAND WEDDINGS

From the fourteenth to the early seventeenth century it was the custom for any bride to be married with her hair hanging down her back, the recognized symbol of virginity.★

> Come, come, my Lord, untie your folded thoughts
> And let them dangle loose, as a bride's hair.
> John Webster, The White Devil, IV, 1 (1612)

Fashionable hair styles were discarded, even sometimes by the bridesmaids, but crowns, jewels and gold circlets might be worn by all ranks. "Married in her hair" was the expression used and this is shown in many illustrations (Pl. 22b).

The marriage of Princess Margaret, Henry VII's daughter, who was only 14 years old, to King James IV of Scotland, in 1503, is very fully described in part of a MS. "written by John Younge, Somerset Herald who attended her on her journey". The following is a short extract.

> The Kyng was in a Gowne of Whit Damaske figured with Gold and Lynned with Sarcenet. He had on a Jakette with Slyffs [sleeves] of cramsyn satin, the Lists [borders] of Blak Velvett, under that sam a Doublet of Cloth of Gold, and a payre of Scarlette Hosys [stockings]. His Shurt broded with Thred of Gold, hys Bonnet Blak, with a ryche Balay [ruby] and hys Swerd about hym.
> The Qwene was arayd in a rich Robbe lyke Hymselfe, borded of Cramsyn Velvet and lyned of the self. Sche had a varey riche Coller of Gold, of Pyerrery [jewels] and Perles, round her neck, and the Croune upon hyr Hed. Her hayr hangyng. Betwixt the said Croune and the Hayres was a varey riche coyfe hangyng downe behynde the whole length of the body.
> Leland, Collectanea, Vol. 4

The bride's "hair hanging" is shown in Henry V's marriage (see Fig. 30).

Anne of Cleves on the day of her marriage to Henry VIII in 1540 was

attired in cloth of gold, embroidered with flowers in pearl, on her head a

★ A queen at her coronation might do the same, even when a wife. Cf. Pl. 39(b).

coronet of gold and precious stones set full of branches of rosemary. Her long yellow hair, no longer confined by a caul, hung over her shoulders.

Archaeologia, XXVII, p. 70. The Loseley MSS. ed. by A. J. Kempe

Stow, in his *Survey of London*, tells of the marriage of three daughters of a wealthy London scrivener, in 1560:

They were in their hair and goodly apparel set out with chains, pearls and stones. Thus they went to Church all three, one after the other with three goodly caps garnished with laces, gilt and fine flowers and rosemary strewed for their home coming, and so to their father's house, where a great dinner was prepared.

The wedding of Princess Elizabeth (daughter of James I) to Frederick the Elector Palatine (later King of Bohemia) was very magnificent. They were married in Westminster Abbey in 1613 when the Princess was but 15 years old. She too wore her hair hanging down and the following describes her apparel.

Upon her head a crown of refined golde, made Imperiall by the pearles and diamonds thereupon placed, which were so thicke beset that they stood like shining pinnacles upon her amber-coloured haire dependantly hanging, playted down over her shoulders to her waiste, between every plaight a roll or liste of gold-spangles, pearles, rich stones and diamonds and withall, many diamonds of inestimable value embroidered upon her sleeves . . .

Leland, *Collectanea*, Vol. 5, 33. Mr Anstis's Narrative

"Her vestments where white, the emblem of Innocency . . ." Her train was borne

by Twelve young Ladies in White Garments so adorned with jewels that her Passage looked like a Milky Way.

W. Kennett, *A Complete History of England*, Vol. 2, p. 690

The number of bridesmaids differs in the various accounts but from the "Warrant to the Great Wardrobe" we learn of the gorgeous material ordered for "eleven bryde maydens". Seven had gowns of cloth of silver, all had "silver loop lase" trimmings and detachable sleeves made of "several colord tyssues" (B.M. MS. Add 575 B, f. 27).

For marriage by proxy ordinary clothes were worn (see Fig. 27).

The fashion for hair flowing loose came to an end in the later seventeenth century. At the wedding of William of Orange, father of William III, and Mary, eldest daughter of Charles I, in 1641

27. Marriage by Proxy of Mary Tudor aged 11 or 12 (daughter of
Henry VII). In 1508 the Sieur de Bergues, Emperor Charles V's repre-
sentative, married Mary by proxy in the royal chapel of the Tower.
The marriage was never fulfilled. The picture shows Mary in a plain,
trained gown and English hood and, presumably in her honour, the
attendants carry a Tudor rose.
Wood-cut in P. Carmelianus Carmen de Sponsalibus, 1508.

The Bridegroom, apparelled in a suite and Cloak of unshorne Velvet richly
embroidered with silver . . .
    The Bride habited in White embroidered with Silver, her Hair tyed up
with Silver Ribbands, not dishevilled about her Shoulders as in former Times
used, her Head adorned with a Garland of Pendant Pearls . . . unmarried
Ladies habited in White Satin immediately following her . . . her Trayne
born by young unmarried Ladies . . .

Leland, *Collectanea*, Vol. 5, 343.

Even in the eighteenth century, however, if a bride had pretty hair she
might wear it unconfined on her wedding day. Narcissa, the bride

was dressed in a sack [a sack-backed gown] of white satin, embroidered on the breast with gold; the crown of her head was covered with a small French cap, from whence, descended her beautiful hair in ringlets that waved upon her snowy neck, which dignified the necklace I had given her; her looks glowed with modesty and love: and her bosom, through the veil of gauze that shaded it, afforded a prospect of Elysium.

Tobias Smollett, *The Adventures of Roderick Random*,
Vol. 3, p. 208 (1748)

The outstanding feature of all wedding garments has always been the bride's wedding dress. In medieval days it followed the contemporary fashion, but was of richer material, and with Royal or aristocratic weddings the accessories were very costly.

Here is Chaucer's delightful description of the wedding dress prepared for Patient Griselda (end of the fourteenth century).

> . . . the marquis bade prepare
> Brooches and rings, all for Griselda lit
> With jewels, gold and lapis; he took care
> Her wedding-garment should be made to fit,
> But by another girl they measured it,
> Who was of equal stature; gems were sewn
> On it to grace a wedding like his own
>
> . . . . . .
> They combed her hair that fell but rudely tressed
> With slender hands as if preparatory
> To coronation, and a crown was pressed
> Upon her head with gems of changeful glory.

Geoffrey Chaucer, *The Canterbury Tales*.
Translated into Modern English by Nevill Coghill

Accounts and illustrations of royal weddings date back to the Middle Ages, and some are very fully recorded.

In a MS. of 1250–9[1] the marriage, in 1236, of Isabella, Henry III's sister, to the Emperor Frederick, is represented. Both bridegroom and bride wear crowns and long gowns and mantles. The Emperor holds a ring ready to put on the bride's finger (Fig. 28).

In the marriage of King Offa I, as depicted by Matthew Paris[2] in the middle of the thirteenth century, the bride is very simply clothed in a mantle over a kirtle and on her head she wears the usual medieval head-dress known as a

28. Marriage of Emperor Frederick to Isabella,
sister of Henry III.
After drawing in 1250–9 by Matthew Paris. B.M.
MS. Roy. 14 C VII f. 123v.

veil or coverchief. It is not a bride's veil in the modern sense. The King wears
a crown and a hooded mantle over a long tunic. He places a ring on the
bride's finger. The two attendants both wear the typical stalked caps of the
period and the man behind the king has on the new style of overgarment
called a garde-corps or herigaut (Fig. 29).

The trousseau of Princess Philippa, daughter of King Henry IV at her
marriage to Eric of Denmark is well documented. The Princess was married
in 1406 at the age of 12. Her wedding dress was:

> a tunic and mantle with long train of white satin worked with velvet, furred
> with pured miniver (i.e. white fur) and purfled with ermine; and the sleeves
> of the tunic also furred with ermine.
>
> *Archaeologia*, Vol. 47

At the marriages of Sir John Nevill's two daughters, Elizabeth and Mary,
a list with the cost of materials and garments is given in detail.

Elizabeth was married to Roger Rockley in 1526 and among the garments
supplied are "a pair of perfumed gloves 3s. 4d.—Item for a pair of other
gloves 4d."

Mary was married to Gervys Clifton in 1530 and her trousseau included
"3 boxes to carry bonnets in 1s." Both daughters were well equipped both
for the wedding day and after. (Whitaker, T. D., *History and Antiquities of
the Deanery of Craven*, 3rd edn., ed. A. Morant.)

Et cum super hoc negocio si
follicitarentur ⁊ alloquerem
ciens ioculando ⁊ talia ilia ai
dia fuisse uanitatis procerū ?

29. Marriage of King Offa I.
Drawing, by Matthew Paris, mid-13th century, B.M. MS. Cot. Nero
D I f. 6v.

Fig. 30 shows the marriage of Henry V to Katherine of Valois, as imagined by a draughtsman working in *c.* 1485. The King wears his crown and robes of estate and his bride a similar crown and a furred gown and mantle. The King is attended by his lords; two are wearing peers' robes and spiked coronets and Katherine is accompanied by her ladies, two of whom are wearing coronets. One holds up the queen's train.

The marriage of Princess Margaret, sister of King Edward IV, to Charles Duke of Burgundy in 1468 is thus described:

> The Duke came in the morninge betwyxt 5 and 6 of the cloke, thei weare weddid by the Bishope of Salisbury and the Bishope of Turnaye . . . And my Ladie was sett in a litter, richelie emparreillide wt. Clothe of Golde

30. Marriage of Henry V to Katherine of Valois. Note the bride's hair
falling down her back. (Depicted in *c.* 1485.)
After B.M. MS. Julius E IV art. 6 f. 22.

cremysine, hir surcot and hir mantell whit clothe of golde, furred wt.
ermyne and she herself richlye corroned.

Archaeologia, Vol. 31, 326

Pl. 22(a) and (b) show royal wedding costumes of the period 1470–80,
though the marriages portrayed are of earlier dates. The nobility of the company is shown by the lavish use of fur, especially ermine, in the gowns of the
wedding couples and the tippets (capes) of the attending peers. Although depicted in the same MS., curiously enough the King-bridegrooms are shown,
one wearing his crown (a) and the other bareheaded (b). In both pictures a
bridesmaid bears up the very long train worn by the bride, who may or may
not wear a coronet. She and the bridesmaids (in (a)) have steeple head-dresses,
without flowing hair. In (b) the hair of the bride and bridesmaids flows loose.

The bishop's cope (in (a)) is particularly magnificent. The youth behind the king (? "best man") in the same picture wears a new style of hat and under his gown, as also under the king's, can be seen a doublet laced across a stomacher in the latest fashion.

Princess Mary, daughter of Henry VII, married Louis XII of France in 1514. They were both apparelled in "goldsmith's work"[3]—very different from her simple Proxy marriage attire shown in Fig. 27.

The marriage of Queen Mary to Philip (later Philip II) of Spain was also very grand. One slightly unusual feature is the fact that the bride's train was carried by men and not maids.

> . . . the Prince, richly appareled in Cloth of Gould imbroydered, accompanied with a great nomber of Nobles of Spaine in such Sorte as the like hath not beene seene, proceeded to the Church and entered in at the West Dore, and passed to his Traverse all the way on Foote: and to the Church he had noe sword borne before him. [Out of deference to the Queen.]
> Then came the Queene's Majesty, accompanied with a great Nomber of the Nobilitie of the Realme with sword being borne before her by the Earl of Darby and a great nomber of Ladyes and Gentlewomen very richly appareled. Her Majestie's trayne was borne by the Marquess of Winchester, assisted by Sir John Gage her Lo-Chamberlaine.
>
> Leland, *Collectanea*, Vol. 4, taken from
> "A Book of Presidents examined in 1634 by William le Neve".

Pl. 23 shows the marriage of Charles II to Catherine of Braganza in 1662. The King wears petticoat breeches, the latest fashion, trimmed with multiple ribbon loops called "fancies". The turnover tops of his boot hose are elegant and conspicuous. His bride on the other hand is old-fashioned for England. Both John Evelyn and Pepys remark disapprovingly on the farthingale worn, which went out of fashion in England in about 1620.

> The Queen arrived with . . . Portugese ladies in their monstrous fardingales . . . Her Majesty in the same habit, her foretop long and turned aside very strangely.
>
> *The Diary of John Evelyn*, Vol. I

Wedding gowns, whatever their fashion, always had long trains (See Pl. 10(b) and 24), except, as a rule, with crinolines.

The noticeable feature of the Princess Anne's wedding dress when she married the Prince of Orange in 1734 seems to have been the train. The Bride in her Virgin robes of silver tissue, having a train six yards long laced round with massy lace, adorned with fringe and tassels; on the sleeves were several bars of diamonds.

The London Magazine or Gentleman's Monthly Intelligencer

The wedding of George III and Princess Charlotte of Mecklenburg in 1761 is fully recorded by the first Duchess of Northumberland. The bride's jewellery was what most impressed her.

The Bride was dressed in a silver Tissue stiffen body'd Gown, embroidered and trimmed with Silver, on her Head a little cap of purple Velvet quite covered with Diamonds, a Diamond Aigrette in Form of a Crown, 3 dropt Diamond Ear Rings, Diamond Necklace, Diamond Sprigs of Flowers on her Sleeves and to clasp back her Robe a Diamond Stomacher, her purple Velvet Mantle was laced with Gold and lined with Ermine.

· · · · · ·

The King was dressed in a Stuff of a new manufacture, the Ground Silver flower with embossed plate and frosted Silver and wearing the Collar.

The Diaries of a Duchess 1716–1776. Ed. by James Grieg

Horace Walpole, who was present at this wedding, gives a similar account of the bride's attire. He was obviously impressed by the weight and length of the train, which needed to be carried by ten bridesmaids.

The Queen was in white and silver, an endless mantle of violet coloured velvet, lined with ermine, and attempted to be fastened on her shoulder by a bunch of large pearls, dragged itself and almost the rest of her clothes halfway down her waist . . . [She wore] a stomacher of diamonds, worth three score thousand pounds, which she is to wear at the coronation too.

Horace Walpole and his World, Select Passages from his Letters.

Ed. by L. B. Seeley

As a change from royalty, there are fascinating details about the wedding of a landed country gentleman, Jacob Houblon, to a future heiress, in the diary of the Rev. Stotherd Abdy who married the couple in 1770.

This was the Day of Days . . . I drest myself in my new Habit ready for the celebration of the Ceremony and everybody except the intended Bride herself, seated at the Breakfast in the Parlour, in new and elegant undresses [morning wear] by ten o'clock. Soon after eleven o'clock, Mr Archer handed his eldest Daughter [the bride] down from Lady Mary's dressing Room. Her apparell was a night gown [day wear] of silver Muslin with silver Blond* Hat and cap admirably adapted to the gown. Mr Houblon in white and silver led his future Mother: Mr J. Houblon [led] the Bride-Maid, Miss Charlotte Archer, who looked enchantingly in an undress of white Lustring† ornamented with Silver Blond, with the serpentine Line of Beauty hanging pendent from her neck in the appearance of a Silver Snake . . .

We past through a Lane of Tenants and a group of servants in new rich Liveries to the Church . . .

After the service and a walk round the garden

we came again into the Drawing Room, where a profusion of Bride Cake was placed ready for refreshment and salvers of rich wine. The Bride and Bridegroom's healths were drank and pieces of cake were drawn properly thro' the Wedding Ring for the *dreaming* Emolument of many spinsters and Bachelors (cf. pp. 74 and 75).

After this we all parted to dress ourselves before dinner and by three o'clock there was assembled below stairs a set of Ladies and gentlemen drest with uncommon elegance. The Bride looked enchantingly in a very rich white and silver sack with a Hoop, a suit of very fine Point Lace and all her diamonds.

The Bridegroom in a rich suit with silver and shaded of colours in the Lace: His Hair drest to the Life and Bag‡ and solitaire§ . . . Miss Archer . . . the charming Bride-maid, the soft emblem of Innocency, was in a Robe of a most beautiful blue and white stripe with flowers of silver and colours.

. . . . . .

Mrs Abdy [the parson's wife] was in a new silk of Brown, with Brocaded Flowers. . . .

Mr Shirley in a handsome suit of Cloaths new for the occasion and an enchanting Wig made by the twister of Crines‖ at Newbury.

Last of all Parson Abdy himself:

After disrobing . . . put on all he had a right to, which was a plain superfine grey Frock¶ and waistcoat that had never been on his back before.

* Blonde = a type of silk lace.
† Lustring = a fine taffeta.
‡ Bag = bag wig.
§ Solitaire = a black ribbon worn with a stock and usually with a bag wig.
‖ Crine = hair.
¶ In the eighteenth century a frock (for a man) was a morning coat, always with a turn-down collar. It was often worn for comfort, being looser than the dress coat.

After we had sufficiently admired each others dresses . . . we were called
to another scene.

Extract from the Rev. S. Abdy's Diary in
Lady Alice A. Houblon's *The Houblon Family*, Vol. 2

Towards the end of the eighteenth century, even for aristocratic weddings,
the bride often wore a hat instead of a wreath and veil. The hat too might
have a veil, but this was optional. Horace Walpole's niece was married in a
hat.

> May 16, 1759. Well! Maria was married yesterday. Maria was in a white
> silver gown with a hat very much pulled over her face.
>
> *Selected Letters of Horace Walpole* Edn. 1926, p. 231

Mary Curzon in a letter to Miss Heber in 1778 writes:

> As soon as breakfast was over we went to Church. Sir George and my sister
> look'd beautiful.
>
> She was dress'd in a white figured Sattin gown, a fring'd silk petticoat
> [skirt], white silk fring'd slippers, a beautiful white hat trimm'd with blond,
> a long figur'd white sattin cloak trimm'd with fur, and arm-holes, and really
> you never saw a more elegant creature than she look'd. He is very handsome
> and was dress'd in a light colour'd suit.
>
> I must tell my own dress, being bride's maid. I had on the same sattin as
> my sister's, an Italian nightgown [day wear] that train'd a yard on the ground,
> a little hoop, leylock* slippers—straw colour'd heels and roses, a white chip
> hat—one row of ribbons, pink satin Cloak trimm'd with fur, a short lac'd
> net apron . . . as soon as the ceremony was over, signing and witnessing
> done in the vestry, Sir G. handed his lady thro' us all. They got in their
> chaise and four and drove away . . .
>
> Lady Smith's clothes are elegant . . . She gave favours. [Lady Smith was
> one of the wedding guests.]
>
> Letter 9 in *Dear Miss Heber, an Eighteenth Century Correspondence*,
ed. Francis Bamford

Again we have this note in the diary of Mrs Charlotte Louisa Papendiek:[4]

> A white jacket and petticoat [skirt], my sattin cloak and a white hat formed
> my bridal attire. (1783)

At a wedding in 1812

---

* Leylock = lilac coloured.

> The bride wore a robe of real Brussels point lace over white satin . . . A cottage bonnet of Brussels lace with two ostrich feathers; she wore a deep lace veil and white satin pelisse trimmed with swansdown.
>
> *The Ipswich Journal*

Perhaps the most famous of all nineteenth-century weddings was that of Queen Victoria to Prince Albert in 1840. Compared with earlier royal weddings simplicity in dress was aimed at. By now it was customary for the royal bridegroom to wear a Service uniform (see Pl. 25). The following is taken from a full report in *The Times*, Tuesday, 11th February 1840. The Queen's

> dress was a rich white satin trimmed with orange-flower blossoms.
>
> On her head she wore a wreath of the same blossoms, over which, but not so as to conceal her face, a beautiful veil of Honiton lace was thrown. Her bridesmaids and train bearers were similarly attired save that they had no veils.
>
> Her Majesty wore the Collar of the Garter but no other diamonds or jewels.
>
> Her attendants were arrayed with similar simplicity.
>
> The Prince . . . wore the uniform of a Field Marshall in the British Army. Over his shoulder was hung the Collar of the Garter surmounted by two white rosettes.

Later *The Times* contradicts the statement that Her Majesty wore no diamonds as jewels and says:

> A pair of very large diamond ear-rings, a diamond necklace and the insignia of the Order of the Garter were the principal ornaments worn by the Queen.

Other sources confirm this. Additional particulars from the *Court Newsman* describe in more detail the Queen's wedding dress.

> The cost of the lace trimming alone . . . was £1,000. The white satin . . . was manufactured in Spittalfields.

The Queen Dowager Adelaide was also in white with a train of rich violet velvet, lined with white satin, and she wore a

> head-dress of feathers and diamonds.

For less privileged spectators feathers, on this occasion, were prohibited. On 10th February 1840 (the day before the wedding):

> The spectators . . . may wear white wedding favours . . . the exclusion
> of feathers is particularly desirable as they would interfere with the view of the
> passing scene.

When all was over and at

> the Departure for Windsor at the conclusion of the breakfast . . . the Prince
> was dressed in a plain dark travelling dress and H.M. in a white satin pelisse
> trimmed with swansdown, with a white satin bonnet and feather.

At a wedding in 1873, described by Laura Troubridge, the bride's wedding
outfit was closely modelled on the Queen's. Then:

> For going away Lady Audrey had on a dark blue velvet gown with a very
> long train, but as she came to the door her maid threw over her shoulders a
> splendid Indian shawl, red embroidered all over with gold, which was a
> wedding present from Lord Bute and had . . . cost £400, but it made her
> look rather old and prevented us seeing her gown.

Flowers and old satin slippers were thrown, and one slipper

> went straight into the bridegroom's hat as he was taking it off to bow.
> *Life Among the Troubridges* (Journal of Laura Troubridge)

The surprising fact that Lady Audrey's going-away dress had a long train
would not have been unexpected at the time, as trains, even for walking
dresses, were the fashions in the 1870s.

The marriage of the Prince of Wales (later King Edward VII) to Princess
Alexandra of Denmark, celebrated in St George's Chapel, Windsor, took
place in 1863. The pageantry of this wedding was remarkable and the garments worn by all were stately and imposing.

> The dress of the Princess . . . the bride was a petticoat of white satin
> trimmed with chatelaines [chains] of orange-blossoms, myrtle, and bouffants
> of tulle, with Honiton lace, the train of silver moiré antique,* trimmed with
> bouffants of tulle, Honiton lace, and bouquets of orange-blossom and myrtle.
> The body of the dress was trimmed to correspond.
>   Her Royal Highness wore a veil of Honiton lace, and a wreath of orange-
> blossom and myrtle.

The eight bridesmaids carried the bride's train.

* A heavy watered grosgrain.

The wreaths of the bridesmaids were formed of blush roses, shamrocks and white heather, with long veils of tulle falling from the back of the wreath. The dresses of white tulle over white glacé* were trimmed to correspond.

. . . .

The Prince of Wales wore his mantle of the Kt of the Garter, with white ribands on each shoulder, over his uniform of General in the Army, which was so concealed by the ample folds of the blue and ermine [mantle] that only a glint of the scarlet tunic and the extremity of his gold-striped overalls [loose trousers of white cord or leather, worn for riding], boots and spurs, were visible.

The Duke of Cambridge wore the mantle and hood of the Order of the Garter, as did all the Knights of this Order.

Among those present at the wedding were

Princess Helena [who] wore a train of white silk with bouquets of the rose, shamrock and thistle, tied with silver cord . . . Headdress wreath of lilac, white feathers and blonde lappets†, diamond ornaments.

The Illustrated London News, 31st March 1863

The bride's mother, Princess Christian of Denmark, wore

a diamond tiara surmounted with white plumes [which] rose over her placid brow.

The Queen's eldest daughter was seen

leading by the hand her son, the little Prince William of Prussia, in his Highland dress. [The Kaiser aged 4.]

Lord Combermere, bearing his gold stick of office,—an old soldier who strode stiffly . . . in glittering cuirass, covered with orders, and in the jackboots which gleamed almost as brightly, had served in Flanders in the last century.

Waiting to see the procession from Castle to Chapel

opposite the grand entrance to the Castle were drawn up the children of Her Majesty's Schools—the girls in scarlet cloaks, the boys in French grey.

Receiving the procession at the West door of the Chapel was

* A plain taffeta with a lustrous surface.
† Silk lace pendents to headdress.

Garter King-at-Arms, in the quaint richness of his official garb wearing a crimson satin mantle and carrying his sceptre . . . [and] Heralds, Pursuivants and Trumpeters, in their State dresses from the splendours of which, it may be remarked, there is some detraction in the appearance below the tabard of the the unromantic *pantalon*.

Yeomen of the Guard in doublet, ruffle and hose . . . halberd in hand were also in evidence.

The ceremony of "throwing the shoe" was not forgotten, and it was flung with so good an aim by the Duke of Cambridge that the Prince of Wales received on his cheek the full force of the missile which, as it belonged to the Princess Louise, may not have been very formidable.

Sir William Howard Russell, *The Marriage at Windsor*, 1863

At the wedding in 1858 of the Princess Royal to Prince Frederick, later Emperor of Germany (Pl. 26), the display of Scottish Highland Costume attracted much attention:

Conspicuous among the peers by his dress and noble appearance was the Duke of Atholl who wore the full costume of his clan, tartan and philibeg,* claymore and heron's plume. It is almost needless to say that his Grace attracted considerable notice, especially among the foreign visitors to whom the sight of a Highland costume is always an event . . .

The Prince of Wales and Prince Alfred follow in Highland Costume . . .

The bridegroom . . . wears the dark blue uniform of the Prussian service and over his breast the orange ribbon of the Order of the Black Eagle; his helmet, of polished silver, and its plume of feathers is carried in his hand: . . . the dress of the bride is composed of a rich robe of moiré antique ornamented with three flounces of Honiton lace, the pattern of which is formed of bouquets of the rose, shamrock and thistle. The train is of a similar material.

The bridesmaids have each a dress of white glacé petticoat covered with six deep tulle flounces looped up with bouquets of roses and white heather— the latter said to have been modelled from a sprig of heather which the Princess gathered during her last walk in the mountains near her Highland home.

Illustrated London News, 30th January 1858

The marriage in 1896 of Princess Maud of Wales (daughter of Edward Prince of Wales later Edward VII) to Charles Crown Prince of Denmark (afterwards King Haakon VI of Norway) is shown in Pl. 27. The following is a contemporary description.

* i.e. filibeg = a kilt.

Her bridal gown of white satin was cut low and square, and was held at the waist by a belt of silver embroidery; the sleeves were short and puffed; and over her head fell a beautiful veil. The perfume of orange blossoms filled the air as she passed along, with her attendant maids who wore white satin relieved with clusters of red geranium—a compliment to the bridegroom, the prevailing red, white and silver of the costumes recalling the Danish national colours.

The bridegroom . . . wore the uniform of the Danish Navy and walked with erect figure.

[On walking] through the doorway into the Bow Library [the bride] gave a backward glance at her train apprehensive of how it would fare at so abrupt a turning . . . her sister . . . stooped down and raised and guided the train.

The royal couple did not escape a shower of rice as they drove away.

Illustrated London News, Vol. 99, Pt. 2,
Royal Wedding Number, 25th July 1896

CHAPTER 8

FURTHER CONVENTIONS IN WEDDING ATTIRE

(a) Bridegrooms

Although descriptions of bridegrooms' costumes have already been included with those of the brides', a few comments concerning the conventions imposed by fashion, especially in the nineteenth century, must be made.

A bridegroom's dress, among the nobility, in the early centuries was always made of rich materials in the fashion of his day. It was also very expensive. Sir William Compton's was so valuable that he left it in his Will:

> To the Abbey Church of Winchcomb in the county of Wigorn Worcestershire] my wedding gown of tinsel satin to make a Vestment to the intent that they shall pray for my soul. (1522–3)
>> Sir Nicholas Nicolas, *Testamenta Vetusta*, II, p. 592

A great deal of care too was often taken in choosing beforehand the correct accessories, not only for himself but for his relations. The following letter from Henry Oxinden to Elizabeth Dallison in 1642 is an example.

> Honored Cozen,
> I forgot to send for a fan and 2 sutes of ribbon and pendents, which I desire to bee of the newest fashion and not to[o] plaine; and a pair of garters and roses [i.e. shoe rosettes] such as you think fitting.
> My mistris hath a desire to have a paire of speciall good gloves for my mother, and a paire for my sister and 3 paire for her sisters, of 6s. 8d. the peice at least.
> The time when we shall use these things is uncertaine; however wee desire to have all things in readiness, and what I have forgot that appertaineth to a privat wedding, I desire you to put me in mind of. I conceive I shall want a paire of plaine perfumed gloves for myselfe and what is most in fashion to hap my sword in. I shall want a plain band [collar] and cuffes and boot hose tops of the newest and best fashion that is.
>> *The Oxinden and Peyton Letters 1642–1670*, ed. Dorothy Gardiner

Boot-hose tops were the decorated borders to boot hose, stockings worn with boots. The tops overlapped the top of the boots and were designed for show. Some boot-hose tops were made of gold or silver lace or linen fringed with silk.

An example of the cost of a country gentleman's wedding clothes, in 1702, is given in *Blundell's Diary*. Nicholas Blundell paid his tailor £1. 15. 0. for making a blue "wedding suite" with silver buttons.

In 1777 we are told that

> Mr Dawson is in want of £400 to buy, I suppose, eight new coats for his Wedding.
> > A letter from Mary Noel in *The Noels and the Milbankes*,
> > ed. by Malcolm Elwin

In a letter from Lady Stormont to Mary Graham in 1776 she describes the grandeur of Lord Stormont's wedding suit.

> I have always forgot to tell you that Lord Stormont's wedding coat was something in the pattern of Mr Graham's, only embroideries with foils upon Brown Cloath and lined with *couleur de paille** with a waistcoat *paille* embroidered with gold and foils.
> > E. Maxtone Graham, *The Beautiful Mrs Graham*

The nineteenth century developed certain definite conventions regarding the bridegroom's wedding suit. Up till about 1830 it was usually a ceremonial "full dress" suit often with a white waistcoat and white stockings.

> The bridegroom wore a plain blue coat with yellow buttons, a white waistcoat, buff breeches and white stockings.
> > *Ipswich Journal*, 1812

By 1830, breeches were replaced by trousers or pantaloons, i.e. close-fitting trousers sometimes called "tights". A bridegroom (Fig. 31) might be

> dressed in light blue coat, double-milled Kerseymere pantaloons, white neckerchief, pumps and dress gloves

or

> blue coat, yellow waistcoat, white trousers and Berlin gloves.
> > Charles Dickens, *Sketches by Boz*, 1835

During the 1850s and 1860s the frock coat came into fashion, although tail coats were still worn.

---

* Couleur de paille—straw coloured.

31. Bridegroom in black tail coat, pantaloons and a gold-trimmed
chestnut-coloured cashmere waistcoat. Bride in robe of blonde lace.
The Weekly Belle Assemblée, May 1835.

Mr P. will not stir a finger without me and even consulted me about his
wedding-coat, whether it shall be a frock-coat which I advised though I
believe not quite correct with a bride's veil. (1853)
The Letter-Bag of Lady Elizabeth Spencer-Stanhope.

Frock coat, blue, claret, or mulberry-coloured, . . . Waistcoat . . . of
white quilting, . . . Trousers of pale drab or lavender doeskin.
    This is suitable for the bridegroom or for any gentleman attending. Un-
fortunately invisible green and even black frock coats are occasionally seen at
weddings but both are inconsistent with the occasion except in the case of the
marriage of a clergyman.
Minister's Gazette of Fashion, 1861

For the bridegroom in 1869:

32. Prince Louis of Hesse, who was married to Princess Alice in 1862,
wears a tail coat. They were married in the dining room of Osborne
House.
Illustrated London News, *July 1862.*

Short frock coat of blue diagonal, velvet collar, edging of fine silk cord;
plain buttons; cuffs with one or two buttons. Silk facings quite out of date.
D-B waistcoat of white drill. Dove grey Angola trousers. Lavender gloves.
Light blue tie. The groomsman wears a frock coat with trousers and tie not
quite so light and gay as the bridegroom's.
   Morning coats are not worn on these occasions.
                              The West End Gazette of Fashion, 1869

However, in the 1870s and 1880s the morning coat was the rule, although
some still preferred the frock coat.

Frock coats are seldom worn even at weddings, the Morning Coat being
preferred on account of its smarter appearance.
                              The Tailor and Cutter, 1884

ELEVEN O'CLOCK A.M. : A WEDDING AT ST. JAMES'S CHURCH, PICCADILLY.

33. A wedding in 1859. The bridegroom and other gentlemen wear
frock coats, the bride a veil.
Illustration in G. A. Sala Twice Round the Clock, *1859.*

In the 1890s the frock coat was back again.

The bridegroom and his best man were dressed alike. Black frock coat faced
with silk. Double-breasted waistcoat of light colour and a dark tie, or a dark
waistcoat with a light tie. Grey striped cashmere trousers. Patent leather
button boots. Pale tan kid gloves or of grey suede. Silk hat. [i.e. top hat.]
The Tailor and Cutter, 1899

34. Bridegroom in smart frock coat, showing the fashion for the last decade of the 19th century. White favour.
The Graphic *2nd Aug. 1889, advert.*

Top hats were the rule all through the nineteenth century, and with "top people" remain so today.

(b) Bridesmaids

It was in the nineteenth century that great care began to be taken over the bridesmaid's dresses which were different from that of the bride and usually coloured. At a wedding in 1847, for example, there were

> . . . the four bridesmaids, two wearing light blue dresses of the most delicate tint and white bonnets, two in lilac dresses of equally delicate shade and white bonnets.
>
> *The Stockport Advertiser*

At a wedding on 17th September 1873:

> The bridesmaids wore pale blue silk trimmed with gauze flounces of the same colour and silk bows edged with dark grena* velvet, long grena velvets round their necks and blue silk stockings and boots with rosettes. The five big ones had blue and grena bonnets, while the three little St. Aubyn girls had white straw hats, high and large-brimmed, lined with blue silk, caught up at one side with blue silk and blue and grena feathers. The five elder ones had silver bracelets with Lady Audrey's initials on them.
>
> J. Troubridge, *Life Amongst the Troubridges* . . ., 1966

(Lady Audrey was the bride.) (See p. 104.)

The boots worn by these bridesmaids were fashionable evening wear in the 1870s. These boots were usually of black silk or satin, they reached the calf and were laced down the front.

At a wedding in 1879:

> The bridesmaids' dresses were—some blue, some pink cashmere, made with yoke bodices, silver belts and long trained skirts: hats of the same material. Hats and caps run each other close for bridesmaids, and they are so much alike, it requires a connoisseur to distinguish them.
>
> *Cassell's Family Magazine*

At the wedding of the Princess Louise of Wales to the Duke of Fife in 1889

> The bridesmaids . . . wore dresses of a lovely shade of blush pink foille with demi trains draped with crepe de Chine over which were arranged broad moiré sashes. The bodices were cut V shaped with elbow sleeves, and trimmed with crepe de Chine. They carried bouquets of pink roses and each also wore a bouquet of pink roses on the hair.
>
> *The Illustrated London News*, 3rd August 1889

Plate 28 shows bridesmaids in 1867 wearing bonnets with short veils and carrying posies.

(c) Children Attendants

Small boys acting as pages often formed part of the wedding procession from the sixteenth to the end of the nineteenth century. They were usually decked in fancy dress and in the nineteenth century might be train bearers (Pl. 29).

Little girls and little boys sometimes formed part of the bridal procession. At the marriage of the Marquis of Kildare with Lady Caroline-Leveson-Gower (Fig. 35):

* Grena = red (? from grenas, old plural of gernet or garnet).

35. The wedding of the Marquis of Kildare and Lady Caroline
Leveson-Gower in 1847. Charity children lined up. The bridesmaids
and bride's mother (on the right) wore long veils.
Illustrated London News *16 Oct. 1847 (detail).*

The centre aisle was supplied by between fifty and sixty little girls educated
in the Duchess' own school, all of whom wore white dresses and straw hats
trimmed with a wreath of green leaves, each bearing a small basket filled
with choicest flowers. All the boys wore white favours.

Illustrated London News, 1847

(d) Late Nineteenth-century Formalities

Finally the correct costume for the occasion in the late nineteenth century is
carefully summed up by Mrs John Sherwood in her *Manners and Social Usages*
of 1884.

The Etiquette of Weddings, Chapter VI.
No man ever puts on a dress coat before his seven o'clock dinner, therefore
every bridegroom is dressed in a frock coat and light trousers of any pattern

he pleases, in other words, he wears a formal morning dress, drives to the Church with his best man, and awaits the arrival of the bride in the vestry room. He may wear gloves or not as he chooses. The best man is the intimate friend, sometimes the brother of the groom. He accompanies him to the church . . . follows him to the altar, stands at his right hand a little behind him and holds his hat during the marriage service.

. . . . . .

The bridegroom is allowed to make what presents he pleases to the bride and to send something in the nature of a fan, a locket, a ring or a bouquet to the bridesmaids; he has also to buy the wedding ring and of course he sends a bouquet to the bride . . .

The bride meantime is dressed in gorgeous array, generally in white satin with veil of point lace and orange blossoms and is driven to the church in a carriage with her father who gives her away . . . A bridal register is signed in the vestry.

Formerly brides removed the whole glove: now they adroitly cut the finger of the left hand glove so that they can remove that without pulling off the whole glove for the ring.

. . . . . .

Wedding favours made of white ribbon and artificial flowers are indispensible in England . . . Such ornaments are used for the horses' ears and the servants' coats in this country. Here the groom wears a boutonnière of natural flowers.

Next come the correct rules for a widow bride.

A widow should never be accompanied by bridesmaids or wear a veil or orange blossom at her marriage. She should at church wear a coloured silk and a bonnet. She should be attended by her father, brother or some near friend. It is proper for her to remove her first wedding ring, as the wearing of that cannot but be painful to the bridegroom.

If married at home, the widow bride may wear a light silk and be bonnet-less, but she should not indulge in any of the signs of the first bridal.

Mrs Sherwood also describes what should be worn by a widow when attending a wedding.

Deep red is deemed in England a proper alternative for mourning black, if the wearer be called upon to go to a wedding during the period of the first year's mourning. At St George's, Hanover Square, therefore one may often see a widow assisting at the wedding of a daughter or son, and dressed in a superb red brocade or velvet, which, directly the wedding is over, she will discard for her solemn black.

CHAPTER 9

THE WEDDING RING

To the ancients there was a mystic significance associated with a ring. Its circular continuity symbolized eternity and therefore the constancy of love. Robert Herrick's poem "A Ring presented to Julia" (1649–50) demonstrates the persistence of this concept.

> Julia I bring
>   To thee a Ring
> Made for thy finger fit;
> To show by this
>   That our love is
> (or should be) like to it.
>   . . . . . .
> And as this round
>   Is no where found
> To flaw, or else to sever,
>   So let our love
>   As endless prove
> And pure as gold for ever.

Greek and Roman rings were often inscribed with mottoes suggestive of belief in the mystical power of the ring. In England, especially in the sixteenth and seventeenth centuries, rings thus inscribed were called "posy-rings" and the motto or "posy" (cf. poesy) was on the flat inner side of the ring, and might read as follows:

> Our contract
> Was Heaven's act,

or

> God above
> Encrease our love.

Rings with these mottoes are generally considered to be betrothal or wedding rings. John Lyly in the second part of his *Euphues* writes:

. . . the Posies in your rings, which are always next to the finger, not to be
seene of him that holdeth you by the hand, and yet knowne by you that
weare them on your hands. (1579)

The mention of a posy occurs in Shakespeare's *Merchant of Venice*, V, i, 147.

About a hoop of gold, a paltry ring
That she did give me, whose posy was
For all the world like a cutler's poetry,
Upon a knife "Love me and leave me not". (1596)

An example of a posy ring with a Latin motto *"Maneat inviolata fides"* is
mentioned in *The Diary of Lady Margaret Hoby 1599–1605.*
Pepys too talks of posy rings:

. . . we sat studying a posy for a ring for her which she is to have at Roger
Pepys his wedding. (1659)

Posy rings were also worn in the eighteenth century.

. . . A young Poetical Lover of my acquaintance . . . promised me to get
the Measure of his Mistress's Marriage Finger, with a Design to make a Posy
in the Fashion of a Ring which shall exactly fit it.
The Spectator, Vol. I, p. 329 (number issued 1711)

In 1748 the widow of Matthew Postlethwaite, Archdeacon of Norwich,
wrote to her stepdaughter as follows:

Mr Page (after courting upwards of twenty young and old) is married to a
young girl of two or three and twenty . . . the Motto of the wedding ring
is in Latin but this is the English "I came, saw, conquered".
Notes and Queries, 6th Series, Vol. 3 (1881)

Mottoes on rings, sometimes very elaborate, continued into the nineteenth
century. The following is an example. Precious stones set round the outside
of the ring were selected so that the first letter of each stone when joined
together would spell a word.

Ruby, Emerald, Garnet, Amethyst, Ruby, Diamond, Lapis-luzuli, Opal,
Verde-antique, Emerald, Malachite, Emerald.
(Regard, Love me.)

These posy rings, however, were usually more in the nature of engagement
rings, just as in the Middle Ages and Shakespeare's day solemn betrothal by
an exchange of rings between lovers often preceded matrimony.

Priest A contract of eternal bond of love
Confirm'd by mutual joinder of your hands
Attested by the holy close of lips,
Strengthen'd by interchangement of your rings:
And all the ceremony of this compact
Seal'd in my function, by my testimony.

Shakespeare, *Twelfth Night*, V, i, 160

The true wedding ring, the ring used at the wedding ceremony, symbolizing the sacredness of marriage, dates back at least to the thirteenth century and possibly earlier. In Chaucer's *Canterbury Tales* (1373–93) Griselda is thus described in the Clerk's Tale:

She stood transfigured in her gorgeous dress
Scarce recognisable for loveliness
The Marquis then espoused her with a ring
Bought for the purpose.

(From Nevill Coghill's translation, 1965)

In the sixteenth century, gimmal or double rings, symbolic of matrimony, were much used as wedding rings.

At the marriage of George III to Charlotte of Mecklenburg in 1761, the wedding ring was noted by the Duchess of Northumberland:

The Duke of Cumberland gave away the Bride and the Instant the King put on the Ring a Rocket was let fly from the top of the Chapel, as a signal for the discharge of the Park and Tower Guns which were immediately fired.[1]

Wedding rings of the seventeenth and eighteenth centuries were often set with precious stones. Pepys describes one in 1668 set with diamonds.

. . . mighty proud she [his aunt] is of her wedding ring, being lately set with diamonds; cost her about £12; and I did commend it mightily to her, but do not think it very suitable for one of our quality.

Nicholas Blundell in 1703 bought two wedding rings, one for his wife "a false Diamond Ring" for 14s. and a much grander one for himself "for his weding ring £1. 5s."[2]

The plain gold ring, the "visible pledge of matrimony" was preferred by some brides as early as the thirteenth century. In 1530 Mary Nevill's wedding ring is listed thus:

Item a Weding Ring Gold, 12s. 4d. [See p. 96.]

Queen Mary I in 1554 "chose to be wedded with a plain hoop of gold, like other maidens".[3]

Dorothy Osborne writes in 1653 (*Love Letters . . . to Sir William Temple*)

> Before you go, I must have a ring from you, too, a plain gold one; if ever I marry it shall be my wedding ring. (Letter 48)

> Here is a ring, it must not be at all wider than this which is rather too big for me than otherwise, but that is a good fault, and counted lucky by superstitious people. (Letter 50)

In default of a ring the church key might be used; even a leather ring cut from the groom's glove was once resorted to [*N. & Q.* 2nd Ser. X (1860)].

At what period the plain gold circle was recognized as the wedding ring and the wedding ring only is a little uncertain. It was, however, accepted as such from the nineteenth century onwards.

Queen Victoria's wedding ring was plain but large. In the procession after the ceremony

> Prince Albert enclosed Her Majesty's hand in his own in such a way as to display the wedding ring which appeared more solid than . . . in the ordinary weddings.
>
>

The Times, 11th February 1840

The Ring Finger

There is some evidence that the wedding ring may have been worn on the right hand in the Middle Ages, though it has been on the left for the last four or five hundred years in England. The change apparently came at the Reformation.

> That the man should put the wedding ring on the fourth finger* in the left hand of the woman, and not on the right hand, as hath been many hundres of years continued.
>
>

Peter Heylyn, *History of the Reformation*
(1st pubd. 1661), Edn. 1849, p. 430

Why this particular finger was chosen was possibly because of a belief that a nerve or vein from this finger was directly connected with the heart. The practice was sanctified in early liturgies as follows:

* Meaning the fourth digit, the thumb being the first.

In the Hereford, York and Salisbury Missals the ring is directed to be put first upon the thumb "in the name of the Father" afterwards upon the second "and of the Son", then upon the third "and of the Holy Ghost" and lastly on the fourth finger "Amen" where it is to remain: *quia in illo digito est quaedem vena procedens usque ad cor.*

Editor, *Notes and Queries*, 5th Series, XII, 408 (1879)

A very strange fashion, however, was adopted by some married ladies in the late sixteenth and seventeenth centuries, when the wedding ring was worn on the thumb. In Thomas Southerne's play the *Maid's Last Prayer*, 1693, the following words are spoken by Lady Susan Malepert:

> Marry him I must, and wear my Wedding Ring upon my Thumb too, that I'm resolved on.

During the Commonwealth many Puritans condemned the wedding ring as of "heathen origin" and preached against its use, but without success. This is referred to in Butler's *Hudibras*, 1663.

> Others were for abolishing
> That tool of matrimony, a ring
> With which the unsanctified bridegroom
> Is marry'd only to a thumb.

This again refers to the practice of wearing the ring on the thumb.

Plate 30 shows portraits of Martha Cranfield, Countess of Monmouth (in *c.* 1620) and Queen Henrietta Maria (in *c.* 1649), each wearing a ring on her thumb. See also Pl. 7.

At what period married women began to wear the ring without ever removing it has not been established. It is an interesting observation that in eighteenth-century portraits where the left hand is shown, the ring is usually absent. It is certain, however, that from the nineteenth century on, the true wedding ring has been worn by married women continuously.

An amusing incident concerning a wedding ring is described in *Catherine Gladstone*, by her daughter, Mary Drew (1919).

> Sir Charles Ryan told me of his lifelong gratitude to her (Mrs Gladstone) for coming to the rescue at the most embarrassing moment of his life. He was being married to Miss Shaw Lefevre in July 1862 . . . in the presence of the usual London crowd. When the time came for him to place the ring on the finger of the bride, it refused to go on—the ring was too small. An awkward

pause ensued—paralysis on the part of the guests—when Mrs Gladstone was seen rapidly making her way through the crowd, and as she reached the neighbourhood of the bridal pair, drawing her own wedding ring off her own finger, she put it in the hand of Sir Charles. He slipped it on, it fitted, and the situation was retrieved. Yet she was always superstitious about her wedding ring and could never bear to be without it.

"With this ring I thee wed", and having been placed on the bride's finger, there it has remained ever since as a badge or symbol of the largest "union" in the world.

CHAPTER 10

COSTUME AND DEATH CUSTOMS

Why do people spend more money . . . upon a death, Mrs Gamp, than upon a birth?

Charles Dickens, *Martin Chuzzlewit*

It is significant that deaths were reported in the press earlier and in much greater numbers than births and marriages. The newborn is unknown to everyone, the married couple will be with us for other occasions, but the dead is known to many and his removal is once and for all. Added to this are the weighty effects of fear, grief and other emotions, as well as beliefs, all confined to the death situation. The customs and ceremonies that have grown up around it are thus far more complex than those connected with births and marriages.

Because the clothing of the dead tends to become a representation of himself, and the clothing of the living a means of self-expression, costume enters into most death customs, and even into the mere symbols to which they have often been reduced by historical, religious and local factors. The present chapter and the next therefore review such practices, dealing first with those in close relation to the dead, then with the general characters of mourning by the survivors.

(a) Dressing the Corpse

Particulars of grave-clothing are discussed in Chapter 12. Here we give a few examples of superstitions and customs connected therewith.

One of these is due to the fear that the ghost of the dead may return to harass the living. It was said in Lincolnshire, at least until the present century, "you must never forget to tie the feet [of the corpse] else the dead may return, or some other spirit may take possession of the body for its own purposes".[1]

But over this matter there have been conflicting influences. B. Puckle tells us "winding sheets were often loosened at hands and feet to aid resurrection".[2] For, in the words of the judgment in a case of shroud-thieving in 1616, the shroud "is bestowed on the body for the reverence towards it to express the hope of resurrection".[3]

Rich. and Cecilie Howard, 1499.   Aylsham, Norfolk.
Husband and wife in shrouds.

36. Husband and wife, in shrouds tied at the head but not the feet.
Monumental brass, Aylsham, Norfolk. 1499
Herbert Macklin Monumental Brasses *1913*.

Folklore often holds that murdered people, being extra prone to restlessness, must be restrained by the removal of their footwear; and as recently as
1889, when a case of murder came to court in Arran, the constable was found

to have hidden the victim's shoes. (Radford *Encyclopædia of Superstitions* edn. 1961 p. 307.)

Whatever the motive, fear or affection, the body itself is nearly always an object of solicitude. Where there was affection, this is natural. As John Weever expressed it in 1767, if the garment or ring of one's father is esteemed in proportion as one held him dear, then our bodies are not to be despised, seeing that "we wear them more near unto ourselves than any attire whatever".[4]

Robt. Alee, 1518, in Shroud, Dunstable, Beds.

37. Figure emerging from shroud at resurrection (?). Feet freed from their tie. Brass at Dunstable, Beds. 1518.
Herbert Haines Manual of Monumental Brasses . . . British Isles (*1861*) Vol. *1*.

In this connection the grave-clothes have paramount importance. The custom is universal of wrapping the body in what would promote comfort if it were living and give it decorum in death. As we shall see, many in our own times have been buried well dressed, and not only the eminent, who lie in state. A modern example is one witnessed among gypsies near Romney as recently as *c.* 1900 and reported in *Jour. Gypsy Lore Soc.*, 1957. Faithful to their tradition they coffined the deceased "fully dressed as in life in the man's best clothes with a new pair of boots".[5]

At Oxford even in 1938 a woman insisted that her little girl be buried in all her clothes with a new coat "to keep her warm".[6]

Even separated parts of the body (often the heart) would be carefully vested before burial. Queen Mary's heart (whether bearing the word Calais or not) after removal was reverently wrapped in red sarsenet (silk) garnished with four yards of passemayne lace, to be interred in a velvet-covered box[7] bound with silver.[8] The bowels of Anne of Denmark, wife of James II, (d. 1618) were sent for burial in an urn covered with a black cloth "and a sheet". Arriving by river this was met at Westminster by, among others, Richmond herald, who carried his royal tabard ceremonially over his arm (cf. Fig. 15).[9]

(b) Burying the Deceased's Accessories and Emblems

The pagan practice of burying with the dead his goods, together with gifts, supposedly for his future use, has never disappeared entirely. For example we know from disinterments that Henry II in 1189 and King John in 1216 were buried with their swords.[10]

In the same way, very personal belongings and emblems of office were buried with the eminent, perhaps sometimes simply because it seemed the safest way to treat what association had made precious. Those that were "costume accessories" concern us.

When the body of St Cuthbert (d. 689) was disinterred in 1104 (see p. 164) there were found with him

> a pair of scissors with which his hair was once cut, according to report, . . . along with his ivory comb.[11]

When, up to the Reformation and again in the nineteenth century, bishops, archbishops and certain abbots had a pastoral staff or crook they would generally be buried holding this in the hand (see pp. 164–5). Alternatively archbishops might have their special staff which is surmounted by a cross.

It was the same with the sceptres of kings. Two of these were bestowed at the coronation, and medieval ordinances[12] for the interment of a king lay down that the sceptre with a cross must be placed in his right hand and that with a dove in his left. When Edward I's tomb in Westminster Abbey was opened in 1774 and the folds of the wrapper thrown back he was found to be lying there with the two sceptres exactly as prescribed.[13]

Humbler staves of office have traditionally been interred. The hospices supported by the Livery Companies of London were administered by members, whose insignium was a green staff. Rules for the burial of an alderman (*c.* 1580) read:

> If the party deceased have been one of the maisters of the hospitall he may have his green staffe layd on the corpse [coffin] . . . and the same broken . . . and thrown into the grave.
>
> B.M. MS. Egerton 6064, f. 102

One is tempted to mention another instance where the "tools of his trade" featured at a man's funeral—although they were in no sense costume accessories. On the coffin of Lord Leighton, P.R.A., in 1896 appeared

> the palette, laid with colours, and the brushes and mahl-stick of the President.
>
> *The Graphic*, Vol. 53, p. 163

Fig. 45 (p. 141) shows that the same thing was done for Millais.

(c) Burying other Tokens

Apparel, really or symbolically laid with the dead, need not be their own. The Rev. F. Blomefield wrote in 1739 about "our ancestors":

> Any man might bequeath his burial to what Abbey he pleased . . . in the hope of some Ease to the poor departed Soul . . . especially if the Corps had some Religious Garment put upon it, as was then usual.
>
> *A History of . . . Thetford . . .*

In the Middle Ages, into his master's grave a herald might cast his own tabard or cote-armour embroidered with the arms of his allegiance; and in the same way a nobleman's highest ranking servants threw into the grave their own wands of office. These wands were always broken first, like the grave goods of most primitive peoples.* An eye-witness gives the following vivid account of both practices in 1502.

The body of Prince Arthur,† whose life was cut off at the early age of 15, had just been lowered into its grave:

---

* The reasons for this are discussed by L. V. Grimsell in *Folklore*, Vol. 72, p. 476 (1961), and by B. Aitken, *Folklore*, Vol. 73, p. 57.

† His christening was described on p. 45 seqq.

His Officer of Armes [herald] sore weeping, tooke of[f] his Coate of Armes and cast it along over the Chest [coffin] right lamentably. Then Sir William Overdale, Comptroller of his Houshold . . . tooke the Staffe of his office by both endes and over his owne Head brake it and cast it into the grave. The Steward did the same and then the Gentlemen Ushers their Roddes . . . This was a piteous sight.

Leland, Collectanea, Vol. 5, p. 380

As well as other ideas, there seems to be expressed here the logic of destroying a dedication symbol that has lost its *raison d'être* but (like the dead man's treasures) must never fall into desecrating hands. Even to this day, as L. V. Grimsell says, "it is the custom for the Lord Chamberlain to break (now, alas unscrew!) his staff of office at the funeral of his sovereign".[14]

There may be something similar in the motives underlying the gypsy custom whereby a widow ties, with a red ribbon, her wedding ring to the wrist of her dead husband.[15]

Another symbol of office, the key of a Chamberlain,* if not actually buried may be symbolically carried at a funeral, as was done for the Margrave of Brandenburg-Anspach in Berkshire, as late as 1806. His two chamberlains followed the bier "with their keys in crape scarves".[16]

Ex officio finger-rings are usually worn by the corpse and examples will be given later. The "mortuary ring" is a true gift to the dead. In Somerset folk-lore when such rings were dug out of graves people wore them as a cure for the cramp.[17] Rings were given to the dead as late as 1865—they were put into Lord Palmerston's grave in Westminster Abbey (see pp. 237, 240).

(d) Parading the Deceased's Apparel and Emblems

As with his servants' keys, the custom of burying with a dead man his "needs" and belongings largely gave place to that of merely parading them, or symbols of them, in his funeral. Down to this day, articles of apparel and insignia of the great are often carried in their funerals, as will be seen.

In medieval and Tudor times one of a dead king's chargers, though not to be slaughtered, as with some peoples, was actually ridden up the nave of Westminster Abbey at his Requiem Mass to be "offered" at the "door of the Choir".† In the same way in the funerals of all ranks from esquires upwards,

---

* The Lord Great Chamberlain of England (not the Lord Chamberlain) has one.

† A gypsy woman's two horses were actually slaughtered at her death in Garsington in 1953 (Radford, *Encyclopaedia of Superstitions*). Some will remember Edward VII's charger and Caesar, his dog, walking in his funeral procession in 1910.

Henry St. George Esqr. Richmond Herald.

Elias Ashmole Esqr. Windsor Herald.

William Dugdale Esqr. Norroy King of Armes.

Sr. Edward Bysshe Kt. Clarenceux King of Armes.

38. Heralds in funeral procession carrying deceased's helmet with crest, shield, sword and coat of arms. *Engraving after Francis Barlow in Francis Sandford* Order of the . . . Interment of George Duke of Albemarle, *1670*.

till the eighteenth century, and in certain state funerals subsequently, a man's apparel was represented by what was called in the sixteenth century his "hatchments" or "achievements".* These consisted of (i) a coat-armour or coat-of-arms, not of metal but a tabard-shaped surcoat, embroidered or painted with his arms, (ii) his helmet and crest. If he was a knight or peer there were a sword and other articles as well (Fig. 38).†

These were all carried in the procession, and then orientated on the coffin as though in wear. The four mentioned here were finally offered to the officiating priest at the altar. They might then by him be "delyverd unto

* In modern heraldic usage both words have changed their meaning. A funeral hatchment is now a painting of the arms of the deceased on a black background, hung up over his doorway. In a contemporary account of James I's funeral "hatchment" is used in both the old and the modern senses (College of Arms MS. I 4, ff. 32–45).

† No shield is mentioned in an ordinance of perhaps early Tudor times (EETS Extra Ser. VIII, p. 30, 1863), but it featured in Henry VII's funeral and onwards.

the . . . heir",[18] even "with reverence".[19] The heir in turn gave them to the church, not actually to be interred but to be hung up over the tomb, as were Sir Peter Carewe's in 1575, "for a memoryall of a right noble gentleman".[20] Those of the Black Prince hang with his spurs and some of his mail in Canterbury Cathedral to this day.

Along with the horse, the hatchments became looked on as a gift to the church or the sexton, and as early as 1334, the Prior of Westminster claimed one hundred pounds *in lieu* when Edward II's son John was buried there without them, after his death in Scotland.[21]

Henry V's "hatchments" were borne only by "captaines",[22] but from late fifteenth century to carry them became the recognized prerogative of heralds.

39. Guardsman in mourning cloak, carrying battle-axe reversed, at Queen Elizabeth's funeral. *c.* 1603.
B.M. MS. Add. 35324 f. 38v.

An interesting point is that the weapons of the dead man and of his soldiers were reversed, as they would be on the battlefield in token of truce for burial. He who actually offered the sword would be "holding the poynte thereof in

40. Small page boy in black military "cassock" and breeches carrying
reversed battle-axe (made to measure?). 1588.
Engr. T. de Bry after Thomas Lant in Funeral Procession of Sir Phillip
Sidney *1588.*

both his handes, the pomell . . . upwards".[23] The rider of Henry VII's
horse in the Abbey (1509) was, in accordance with tradition,

> armed complete with the King's harnes [armour] his face discovered, bearing
> in his hand the King's battle axe the head downwarde restinge on his foote.[*]

A century later Sir Phillip Sidney's small page carried an emblematic battle-
axe in the same way (Fig. 40).

By assimilation we have the practice of leading a cavalry-man's horse in the
procession with his riding-boots hanging from the saddle in reverse. 'But
not always thus? See Pl. 31. Perhaps the artist was at fault here.)

[*] The axe was also offered; its rider's armour, always stripped off in the vestry, sometimes
followed. B.M. MS. Harl. 3504.

41. Cap and feather of the Order of the Garter, as paraded at funerals
of the Knights.
*Engr. W. Hollar in Elias Ashmole . . . Institution . . . of the Order
of the Garter pp. 202/203 (1672).*

That the boots are paraded at all is perhaps another derivative of the
notion of providing the dead with his "needs". For an officer of state, other
articles may be pressed into service. At the funeral of General Ireton in 1652,
as well as his own sword, etc.:

> the mace and sword with other marks of his charge in Ireland were carried
> before [him] in black scarfs.

John Evelyn, *Diary*, Vol. I, p. 275

And at the funeral of a Lord High Chancellor of Scotland, e.g. the Duke of
Rothes in 1681, a man walked in the procession with his arms full of the
Chancellor's enormous ceremonial gown of office (Pl. 32).

Headgear being, as it were, nearest to the person himself, appears at the
obsequies more persistently than any other apparel: hence for example
Wellington's famous cheese-cutter cap on his coffin, and throughout history

the carrying of ducal coronets on velvet cushions sometimes even in the rain (Pl. 33).

A cavalry-man who was also a knight of the Order of the Bath would be accompanied on his last journey by a special *hat* (as well as *two* pairs of "reversed" boots!). It is hard to imagine the funeral of Sir W. Fawcett K.B. in 1804. Behind the coffin plodded the Prince Regent. In front went two chargers, one bearing the dead man's "military boots and spurs", the other a

> State Horseman bare-headed carrying the insignia of the Order . . . *i.e.* crimson velvet cushion with gold fringe, white satin hat and white plume of feathers; the boots and gold spurs, reversed.
>
> *The Statesman*, 1804

The ladies of royal and noble families sometimes had "hatchments" carried at their funerals, exactly as did men. Queen Elizabeth of York (d. 1503) did not,[24] nor did Henry VIII's wives, even Anne of Cleves, who was "buried prince-like" in 1557.[25] But being a reigning monarch, Queen Mary I (d. 1553) had the entire outfit. (There was even a horse and battle-axe.)[26] So did Mary Queen of Scots when, six months after her death in 1587, Queen Elizabeth gave her a respectable second funeral.[27] An illuminated manuscript of about this time[28] showing the "Funeral of a Duchess" depicts heralds with a shield, coat-of-arms and coronet but no weapons; and a later Elizabethan ordinance would appear to settle the matter:

> it is not convenient that a woman should have [borne at her funeral] a Coate of Armes or Shielld helme and creste, the which is not lawful today.
>
> B.M. MS. 2642, f. 205

In explanation it adds: "yt agreeth not to saye 'a woman of Armes' ". But a woman of Armes is just what Queen Elizabeth herself was apparently counted to be. Everything was carried in her procession except gauntlets and spurs.[29]

At the death of the next queen, Anne of Denmark, wife of James I,

> Question was made by ye lls [Lords] Comissrs. of the difference betweene a quene a kinges wife and [a queen who was] an absolute Sovereigne . . .
> Standerte Cote of Armes crest sword and target and such like, as also the Leadinge a spare horse . . . were thought due to sovereignes [only] and so it was concluded all theis should be omitted at this funerall.
>
> College of Arms MS. I 4, f. 7v

In fact the custom, where women were concerned, was moribund. By the

42. Pall with white cross and embroidered escutcheons. Pall-bearers,
one at each corner, in gowns and hoods; underbearers, without these,
carrying the coffin. Heralds with banners. *c.* 1565–75.
College of Arms MS. M6 f. 74 by courtesy of the Chapter of the College.

time Mary II died (1695), despite her sovereignty, her only possessions displayed at the funeral were a crown and sceptre lying on the pall.

(e) Palls

The pall that has always been spread over a coffin concerns us, for it takes the
place of a cloak (*pallium*) which might cover the dead before the days of
coffins, or again on the battlefield. For the rich it was often of red velvet like a
ceremonial mantle—examples of red ones range from Henry V's in 1422 to
Millais's in 1896. George II had royal purple.

Most palls bore a white cross. Heraldic "escutcheons" might be embroidered at the sides or on the holland sheet extending beyond (Fig. 42.)
Wellington's pall had his orders and decorations pinned all over it.

Palls may originally have been buried with the dead. A modern example
of this was when at St. George's Chapel, Windsor, four bearers, "his friends",
held the corners of Charles I's black pall until the coffin was lowered into the
vault—"in sorrow and silence"—and then they cast the pall in after it.[30]

These coverings developed great beauty and magnificence, especially those
of the London Guilds. Each was embroidered with the company's arms and
lent out, for its members, as an honour. At least four of these still exist: that

of the Saddlers, crimson and gold, dates from 1508 and must have seen many a city magnate into his grave.

For the poor, the Parish would lend or hire out a pall. We are told by J. E. Smith, in his *History of St. John-the-Evangelist, Westminster*, that until 1807 this church's pall for paupers bore the words "Buried at the expence of the parish".

Misson, writing in 1698, says that in England even for "middling" people

> The Parish has always three or four Mortuary Cloths of different Prices . . . These cloths, which they call Palls, are some of black velvet, others of Cloth with an Edge of white linnen or silk . . . For Batchelor or Maid or for a Woman that dies in Child-bed, the Pall is white.[31]

Not unnaturally the pall was often treated as though it represented the dead person's apparel and thus himself. An early sixteenth-century manuscript on "The Manner of Ordering" a funeral[32] says that a man "must be supporting" each corner of a person's pall "as if they bare him". Thus the terms "bearers" and "pall-bearers" are synonymous. Of Queen Mary I's pall-covered coffin a contemporary wrote that four noblemen as they walked beside it "touched it with their hands".[33] Plate 34 shows an eighteenth-century example.

Generally pall-bearers have been chosen for their close association with the dead in rank, sex, sometimes age and as far as possible friendship.

Misson (loc. cit.) shows that the sex would correspond.

> The pall . . . is so brord that the six or eight Men [later called "underbearers"] that carry the Body [coffin] upon their shoulders are quite hid beneath it to their waste and the corners and sides of it hang down low enough to be born by those six friends, *Men or Women according to the Occasion*★ who are invited for that purpose.

In the following example, age affected the choice:

> Calverley departed this life . . . aged 18 . . . there were white gloves and scarfes for the boys that wer the bearers. (1702)
> *Yorkshire Diaries*, Surtees Soc. pubns, Vol. 77

'The use of white for scarves, as for palls, at bachelors' funerals is mentioned on p. 147.)

★ Italic ours.

For Sir Phillip Sidney, certainly, the link was one of affection. Thomas Lant, who was present, says

> The corners of the Paule were houlden by four Gentlemen his deer lovinge frendes.[34]

Sometimes friendship made for a very close match, as when John Evelyn was invited to "hold up the pall" of Samuel Pepys.[35]

Pall-bearing may be an opportunity for a social group to assert its solidarity. A somewhat bizarre example may be worth quoting, since costume plays a conspicuous part in it. The report was in the *Old Whig* for 14th August 1735:[36]

> On Thursday night was interr'd in Covent Garden Church Yard . . . the Head Cook of the Rose Tavern, the Pall being supported by six cooks dress'd in white napkin Caps with white favours, white stockings and white gloves, green Aprons with white ones tuck'd up half-way; the novelty of which . . . drew . . . a vast crowd of spectators.

It was the custom, at least until the Reformation, for the well-to-do to make symbolic gifts to the dead, in the form of additional palls, which were pieces of silk in decorative colours. These were ceremonially laid on the coffin during masses, before burial. Edward II in 1318 gave fourteen of them at the death of his stepmother Queen Margaret, and in 1320 for a lady cousin's coffin he ordered "v pieces of silk powdered* with birds".[37]

These palls appear to have taken the place of today's funeral flowers, but were truly seen as gifts to the dead: at the funeral of the Earl of Salisbury, in 1462/3, the Ladies and the Barons each "*offered up to the cor[p]se a clothe of golde*".[38] The number offered varied. An unusual example was for Queen Elizabeth of York, to whom, in her coffin in 1503, twenty ladies gave palls to the number of her years—thirty seven.[39]

Strict protocol came to be observed in the matter of numbers. An ordinance, probably of the early sixteenth century, lays down a minimum for Earls:

> yf it bee an Earle, there must bee . . . too [two] Clothes of bawdkyn† to be offered. Some men calles these clothys pawlles.
>
> Bodleian MS Ashmole 837‡

* Dotted over, in embroidery.
† A very rich brocade-like silk.
‡ A copy made in Stuart times from a Pre-Reformation ordinance.

And another reads firmly "that no gentlewomen have any Paulles . . . offred at the Masse [if she be] under the degree of Countess" (B.M. MS. Egerton 2642 f. 205).

An ordinance of 1616 surprisingly states: "Be it noted that noo gentle-women are to offer at the funerall of a man."[40] This may mean Mass penny or palls or both.

Comparing Henry VIII's and Catherine of Aragon's takings we see how sex and rank influenced the number of palls. For Henry VIII (1547):

> the Lordes moreners brought sundry peeces of silke of diverse colors some moo some lesse according to their degreyse and laid all the same uppon the legges of the King his picture [i.e. the wax effigy on his coffin].[41]

The chief mourner, a Marquis, laid four; earls three each; barons two.[42] But for Catherine of Aragon (1536) it was only Duchesses three, Countesses two, Baronesses one.[43]

What the palls meant was expressed in a MS. of 1509. Henry VII's mourners offered them "in token of their Homage which they in Dutie ought to doe".[44]

The ultimate use of the palls, which in practice became an offering to the Church, was to make vestments.[45]

(f) Foliage, Garlands, Wreaths

Tokens like these were probably, as B. Puckle[46] suggests, originally "an offering to the dead rather than a condolence for the living"—were even seen as another of his needs. In confirmation he quotes a statement of Sir Walter Besant's that in Yorkshire it was still the custom (late nineteenth century) to *bury* in the churchyard a girl's funeral garland; further, it would be unlucky to remove even a fragment of its ribbon before it was thus handed over.[47]

"Tributes" in the form of vegetation are now of course usually only displayed at the funeral (though flowers have been put *inside* the coffin within living memory).[48] We need only concern ourselves with what was wearable, namely posies and garlands or wreaths.

Rosemary was early used as a mourning posy,* worn and then given to the dead. Two writers show that in their day (about 1600) it was associated with funerals and weddings simultaneously, just as are flowers today. A character of Dekker's, at a wedding, says:

---

* From *poesy* (cf. "saying it with flowers"; cf. also mottoes on rings).

Bedloes funeral

43. Men in mourning cloaks carrying sprigs
(of rosemary?). Woman in mourning veil. *c.* 1680.
From a set of playing cards celebrating the over-
throw of the Popish Plot in 1678, attributed to
Francis Barlow. Reitlinger Collection, B.M.

and looke this Rosemary (a fatall hearbe) this dead man's nose-gay.
Satiro-mastix (1602) Act I, l. 110

And in a letter, one William Woad says:

The streets strawed with flowers when maids of any sort are buried . . .
and for batchelors they wear rosemary, as if it were a marriage. (1603)
Calendar of State Papers, Domestic, Jas. I, Vol. 3

Misson (loc. cit.) says:

A servant presents the Company with Sprigs of Rosemary: Everyone . . .
carries it in his Hand till the Body is put into the Grave, at which time they
all throw their Sprigs in after it.

Exactly the same custom prevailed in Norfolk right down to 1856.[49]

But there was perhaps an alternative. Another Frenchman, de Rocheford, who had been studying the habits of the British, wrote in 1672: "I met nothing more pleasing to me than the funeral ceremonies at the interment of a My Lord", at which everyone carried a "bough" in one hand, including the parson, and all "threw them into the grave at the end".[50] Unfortunately history does not relate what the French word was that is here translated "bough".

Moral attitudes have made their mark on the use of some of these "tributes". Rosemary for bachelors, in esteem for their chastity, was rather soon given up. By the eighteenth century anyone, even a harlot, could have it (see Pl. 41). But special chaplets or garlands for girls' funerals have persisted all through our period. A writer in Picart's *Ceremonies*[51] says that for a child who died baptized but under the age of discretion, in the Catholic Church of his own day,

> a Crown of Flowers or odoriferous Herbes [must] be set on his Head as a token of Innocence and Purity.

Shakespeare uses the word "crants" for a virgin's garland: Ophelia, suspected of suicide, was denied a Christian burial but "allowed her virgin crants, Her maiden strewments".[52] With a normal funeral she would have been attended by girls all wearing floral chaplets, as it were vicariously. Such a charming chorus is well described in connection with Queen Elizabeth of York's funeral in 1503. For when a woman died in childbed, as did she, she was treated like one who retained her virginity—perhaps because she had paid so high a price for parting with it. The Queen was 37 at her death.

> att fanchers [? Fenchurch] were set xxxvii Virgins all in white linnen having Chaplettes of white and grene on their heads. In Cheap . . . the lady Mayoresse ordeyned also xxxvii other virgins in their heires* houlding likewise pretty tapers.
>
> *Antiquarian Repertory*, Vol. IV, p. 659

By the seventeenth century it was customary for a single garland to be carried in a girl's funeral (Fig. 44) and then hung up over her pew, or in the chancel of the church (like the knight's helmet) until it disintegrated or was buried.[53]

In time, the simple chaplets of fresh flowers were replaced by eleborate

---

* Loose hair implied innocence (see pp. 92–3).

44. *"The Bride's Buriall"*
"A garland, fresh and faire
of Lillies there was made
In signe of her Virginity,
and on her coffin laid:
Sixe maidens all in white
did beare her to the grounde . . ." *c. 1640.*
From woodcut in Roxburghe Ballads *ed. C. Hindley (1874) Vol. 1, p. 246.*

artifices. A contributor to the *Gentleman's Magazine* for 1747[54] tells us that the Parish clerk of Bromley, Kent,

> in that churchyard . . . dug up one of these crowns or garlands which is most artificially wrought in filigree work with gold and silver wire in resemblance of myrtle . . . it was also lined with cloth of silver.

Worse was to follow. In the *Antiquarian Repertory* (1807–8)[55] there is a description of what the garlands had become by that time—a fantastic conglomerate of wood, wire, paper, flowers, dyed horn, silk, even painted eggshells, with a paper glove, bearing the girl's name hanging in the middle. A far cry from the wearable chaplet!—But note that another garment has made its appearance, the glove—something which, as a costume symbol for the person, is second only to the headgear. A "crown" with a glove like this is still to be seen in Trusley church, Derbyshire,[56] and there are others elsewhere. Some are shaped like bird-cages. Despite all this, the original idea of a fresh, not artificial, garland was locally retained. The Rev. J. E. Vaux recalls seeing

45. Funeral of Sir John Millais. Huge wreath contributed by Royal
Academy. The painter's palette and brushes on the coffin. (Pall-bearers
include Lord Rosebery on extreme left and Holman Hunt on extreme
right.) 1896.
Contemporary print (detail), Guildhall Library Noble Collection C 22.83.

in *c.* 1892 at Teignmouth a "much beloved maiden lady" who "lay in her
coffin with a chaplet of eucharis and lilies of the valley". These were not only
living flowers, but were actually "on her brow" like Ophelia's.[57]

It is only at the beginning and end of our period that wreaths have been
regularly sent to the funerals of people other than girls. Yet the giving of
these seems well to represent the provision, for the dead, of vegetation and
apparel simultaneously, and they were almost certainly in use in Saxon times.
The Rev. W. H. Sewell in 1883 spoke of the custom as "revived of late years"
and considered that it had already got out of hand:

What shall be said in favour of a weighty wreath of flowers dank with

> moss . . . as large as a carriage wheel, procured by some public Body or other.
> *Practical Papers on Funeral Reform*

The wreath contributed by the Royal Academy when a Victorian P.R.A. died was an example. As the coffin of Lord Leighton was lowered into its vault in 1896, Millais handed in with it, on their behalf, a wreath of laurels and white satin ribbon that was five feet across (Fig. 45). Six months later he received an exactly similar tribute himself.

As to the colour of Victorian funeral flowers, here ideas about mourning got mingled in. Evergreens would do, but flowers, since they could not be black, had to be white or purple. A propos of the picture in Pl. 55 the *Illustrated London News* wrote:

> We ask . . . whose lifeless form it is that they will deck with these flowers—
> the lily, the rose, the azalea; all white save a few violets; all appropriate to
> scatter over the dead . . .

Even in the present century florists would cut off the stamens of white madonna lilies lest the golden pollen should mar their appropriateness for a funeral.

(g) Bedesmen and Bedeswomen

Even thoughts for the welfare of the soul and its duty to express humility and virtue, have made their impress on costume.

There have always been those who like Queen Elizabeth Wydeville, widow of Edward IV, wished, for religious motives, to be buried "without any worldly pomp".[58] If the identification of her tomb in 1810 was correct,[59] the dowager queen (d. 1492) was simply "wrapped up in waxed canvas of fifty folds" instead of being laid to rest, as was usual for royalty, in her state robes.

Again, it is said that Queen Mary I, at her own wish, lay in state at St James's Palace dressed in the garb of a religious order.[60]

Monks and nuns were (and still are) buried in some of the garments of their rule, and the note of humility is pronounced. One of the "additional Regulations" for the Brigettine nuns, promulgated in *c.* 1415 (when their convent opened at Syon) reads:

> When any sustir [sister] is dede . . . they schal clothe the body withe
> stamen.* cowle. and mantel. wymple. veyle. and crowne cap . with oute

* An undergarment made of the coarse worsted, "stamin".

rewle cote [her dress]. but with hosen and schone tanned and with a gyrdel whiche al schal be of the vilest gere. and in al these excep the mantel sche shal be buryed.

B.M. MS. Arundel 146, f. 172

The body was exposed in a lattice-work coffin for all to see. The founder of this very convent at Syon, Henry V, had a life-like effigy carried at his funeral which, for a similar purpose,

> was raised on a chariot that he might be seen of all, that by this means mourning and grief might grow and his friends and subjects might the more kindly beseech the Lord on his soul's behalf.

46. Bedesmen with rosaries at the funeral of Anne of Cleves, 1557. These are shown in coats; contemporary accounts mention poor men with torches who had the usual gowns.
B.M. MS. Add. 35324 f. 9.

Prayers for the soul, in pre-Reformation times, were ensured for those who could afford it by the employment of Bedesmen and Bedeswomen.* These were recipients of the deceased's charity, sometimes inmates of almshouses. They generally walked in the funeral, sometimes carrying their beads and always provided with mourning garb.

An early example relates to the Duke of Exeter whose will (proved in 1426) provided that poor women of good character and poor men (character not specified), each to the number of the Duke's years at death, should receive and wear at his funeral gowns and hoods of white wool cloth in return for their prayers for his soul. The men were to bear torches, which may account for their being in white[61] (cf. p. 146).

Almsfolk, still often to the number of the defunct's years (Sir Phillip Sidney had thirty-two but Queen Elizabeth had two hundred and sixty), remained a feature of funeral processions long after prayers for the dead were frowned on. Their gowns, and hoods if any, were not like those of the mourners,

* Bede = prayer, a rosary being a string of beads.

being cruder in cut and cloth, and for practical reasons exceptions were sometimes made as to the colour. Henry Machyn, that inveterate attender of
funerals, says that in the funeral of an ex-Lady Mayoress in 1556 poor men
and women had "gownes of sad mantyll fryse"* and in another (1563) the
women even wore russet.[62]

Bedeswomen always had old-fashioned headgear, hoods giving place in
the sixteenth century to veils ("coverchiefs" or "head-rails"). The effect was
essentially humble.

47. Alms-women at the funeral of Mary
Queen of Scots. Old-fashioned gear, mourning
veils. 1587.
B.M. MS. Add. 35324 f. 15v.

Yet some people felt that it was humbler still, not to make a show of their
charities at all. Queen Elizabeth Wydeville at her own wish, only had a
dozen "old men holdyng old torches ends", who did it in return, not for
gowns but just for their dinner.[63]

A great contrast was the display at Henry VIII's funeral (1509). In the procession

> went two hundred and fifty Poor Men in long Mourning gowns and Hoods,
> with royal *Badges on their left shoulders*, the Red and Whyt crosse in a sonne
> shining and the Crown Imperial over that.
>
> College of Arms MS. I II (italic ours)

If Thackeray is to be relied on, the practice of getting almsfolk to attend a
noble funeral in return for their garb was still usual in the 1840s: at Sir Pitt
Crawley's funeral "old women of the Alms House . . . were habited in
sable" (*Vanity Fair*).

* Sad = drab; frieze = a coarse wool fabric.

CHAPTER II

CHARACTERISTICS OF FUNERAL AND
MOURNING WEAR

Mourning costume has varied so much, even in colour, that the only generalizations one can make about it are, first that it deviates from normal dress and, secondly, that it has something suggestive of a garb of humility.

(a) Mourning Colours
Black seems the natural mourning hue, having associations with night and gloom.

> Hung be the heavens with black: yield day to night,
> We mourn in black.
>
> Shakespeare, *I Henry VI*, I, i, 17

It was in the latter part of the fourteenth century (rather earlier abroad) that black was adopted as the definite convention for men's funeral and mourning wear. It was already in use in the medieval church for vestments at the offices of the dead (Pl. 35). Black copes we are told, were worn by the "Abbots of Westminster and Barmesey", who were *in pontificalibus* at the Queen's funeral in 1503[1] and churchwardens accounts (1512–53) show that a "black suite"* used to be hired out by the Parish of Stratton, Cornwall.[2] The custom must have been dishonoured at times, for the clergy in York in 1519 had to be reminded that

> We thinke it were convenient that whene we fetche a cor[p]se to the churche that we should be in our blake [h]abetts mourningly wt our hodes of the same.
>
> Quoted by G. Tyack in *Historic Dress of the Clergy*

The Catholic church retained this view. In Picart's . . . *Religious Ceremonies* . . ., in discussing customs in England in 1723, it is stated that even if Mass cannot be said over the dead body it is "sprinkled and incensed by a priest clothed in his black chasuble". In the Reformed Church, even when

---

* "A whole suit of black" is defined in the same Lady Hungerford's will as a chasuble, two tunicles and three copes.

"ornaments" were approved, the use of black vestments declined. But for Henry VIII

> there were sung three Solemn Masses by Bishops . . . in sundry suits
> the first of Our Lady in white
> the Second of the Trinity in blew
> the Third of Requiem . . . in Black.
>
> College of Arms MS. I 11

For the poor, drab, often called "sad colour", remained for a long time a practical alternative to buying black.

Queens, especially if they were French ladies, tended to be a law unto themselves. When the Dowager Queen (Elizabeth Wydeville) died in 1492, a contemporary wrote:

> The queen her daughter [Elizabeth of York] toke to her chambre, wherefore I cannot tell what dolent [dolorous wear] she go'th in but I suppose she went in blew in lykewise as qwen Margaret [of Anjou] the wife of King Henry the vi went in whenne her mother . . . dyed.
>
> B.M. MS. Arundel 26, f. 29v.

White differs from colours as conspicuously as does black, and has likewise been used in mourning. Being also a symbol of virginity and innocence (cf. p. 60) it has specially characterized mourning for, and by, women and children. Men seldom wore it when mourning for a man, but in the Middle Ages the torch-bearers at his funeral might do so, perhaps to show up in a dim light. When the body of Richard II (1399) was brought to St Paul's "the Londoners" had thirty torch-bearers all clothed in white[3] and again at Elizabeth of York's funeral (1503)

> torch-bearers of certain crafts of London . . . had gownes and hoods of white wollen cloth.
>
> *Antiquarian Repertory*, Vol. 4, p. 660

Men did, quite often, use white when mourning for a woman. Of Henry VIII we read that after beheading Anne Boleyn on 19th May 1536, "Assencion day folowynge [26th May] the Kynge ware white for mournynge." (But during the next week he married Jane Seymour.)

The Almswomen at funerals were frequently in white (or at least in white veils); so were the virgins at the burials of unmarried women and children. Even in 1803, Mrs (Bott) Sherwood, the novelist, tells us, her servant-girl was actually "carried to her grave" by "six young women in white gowns and white hoods";[4] and in 1808, even though she died at the age of sixty-six, Angelica Kaufmann, being a spinster, had her "pall supported by young Ladies in white" (*The Times*, 11th January).

Steele satirizes the whole idea as follows:

> *Sable* (an undertaker) speaks:
> "Goody Trash . . . I told you I wanted you and your two daughters to be three Virgins to Night to stand in white about my Lady's . . . Body . . . you were privately to bring her home from the Man-Midwife, where she died in childbirth, to be buried like a maid."
> R. Steele, The Funeral, I, i

Even a bachelor's chastity was celebrated in the seventeenth[5] and eighteenth centuries by the use of a white pall, favours and scarves (as with rosemary) at his funeral.

White for widows and for children is discussed on pp. 263, 270 respectively. Finally, white trimmings have been used to denote mourning on a costume that was black all over in the ordinary way, for example the white "weeper" cuffs which a Q.C. must don when the Court is in mourning.

Purple as a mourning colour was restricted to royalty for a long time. An inventory of Queen Elizabeth's wardrobe in 1600 records a set of "Mourning Robes" comprising mantle, kirtle, "surcote"* and bodice, all of purple velvet (trimmed with ermine and details of gold).[6]

John Ward in his Diary speaks of the death in 1643 of Louis XIII of France "for whom King Charles I mourned in Oxford in purple, which is Prince's mourning",[7] and according to Pepys, Charles II went into "purple mourning for his brother" in 1660.

Curiously enough in 1815, when George III was believed to be dying, Lady Charlotte Campbell, a Lady-in-waiting, wrote

> people are already talking of what mourning will be worn for the poor old King and some say it is to be *purple and grey*. Is not this an odd idea?[8]

(In the event, in 1820, people simply wore black.)

Purple and mauve for *half* mourning became quite usual in the nineteenth century.

Even red is not unknown as a mourning colour. In certain gypsy tribes it

---

* Compare Fig. 78, p. 209.

is the norm. Writing of a gypsy funeral in about 1900 (mentioned above), Charles Payne records

> Red was much in evidence in the dress of the attendant women, and several of the men wore red neckerchiefs similar to the one round the dead man's neck.
>
> *Jour. Gypsy Lore Soc.*, Vol. 36, p. 78 (1950)

It is stated in *Folklore* (1926)[9] that "when anyone is at a wedding in black it is bad luck for the bride and bridegroom".* Hence the curious convention, in the nineteenth century, for a widow to substitute red when attending a wedding.

Whatever colour is customary, society has generally been highly intolerant of any deviation from it.

> What d'yer fink 'e wore? Why
> Brahn boots! I ask yer! . . .
> Fancy coming to a funeral in brahn boots!
> I will admit 'e 'ad a nice black tie . . .
> But yer can't see people off when they die
> In brahn boots!
>
> "*Brahn Boots*", song by R. P. Weston and Bert Lee, pubd. by
> Francis, Day & Hunter, 1941, and immortalized by Stanley Holloway

(b) Materials for Mourning

The texture of materials used in mourning is almost as important as their colour. For deepest mourning they must have a matt surface so as not to be relieved by high-lights,—"the dead black lustreless look" enjoined by Mrs J. Sherwood in *Manners and Social Usages*, 1884.

This sooty appearance, typical of black crape and bombazine, explain their being chosen. A stricture on an ill-bred widow who wore black *silk* was:

> Bombazine would have shown a better sense of her loss.
>
> Mrs Gaskell, *Cranford*, 1851–3

According to Mrs Delaney, in 1747, dark grey poplin was correct for (informal) full mourning, whereas black silk could only be worn after three months[10] because of its gloss. Even when bonnets and veils were white, crape was preferred for making them.

Similarly (from the sixteenth century onwards), cypress or sypers, a mix-

* A warning once honoured in the breach by the bride herself (see p. 148).

ture of silk and linen, was much used for mourning when made in the dull quality called "currelled" (curled), which was rather like crape. Being light in weight it was favoured for draping flags and drums in processions. Again, Judges, and barristers who have "taken silk" must wear a matt gown specially made for court mourning, although their ordinary gown is black.

The necessary texture and blackness have always been available in wools. Bombazine,★ which was a silk and wool mixture without gloss, was introduced in the sixteenth century. Ordered for the Earl of Rutland's family mourning in 1587,[11] it was an imported luxury; but such foreign silk-containing fabrics were increasingly used, despite a proclamation in 1622 that all mourning wear must be made of English woollen cloth.[12]

The slightly stiff ("hard") type of real crape, the one most used for mourning, is of pure silk but has a matt surface. For its qualities and manufacture see Appendix 9.

Until the middle of the eighteenth century this sort of crape was only successfully produced in Italy, and efforts were made to popularize English materials instead.† Just as the English wool trade received a boost by the "Buried in Woollen" Act of 1678, now it was the silk industry, learnt since then from the Huguenots, that was officially promoted. One of its products was as good as crape in its lightness of weight and became popular for mourning.

> For the encouragement of our English silk called Alamode, H.R.H. the Prince of Denmark, the Nobility and other persons of Quality, appear in Mourning Hatbands made of that silk . . . in the place of Crapes which are made in the Pope's country . . .[13]

Another substitute, "Norwich crape" (partly wool), was prescribed for court mourning in 1760.[14] English Silverets (silk and wool), made in the mid-eighteenth century, was one of the cheaper alternatives.[15] Cheapest of all was bombazet (eighteenth and nineteenth centuries), a wool and cotton imitation of bombazine.

Nice correlations were sometimes made between materials used and the importance of the wearer. In 1810, at a London surgeon's funeral (John C. Saunders) the hatbands of close mourners were crape, those of his colleagues

★ From *Bombyx*, the silk-worm.

† O.E.D.'s earliest example of the word *crape* is dated 1633. D. C. Coleman in *Courtaulds . . .* (1969) says Italian crape and its association with mourning reached northern Europe in the sixteenth century.

and friends were silk, while "medical practitioners and students" had only "half crape".[16] Humbler still was black cotton. When a cousin of a (fictional) Scottish minister died in 1820 his wife wrote:

> Get swatches of mourning print [calico] with the lowest prices . . . they are for the servant lasses.
>
> John Galt, The Ayrshire Legatees, 1821

48. "Widow's first mourning: this dress is made of a peculiar silk called '*radz de mort*' manufactured in Spitalfields for this class of mourning. It is trimmed with quadruple crape which is proof against . . . heat or rain . . . both durable and dressy." Mourning handkerchief.
After an advert: by Messrs Jay in The Queen, *6 May 1872.*

With the 1830s came the rise of the firm of Courtauld's whose huge commercial edifice was built up almost entirely on bales of crape. They developed a secret process (see Appendix 9) and in twenty years had increased their output by fifteen hundred per cent. Industry and the Victorian vogue for mourning played into each others hands. As D. C. Coleman remarks in *Courtaulds* (1969), from which these facts come, "there was money in mourning".

A basic material for a Victorian dress on which festoons, frills and tucks of crape would be mounted was generally a paramatta, silk and wool (later silk and cotton). This is the material from which, to this day, a judge in court mourning must have his gown made.[17]

Jay's, in the 1880s, also advertised cashmeres and gauzy grenadines and *tulles* as mourning fabrics[18] and there was spot crape (with flat dots) for a change (Pl. 36).

By 1884, Mrs J. Sherwood (op. cit.) could recommend an even wider choice. For winter there were "Henrietta cloth and imperial serges", duly matt but "pleasanter than crape" and for lighter weight "Tamise cloth, Bayonnaise, grenadine, nun's veiling and American silk".

With trimmings and favours care had to be taken. Black, or in some circumstances white, *ribbon* was often correct. A transparent silk called "love-hood" or simply "love" was much used: hence "love-ribbon" which decorated caps. "Lace" says Mrs J. Sherwood firmly "is never mourning" (loc. cit.).

Jet, because of its highly reflecting surface, was eschewed until the mid-nineteenth century. It then became the rage and adorned every imaginable outer garment until the Whitby source dried up and jet had to be artificial.

But the rule about avoiding reflecting lights from *metals* has, in particular contexts, been kept to the present day. During periods of court mourning, for example, sword-hilts, shoe- and breeches-buckles and metal buttons had to be made of dull material or else covered with black cloth, lacquer or heelball. This still goes, not only for gentlemen at court but for judges and Q.C.s wearing ceremonial dress. With the same idea, at the death of Charles II the order went out that Privy Councillors should not only put their servants, coaches and sedan chairs into mourning cloth but "none to presume to use any varnished or Bullion Nails" (College of Arms MS. I 4, f. 74).

Gloves at funerals, as late as that of Queen Elizabeth I, were of natural coloured skins, but in the eighteenth and earlier nineteenth centuries they were usually black and of "shammy" leather, perhaps because it had a dull suede-like surface. Shammy was also required for shoes, in court mourning (p. 256).*

* The chamoised skins called "shammy" today are treated with oils and would not lend themselves to dyeing. It is uncertain how the earlier shammy was prepared.

(c) Mourning and Humility

In many ways the mourner in his garb and demeanour seems to be showing humility and submission both towards the dead and to the Deity.

The attitude of the body and lines of the drapery suggest yielding, drooping, as well as weeping. Hence, possibly, the long association of the willow with sadness, reinforced by its greyish colour*—and so the expression "wearing the willow" which means mourning a lost love or lover.

> I'll wear the willow garland for his sake.
>
> Shakespeare, *3 Henry VI,* III, iii, 228

The impression of drooping is conveyed by the long veils of widows and the hanging "weeper" scarves, like black cobwebs, in men's hats.

A bowing attitude was not always enough. At Elizabeth of York's Requiem Mass, which was typical, Lady Mountjoy, as she offered the first pall, "made an obeysance to the coffin".[19] The humility of the chief mourner in relation to the dead is also emphasized in all ceremonious sixteenth-century funerals at the offertory proper. The chief mourner first offers the "Mass Penny" *in the name of the defunct,* proceeding with his or her train "borne up" and with an escort. Lord Derby, doing this at his father's funeral in 1572, was accompanied by two ushers, a herald and three Kings-of-Arms.[20] After returning to his seat he advanced again, now in the role of humble mourner, with an escort of only two and with *his train not borne up.*

Such is the strength of the submission motive that the appearance of mourners has had much in common with that of penitents in medieval times. Thus Wyclif says the hypocrite who wishes to seem "more holi than othere men, bosten thereof in outward signes . . . [such] as mourning [h]abite".[21]

The very use of black and of white bears out the comparison. In the Catholic Church the same black vestments were worn on penitential days as at funerals. Again, in 1361 Edward III decreed that the surcoat colour of the Knights of the Garter should be changed from blue to black as a symbol of humility before God. Elias Ashmole explains (italic ours):

> We conceive this mourning colour was then assumed because the Pestilence Black Death began then to increase . . . the dreadful remembrance of that great Pestilence, which so furiously raged eleven years before, inviting to *all kinds of humiliation.*
>
> *Institution . . . of the . . . Order of the Garter,* 1672

* Even before the introduction of the typical "weeping" variety, Thomas Fuller called the willow a "sad tree".

49. M.A. black academic gowns, late 17th century. (*Left*) ordinary
gown with hanging sleeves and (*right*) mourning gown (*toga lugubri*)
with "pudding" sleeves; both as worn at Oxford and Cambridge.
After David Loggan. (*Left*) Cantabrigia Illustrata *1690.* (*Right*) Oxonia
Illustrata *1675.*

As for white, the proverbial penitential sheet that had to be worn in public
by sinners was always white.

The black, white, grey and drab of mourning are all colours characteristic
of monastic dress, which was designed to express humility. Indeed, a funeral
gown was so like the everyday black academic gown inherited by members
of universities from religious forebears, that they themselves had to adopt a
gown with a specially shaped sleeve when they wished to show they really
were in mourning. Moreover the "pudding sleeve" they then chose was one
that was described in 1560, as "priest's shape" and was typical canonical
wear for the clergy in the seventeenth and eighteenth centuries,[22] as can be
seen in Pl. 34. The academic mourning gown is shown in Fig. 49.

It was the same with styles; a widow often looked like a nun because both
eschewed contemporary fashions, and dressed like their ancestors. Mary

Queen of Scots, when in mourning at the age of 16, wore the "barbe" that had gone out of fashion nearly two centuries before. Just as nuns shaved off their hair, widows often hid it. And it is not fortuitous that "nun's veiling", as we have seen, was recommended for mourning.

50. Mary Queen of Scots, aged 16, in mourning barbe, 1561.
After the portrait by François Clouet.

Long after the days of penance, it still remained true that mourning and modesty of appearance had much in common. Boswell, when wanting to look a very humble man, disguised himself in a tarnished hat and a "suit of second mourning" (1762/3).[23] And the *Spectator* for 1712 laughs at "Creatures of the Town" who "at once consulting Cheapness and Pretension to Modesty" appear to be wearing "an agreeable Second Mourning".[24]

A submissive attitude, even an approach towards "participation of the living in the mortuary state",[25] is expressed in the way mourners tend to cut themselves off from the world by covering the face. The dark veil which has been aptly called "a shroud for the widow" is an obvious example.

A face-covering *par excellence* was the medieval-style hood, used both by men and women from the fourteenth century till the end of the seventeenth.

What distinguished it was not merely blackness but the way it was worn *over the face* at funerals by all the important participants, even when on horseback. At the re-interment of Richard Duke of York, in 1466 (further described on p. 179), the litter was drawn by seven horses. Each rider was "a yeoman clothed in a blacke gowne and with a hoode over there faces"— this despite the fact that each had "to guyde the other horsse before hym . . . with a whipp and a Rayne".[26]

Sixteenth-century Ordinances insist on this mode of wearing the hood, for example:

> For the buriall of a Prince of the Blood Royall: as many Lordes as do accompany the corps must be cladde all in blacke . . . w'th their hoodes hanginge farre over their eyes.
>
> B.M. MS. Harl. 6079, f. 25v.

Hoods like this are strikingly shown in Plates 53 and 58, and ladies' head-dresses worn in a similar way in Fig. 51.

51. Mourning ladies whose head-dresses cover the eyes. 1453. Two of the gilded "weepers" round the tomb of Richard Beauchamp, Earl of Warwick, at Warwick.
After C. A. Stothard Monumental Effigies of Great Britain *1876.*

CHAPTER 12

GRAVE-CLOTHES AND FUNERAL EFFIGIES

In considering historically costumes proper to funerary rites it seems logical to start with what was worn by the protagonist, the corpse itself. The apparelling of the body generally aimed at giving it both physical protection and a good appearance. Treatment varied of course greatly with the status, sex and age of the deceased, with local tradition, with changes in availability of materials, and as we have seen, with ideas of the after life.

(a) Ordinary People

Contemporary descriptions show, according to Joseph Strutt,[1] that in Saxon times the body would be "covered with a *camisia* or *shirt*" and then clothed in accordance with the person's rank. For a time before burial the face was left exposed; then it was covered with a napkin, the *sudarium*, and the whole wrapped in a *sceat* or winding sheet. Illuminations in an eleventh-century Saxon MS. (B. M. Claudius B IV) bear out this account. The sheet, which is often coloured, is generally wound so as to look like a cocoon but can be arranged as in Pl. 37(b). The "Winchester Psalter"[2] (1150–60) affords several examples of the *swaddling* of a corpse. A delicate white shroud tightly invests every part, sometimes the arms separately, and then bands, which may be coloured, are wound spirally around the whole (Pl. 38). The faces are shown uncovered because the bodies are in process of resurrection.

After the twelfth century, winding sheets without swaddling seem to have been usual when there was a coffin. The Queen Mary Psalter[3] (*c.* 1320) affords examples and also shows that a young woman would be buried with her hair loose (folio 302).

Linen was preferred for the inner shroud or winding sheet* even with the poor and there might be an outer wrapping of stouter material as well.

Expenses at the death of a squire in Kent in 1488 included charges for "his leystowe† lynnen and wollyn cloth".[4]

Until the seventeenth century the poor were buried without coffins and

---

* So called by 1541 (Willoughby Household Accounts, p. 473).
† Grave (from *lay* and *stow*, a place).

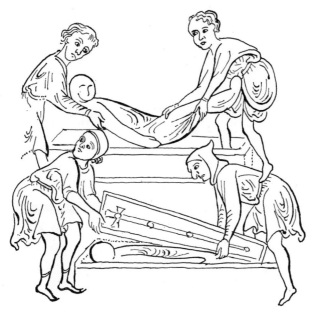

52. (*a*) Corpse in a clinging investment (cere cloth ?) the limbs separate;
no swaddling bands.
Entombment of King Offa I (in two stages) depicted by Matthew
Paris, *c.* 1250.
B.M. MS. Nero D 1 (1st part) f. 4v.

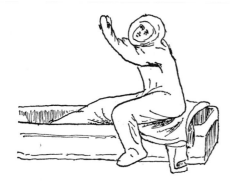

(*b*) Raising of Lazarus Corpse in similar investment. Outer shroud thrown back. *c.* 1320.
*Queen Mary's Psalter (B.M. MS. Roy. 2 B VII)
f. 211.*

for transport might borrow the "parish hamper". It was not until the
eighteenth century that coffins became usual, and even in the 1860s burials
without them were not unknown. This made graveclothes all the more

53. John Donne, when nearing his end, in 1631, posed for his own monumental effigy (which survives at St. Paul's). ". . . having put off his clothes, had this winding sheet put on him, and so tied with knots at his head and feet . . . as dead bodies are usually . . . shrouded and put into their coffin or grave . . . He thus stood . . . with so much of the sheet turned aside as might show his . . . death-like face." (Isaac Walton *Life of John Donne*, 1640.)
Engr. by Martin from part of the original drawing. Frontispiece to Donne's Death's Dvell, *1632 (detail).*

important, especially since to cover the face of the dead is universally felt to be necessary except just while the living take a parting look. (See Misson's account below, and an illustration where a woman holds the little square *sudarium*, Fig. 55.)

The Parish Register of Poynings, Sussex, has an entry for 1608:

Was buried . . . a poore man that died in the place stable [stable of the big house], and being brought half naked with his face bare, the parson would not bury him soe, but first he gave a sheete and caused him to be sacked therein, and they buried him more Christian like.

J. C. Cox, Parish Registers (1910), p. 120

A shrouded but coffinless corpse would often, for convenience in carrying, still be bound round with canvas swaddling bands. The Commonplace Book of a Mr White Watson of Bakewell tells us:

> The custom of Interment in Wooden coffins was on the Rev. Mr Monks coming to reside here [vicar 1678–1724]. A corps . . . was brought in Swaddling Clothes which was abolished in 1697 and was detained in church until a coffin was made, and the wife then took off the flannel for her own use.

Ibid.

It was in the sixteenth to eighteenth centuries that shrouds were often tied up at each end like a cracker (Fig. 54, but cf. p. 123). A ballad published in about 1640 puts in the mouth of a dying bride the words:

> And, gentle mother be not coy
> to bring my winding sheet.
>
> . . . . . .
>
> My bride-laces of silke,
> bestow'd on maidens meete,
> May fitly serve, when I am dead,
> to tie my hands and feete:

Roxburghe Ballads, ed. C. Hindley (1874), Vol. 1, p. 246

Grave-clothes were much affected by an Act of Parliament which came into force to promote the English wool trade, in 1678 (after a similar but abortive Act in 1666).

> Noe person . . . whatsoever shall be buryed in any Shirt, Shift or Sheete made of or mingled with Flax, Silk, Hempe, Gold or Silver or other than what be made of Wooll onely—upon forfeiture of the summe of Five pounds.

(18 and 19 Car. II cap. 4)

An affidavit to the effect that the law had been observed had to be produced by the executors (Pl. 39).

Extreme poverty became an advantage. Flowers or hay replaced grave clothing and a number of entries in Parish Registers read like this one, dated 11th August 1678:

> Noe affidavit made, he being buried in Herbs.[5]

54. Funeral invitation. Corpse in winding sheet, tied at both ends,
otherwise naked. 1696.
Guildhall Library, Noble Collection, C.22. 83 T 1695/6.

The minister at Helmdon, Northants, in 1682 mildly pokes fun at the new regulation:

> Frances Pickeings was shrowded only in a winding sheet made of the Fleece of good Fat Mutton.
>
> J. C. Cox, op. cit.

The Act even applied to children, for example a labourer's child at Frant in 1678 and Lady Chicheley's little girl "wrapped in woollen" at Wimpole in 1681.[6]

Misson (1698)[7] was much struck by this law that ordained burial in "a woollen stuff, which is a kind of a thin Bays, which they call Flannel". He goes on:

> nor is it lawful to use the least needleful of Thread or Silk . . . This Shift is

always white but there are different sorts of it as to Fineness . . . To make
these Dresses is a particular Trade . . . they are always to be had ready
made, of what Size or Price you please . . . They put on the body a
Flannel Shirt, which has commonly a Sleeve purfled [ruffled] about the
Wrists and the Slit of the Shirt down the Breast done [trimmed] in the same
Manner. When these Ornaments are not of woollen Lace they are at least
edged . . . with black Thread. The Shirt should be at least half a foot longer
than the Body, that the Feet of the Deceased may be wrapped in it as in a
Bag . . . they tie the part that is folded down with a Piece of Woollen
Thread, as we do our Stockings.

The outfit is completed by gloves, cravat, "a little square Piece of Flannel
which covers the face", a cap with chin-cloth for a man or a head-dress with
forehead cloth for a woman—all of wool.

An advertisement in the *London Gazette*, 12th–15th August (1678) reads
(italics ours):

Decent and fashionable laced Shifts and Dressings for the Dead *made of
Woollen* have been presented to her Majestie by Amy Potter Widow (the
first that put the making of such things in practice).

The rich often preferred to be fined than see their dear ones "buried in wool".
In 1708 a typical entry appears in the Register of Gayton, Northants.

Mrs . . . Bellingham was buryed . . . in Linnen and the forfeiture of the
Act payd [viz.] fifty shillings to ye informer and fifty shillings to ye poor . . .

J. C. Cox, op. cit.

The merry widow in Steele's "*The Funeral*" (V, i) looks ahead with the
remark:

if you shou'd, as I hope you won't, out-live me, take care I an't buried in
Flannel, 't would never become me I'm sure.

Mrs Oldfield, the famous actress (d. 1730) who delighted in dress, was laid
to rest, according to her maid Mrs Saunders, wearing a very fine Brussels
lace head-dress, holland shift with tucker and double ruffles of the same lace,
new kid gloves and "her Body wrapped up in a winding Sheet".[8] Pope, in
his *Moral Essays*,[9] puts these words into Mrs Oldfield's mouth:

Odious in woollen! 'twould a saint provoke . . .
No, let a charming chintz and Brussells lace
Wrap my cold limbs, and shade my lifeless face.

DuBourg delin.

55. Gathering, before an English funeral. Corpse in white flannel (wool) shirt or shroud, and cap. A woman removes the flannel face-cloth (formerly *sudarium*), to take a last look. Another woman offers rosemary to a guest. 1736.

Engr. after du Bourg in B. Picart Ceremonies and Religious Customs . . . *English trans. Vol. 6, 1737 (1st French edn. 1736).*

Mrs Oldfield was not alone in her vanity. Her contemporary, the writer of *Tricks of the Town*,[10] remarked that "Bills for ordinary Funerals" had of late become "exorbitant" not only because of undertakers' rapacity:

> I believe every Corpse above ground will desire as decent an Interment as its circumstances will admit of; but the extravagant Pride of some People, in going to their graves dress'd in *Lace* and *Velvet* has greatly enhanc'd the Price of Interment.

Gradually resistance to woollen grave-clothes broke down and they became usual for ordinary people; but for a wealthy City coal-merchant in 1785, the time-honoured fine was paid and he was "buried in linen" with a superfine crape shroud, winding sheet, pillow, etc. (*Benenden Letters*, p. 222).

The Burial in Wool Act was not repealed until 1814/15.

According to E. & M. A. Radford (*op. cit.*), "many people in the past used to make up their own funeral garments long before old age. The shroud, cap and stockings needed were carefully sewn and knitted . . . In Northumberland they were included as a matter of course in the wedding trousseau. Shrouds were . . . the usual grave garments" but sometimes other clothes were used, often white for women—a white nightdress was a common choice. A bride dying soon after marriage was buried in her wedding dress.

However, undertakers have been the main source of supply since about 1700. An advertisement of one of them in 1838 lists shrouds in twenty lengths and four qualities ("Common, Middle, Fine Rose, Sup. Rose full trimmed"); also ruffling per yard and winding sheets in nineteen lengths.[11]

It is surprising how persistent was the liking in some places for burying people in their ordinary, or best, day clothes. An American medical journal reproduces illustrations dated 1868 and 1908, showing men's bodies dressed in coats, the first with the feet wrapped but the second in trousers and shoes.[12]

Mrs Sherwood (1884, *op. cit.*), again American, but basing her etiquette on the English, has this to say:

> the body . . . [to be viewed in an open casket on the day of interment] is often dressed in the clothes worn in life . . . a man . . . usually in black . . . A young boy . . . in his everyday clothes; but surely the young of both sexes look more fitly clad in the white cashmere robe.

Here is an example of the use of white—oddly enough in wool for choice! White stockings have along been preferred for women.

A fine specimen of a white wool *grave suit*, heavily frilled with satin, was exhibited as a piece of Victoriana at an Exhibition in the Brighton Art Gallery and Museum in 1970. Reminiscent of a very early example we give on p. 166 one of these garments, though it appears like a nightdress, is really only a front, tied with tape across the back.

The face-cloth continued in use, and the Rev. W. H. Sewell (1882) comments on the necessity of always having to admire its fine workmanship when he was invited to "view the body".[13]

(b) Ecclesiastics

As is true today, men and women following a calling with a characteristic dress of its own, have generally been buried wearing this. Thus soldiers wore military dress, sailors wore their uniform (when they had one), and monks, nuns and priests wore at least some of their ecclesiastical garments.

Because lying in state was the custom where the great were concerned, prelates wore full liturgical vestments, sovereigns and peers their ceremonial robes.

Catholic priests often, and prelates usually, were buried in Mass (Eucharistic) vestments.* "Mitred abbots", like bishops, when *in pontificalibus*, wore certain episcopal vestments as well (cf. Fig. 56). They included a tunicle and over it another tunic, the dalmatic; buskins (loose ornamental silk boots); "sandals" over these (silk, sometimes like ankle-shoes); mitre, gloves, ring of office and pastoral staff (crook). Matthew Paris describes William de Trumpyngtone, Abbot of St Albans (d. 1235) as being dressed in all these for his grave.[14] However, Wigmore, Abbot of Gloucester (d. 1337) wore not sandals but "leather boots" in his coffin.[15]

The history of bishops' grave-clothes goes back at least to St Cuthbert, who died *c.* A.D. 687. A wonderful account of his exhumation in 1104 has come down to us from an eye-witness, Simeon of Durham.[16] The bishop's vestments had retained astonishing beauty and there were elaborate grave wrappings as well.

> His body is everywhere enveloped in a thinly-woven sheet of linen . . . This is the winding sheet.

The head and face were similarly invested by an extremely clinging fine cloth

---

* A priest at Mass wore: a long white linen *alb*, an *amice* at the neck, a scarf-like *stole*, a *maniple* or *fanon* hanging on the fore-arm, and over all a closed cape the *chasuble*. These are shown in Fig. 56.

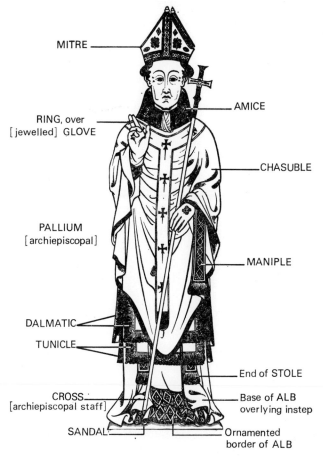

MITRE ——

RING, over
[jewelled] GLOVE

—— AMICE

—— CHASUBLE

PALLIUM
[archiepiscopal]

—— MANIPLE

DALMATIC

TUNICLE

—— End of STOLE

CROSS
[archiepiscopal staff]

Base of ALB
overlying instep

SANDAL

Ornamented
border of ALB

56. Archbishop in full vestments. The Eucharistic (Mass) vestments
worn by all Catholic priests are labelled on reader's right, those proper
to bishops and archbishops only, on left. (Brass effigy of Archbishop
Thomas Cranley, at New College, Oxford. 1417.)
Herbert Haines Manual of Monumental Brasses . . . British Isles
(*1861*) Vol. *1.*

and over it was "a purple face cloth" covering the head and its mitre. At the
neck was the amice; at the feet the alb, and the ends of the stole showed
below the tunicle and dalmatic. These last were "of great elegance and the
costly colour of purple" variegated with citron colour interwoven with

designs of birds and beasts, the borders stiff with gold thread. The chasuble had been removed eleven years after burial but the maniple was there. No ring or staff are mentioned, but the head bore a jewelled gold fillet and on the feet were the episcopal sandals.

A huge fringed linen sheet with raised designs was wrapped round the whole figure and over this was a three-fold "cloth of thicker substance."*

It appears that Bishops were sometimes buried in canonical (processional) instead of Eucharistic vestments. The most obvious difference would be the cope (open in front) in place of the chasuble. In the Queen Mary's Psalter[17] (*c.* 1320) a bishop, with mitre, is seen in his tomb dressed in exactly the same way as two attendant bishops. All wear copes.

The mitre was essential. Machyn records in his diary that in 1556 Dr Belle, sometime Bishop of Worcester, "was put in ys coffen . . . witt myter and odur thynges that longyst to a bysshope".

For an Archbishop the special insignium is the *pallium*, worn over the shoulders, a band of white wool hanging Y-shaped in front and behind. This, too, he took with him to the grave. The whole set of archiepiscopal vestments is shown in Fig. 56.

According to Fitz Stephen,[18] Archbishop Thomas à Becket (in 1170) was buried with all these vestments on top of his ordinary harsh monastic clothes, namely a habit, a hair shirt, and braes (drawers) made of linen lined with sackcloth.

In 1890 the stone tomb of an Archbishop was opened at Canterbury— almost certainly that of Hubert Walter who died in 1205. The linen and woollen parts of the vestments had perished, but of the precious woollen pallium there remained the two lead plummets for its ends and the two pins for the shoulders. The chasuble was of amber damask with designs covered in gold leaf and with ornaments of lace. The buskins, "sandals", mitre, beautifully ornamented crozier and jewelled gold ring were all present in their proper places[19] (Fig. 57).

Wasting too many good vestments by burial was avoided. Walter's mitre (in the new style introduced by himself) was comparatively simple and evidently made for the funeral only; and the tunicle and dalmatic were "represented not by actual vestments but by pieces of silk damask, cut from a length of material and sewn . . . like long bags with an opening for the head". The

* The remarkable preservation may have been partly due to a heavily waxed cloth which had been applied at some unknown date to the outside of the inner coffin.

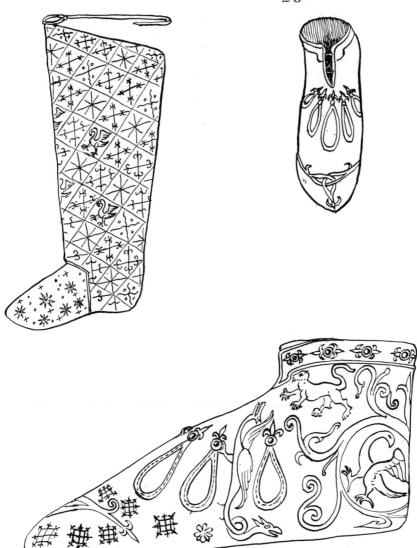

57. Footwear actually found on the body of Hubert Walter, Archbishop of Canterbury (d. 1205) in 1890. Green silk, embroidered in
gold and silver. (*a*) Buskins (fastened by a silk lace) folded flat. (*b*) and
(*c*) "Sandals", jewelled.
After plates in Vetusta Monumenta *Vol. 7 (1893)*

chasuble would hide all but the lower ends of these and the economy did
nothing to detract from the magnificent appearance of the body.

An episcopal ring is worn in the grave; but since a letter from the Archbishop of Canterbury in 1310 shows that he claimed as his own the official
rings of all his predecessors,[20] the grave ring must often have been a "second
best", or one made for the purpose. This is confirmed by an entry in the
accounts of the funeral expenses of the Archbishop of York in 1508.

> For a pontificall ring put upon my lorde's fynger . . . xvi d[21]

A "whitt cotte" for the body cost 3s 3d, which makes the ring look cheap at
1s 4d!

After the Reformation, many of the vestments having been discarded (or
only recently revived), a bishop would generally be buried with little besides
his mitre, cope and episcopal sleeved surplice, the rochet.

There was an important exception to the custom of burying the great in
their most ceremonial dress. In late Medieval and Tudor times funerals
became so elaborate that the lying-in-state could not continue through the
long period of preparation. Instead, after a few days, the body was "chested"
and on the coffin was laid a life-size wax or wooden portrait effigy which
would wear the apparel in its place. Descriptions and relics of these funeral
effigies are therefore a guide to the costumes actually worn in the grave in
earlier times.

A pre-Reformation heraldic ruling reads

> *Beryinge of a bushop or Cardinal:* the corse [body in coffin] to be laid in the
> foresaid chare [chariot] and upon him a figure in a busshoppes array and
> miter, in his hand a croisser [crozier] and on his feete Rede Showes and on
> his handes red gloves garnished with ringes . . .[22]

Machyn tells us that for Bishop Stephen Gardener, Queen Mary's Chancellor (d. 1555/6), over the corpse on its funeral chariot was "ys pyctur
mad(e) with ys myter on ys hed".[23] Bishop Islip's "presentac'on" was set up
over his grave at Westminster the night *after* his funeral.[24]

(c) Kings and Princes

The dressing of the body assumes enormous importance when it is that of a
royal personage, especially when he has been consecrated (anointed) at a
coronation.

The winding sheet which wrapped the body of Edward the Confessor, as seen in the Bayeux tapestry, concealed regal apparel. When his coffin was opened in 1183, such was the splendour of the robes or cloths within it that they were made into three copes for use in Westminster Abbey.[25] Examined again in James I's reign, the body was described as wearing a golden jewelled

58 (*a*) Monumental effigy of King John (1216), Worcester Cathedral. Coronation robes, as he wore them in the grave: crimson supertunic, with gold and jewelled borders; gold tunic; green-lined gold mantle, fastened behind shoulders and draped over right arm; jewelled gloves; finger-ring; sandals (with spurs) over red buskins; crown. He holds a sword. (*b*) Sandal of the same.

After C. A. Stothard Monumental Effigies of Great Britain. *1832.*

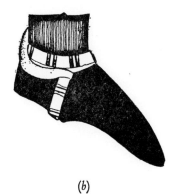

(*a*)   (*b*)

crucifix and locket on a chain and "his skull had on it a . . . gold . . . diadem one inch in breadth".[26]

With Henry II's death in 1189 the custom was first established for the king's body, with his coronation vestments and insignia, to be put on display before being buried. Descriptions of his sepulchral costume have come down to us from three of his contemporaries. "Benedict of Peterborough" says:

> on the morrow of his death when he was to be carried clothed in royal apparel, wearing a golden crown . . . and having gloves on his hands and a golden ring on his finger, a sceptre in his hand, footgear woven with gold, and spurs on his feet, girdle with a sword, he lay having his face uncovered.
> Quoted (in trans.) by W. H. St J. Hope in *Archaeologia*,
> Vol. 60, p. 525

Henry II's son Henry (d. 1183) who was crowned and died during his father's lifetime was buried in the linen garments still impregnated with holy oil, which he had worn for his actual anointing before donning the outer coronation robes. The body was salted and "wrapped in lead and bulls hides"—an early example of the use of lead—for transport across France.★

Valentine Green describes the opening of the tomb of King John (d. 1216) in Worcester in 1797. The body was dressed in coronation robes, just like those sculptured in marble on the tomb, except for

> the gloves on its hands and the crown on its head . . . On the skull in the coffin was found to be the celebrated monk's cowl in which he is recorded to be buried, as a passport through purgatory.
> *An Account of the Discovery of the Body of King John,* (Pamphlet) 1797

Apart from the additional sword, spurs and crown, coronation vestments were, item for item, like the clothing of a bishop, for the good reason that "Kings by their coronation are admitted into a sacred as well as a civil character" (H. Haines).[27] The mantle resembled a cope in being a large ornamental cape without fur (Fig. 59).

The body of Edward I (d. 1307) was carried about with his army, at his own wish, and probably often displayed. His final resting place in Westminster Abbey was opened in 1774 and a very full account of his appearance is given by Sir J. Ayloffe.[28] The body had been invested, like St Cuthbert's, in a fine clinging "cerecloth" (waxed linen), then dressed in the vestments and

★ His great-grandfather Henry I for a similar journey had been wrapped in bull's hides only (Henry of Huntingdon).

The First Plate
of the Regalia.

The Open Pall.

A

59. Coronation mantle (brocade) of cope-like form, worn by James II,
1685.
Francis Sandford A History of the Coronation of James II . . . *1687.*

finally wrapped in a square of coarser cloth, also waxed. The white stole
was covered with designs in "gilt and beautiful transparent glass". Similar
ornaments for the (now perished) gloves remained★ and a sceptre lay in each
hand. The only concession to economy was that the crown was "of inferior
workmanship" and in place of other garments, a piece of cloth of gold covered
the legs and feet. But the MS. *Liber Regalis*[29] (*c.* 1382) even insisted that a dead

★ Coronation gloves had to be of linen because the hands were anointed, as with bishops.

60. Other coronation vestments on traditional lines, worn by James II.
Brocade supertunic or dalmatic; stole to match mantle; sandals and
buskins matching supertunic.
As for Fig. 59.

king's body should wear his coronation buskins and "sandals" as well as all
else.

Richard II, whether from humility or unwonted thrift, willed that
although he was to be buried with the customary jewelled ring on his finger
the crown and sceptre must be without precious stones.[30] (In the event, of
course, his body met with total ignominy. It was displayed at St Paul's simply
wrapped in lead,[31] all but the face, "that they might believe for certain that
he was dead".[32]

Despite the *Liber Regalis* it became customary from Edward II to James I

61. Inner coronation vestments. (*a*) Open tunic slashed at back, shoulders and sleeves. The gaps, "closed with ribbands, being first opened by the Archbishop", the skin is anointed through them.
(*b*) Linen *colobium*, a sleeveless shirt or surplice with lace.
As for Fig. 59.

for the regalia to be put upon a funeral effigy of wood or wax, etc. (cf. Bishop Gardener's above), instead of on the corpse itself—with consequent saving.

At Edward II's funeral (1327) a carved figure of the king wore all the outer robes and insignia, which were returned to the Wardrobe afterwards. His body, like Prince Henry's above, was buried only in the inner garments of his anointing: the headcloth, shirt, tunic and gloves. (The shirt and tunic had to be slit to get them on to the stiff body and were then sewn up again.)[33]

With an edict on the "Burial of a Prince of the Blood Royall" it became properly established that the funeral effigy (called image, picture, figure, personage or representation)

> shal be endowed with the same robes that he ware when he was Kinge or created prynce.
>
> B.M. MS. Harl. 6079, f. 25v.

The wording allows for coronation vestments or, alternatively, robes of estate, or Parliament robes. The latter, being less precious, could be left on display long after the funeral—hence the relics of effigies still at Westminster Abbey.

Above the coffin of Henry V, transported to England in 1422, was "his Figure made of boyled Hides or Leather".[34] This was

> an image very like in stature and face to the dead King arrayed in a long and ample purple mantle furred with ermine . . .
>
> Thomas Walsingham[35]

It bore all the sovereign's accessories. Although the effigy wore "the royal sandals", the description of the mantle shows that the robes were those of estate, not coronation.

Regulations at the time of Edward IV prescribed parliament robes both for the body's lying-in-state and also for the effigy.

> *What shall be done on the demyse of a King annoynted* . . . the body must be [em]barmed, wrapped in laun . . . then hosen cherte and a perer of shone [shoes] of rede lether, and do on his surcote of cloth, his cap of estate . . . a septer in one hande and on his face a kerchief and so shewed to his nobles.

For burial:

> wrappe hym in raynes* well trameled in cords of silk, then in tarseryn tramelled, and then in velvet and so in cloth of gold.

Finally at the funeral

> make an ymage like hym clothed in . . . a mantell of state . . .[36]

An eyewitness recorded that at Edward IV's funeral there was indeed a "personage" like this lying on the coffin; but the King's body was displayed nearly naked to Lords and the Mayor.[37]

Lying on the coffin at Henry VIII's funeral was a bulky and gorgeous figure that might, for all the world, have been the king himself. This time the robes were crimson over a scarlet doublet and hose.[38] The effigy was

> wonderfully richly apparelled with velvet, gold and precious stones of all Sorts; holding in his left hand the Bal of the World with a Cross, upon his Head a Crown Imperial of inestimable value a Collar of the Garter about his neck and a Garter of Gold about his Leg.
>
> College of Arms MS. I, 11[39]

* Very fine linen.

The body itself was wrapped almost exactly in accordance with the instructions for burial quoted above (ibid.).

Edward VI's effigy (1553) unlike his father's, wore Garter Robes. Machyn himself saw it "lyeing recheussly [wretchedly] on the coffin".[40] Another moving sight was the effigy of the young Henry, Prince of Wales, brother of Charles I (d. 1612),

> apprelled . . . with his Creation Robes about the same [purple investiture robes] with crowne [coronet] and capp of Estate.[41]

A contemporary engraving showing the effigy may be seen at the National Portrait Gallery. The figure with parts of its rich doublet and trunk hose and its white stockings, still existed in 1907.[42] The body itself was "wrapped in lead and the heart inclosed in lead upon his breast in the form thereof" (Francis Sandford).[43]

For Henry's father James I (d. 1625) a temporary effigy was made for the lying-in-state, its crown having "Divers counterfeit Stones"; but even for this a Daniel Parkes was ordered to make "one periwigg, beard and eyebrows".[44] The funeral effigy's robes came from the Royal Wardrobe.[45] The crimson ermined mantle covered a garment of green powdered with gold, just as in Richard II's portrait at Westminster Abbey.

No success was met with in efforts to preserve the body of Cromwell, in 1658, and according to James Heath "they were forced to bury him out of hand."[46] His wax "effigies"* played the part of the corpse during prolonged lying-in-state.

It comes as something of a shock to learn what a regal figure this was—"in robes of purple velvet . . . with rich gold lace, Furr'd with Ermins"; a sword hung from an embroidered belt and there was a typical royal sceptre in each hand. After some weeks "this brave thing" was placed upright and its velvet cap "changed for a Crown".† Wearing this it formed the centre piece of a very magnificent funeral.[47]

Cromwell's was the last effigy of a British ruler actually borne in his funeral procession.‡

* The plural form of the word was usual.

† This would seem to justify our putting Cromwell with the kings, "bauble" though he would probably have called the crown himself.

‡ The remarkable waxwork of Charles II, wearing genuine Garter robes and still to be seen at Westminster Abbey, was completed shortly after his burial (Official Guide, edn. 1966, p. 113).

(d) Queens

When the grave of Henry I's wife, Matilda (d. 1118), was opened in 1562 she was found to have been buried in "robes of estate" and wearing a royal finger ring.[48] This set of robes—a long furred mantle and a surcote or a gown— seem to have been the usual burial dress for a queen, until they came to adorn her effigy instead. The hair would be loose, just as she wore it at her corona- tion.*

Anne of Bohemia (d. 1394) was perhaps the earliest queen to have an effigy.[49] Parts of the wooden and stuffed leather figure of Elizabeth of York (d. 1503) have survived till now, with the gold satin ofits bodice and the carved holes for its ear-rings.[50] It still had dark cloth stockings in 1890.[51] It was an

> Ymage . . . clothed in the very Roabes of Estate of the Queen, having her very rich crowne on her Head her heire aboutt her Shoulders her septer in her right Hand and her fingers well garnished with Gould and precious Stones.
>
> *Antiquarian Repertory*, Vol. 4, p. 654 seq.

The Lord Chamberlain's Accounts show that a crimson satin "garment" bordered with black velvet was made for this effigy (a kirtle under the robes?) and the hair was "hired".[52]

Meanwhile "the sergeant of the Chandry", embalming the body was allowed "xl ells of lynning holland cloth for the cerecloth" and then "the King's Plum(b)er closed her in lead".[53]

Catherine of Aragon[54] when she died in 1536, Anne Boleyn in the same year, and Jane Seymour in 1537[55] were all allowed effigies very similar to that of Elizabeth of York, loose hair and all. The last two, we know, even had shoes of cloth of gold, hose, a chemise "and all other ornaments".[56]

There was no effigy for Katherine Parr, but we know something about her grave-clothes, which were very simple. She was buried in Sudeley Castle chapel, and in 1782 "some ladies" had the ground in the ruin opened up. There was an inscribed "leaden envelope"

> which they [caused to be] opened in two places . . . and found . . . a human body wrapped in a cere cloth consisting of many folds of coarse linen, dipped in wax, tar and perhaps some gums. Over this was wrapped a sheet of lead fitted exactly to the body.
>
> *Archaeologia*, Vol. 9, p. 2 (1789)

* Compare the bronze figure of Queen Eleanore at Westminster Abbey.

62. The lead coffin of Katherine Parr (d. 1548) after opening in 1752.
See text.
Archaeologia *Vol. 9, opp. p. 1.*

Fig. 62 shows how they had uncovered one of the (individually wrapped) hands.

Queen Mary I's body was simply cered, after embalming and separation of the heart, but her effigy was elaborate. Fitted with sabatons (footwear) made of "cloth of gold incarnate" lined with satin, it was

> adorned with cremesun velvett . . . [and had] mony good rynges on her fyngers.
>
> Machyn, *Diary*, p. 182

The crown and sceptre were jewelled.

Queen Elizabeth's effigy (in 1603) apparently wore her ermine-edged *white* mantle and combined an ermine-cuffed traditional surcoat with a large up-to-date ruff.★ There was no true head-dress, but the hair was plaited and coifed, possibly in deference to the Queen's age—she was 70. Specially made for the "Representac' on" were a robe of crimson satin, a bodice, a pair of drawers, bumbast (padding), sabatons and a coif of cloth of gold.[57] The effigy was a perfect success, for Stow, who saw the funeral himself, says of the crowds

> when they beheld her statue, or picture lying upon the coffin . . . having a crown upon the head and a ball and sceptre in either hand, there was such a general sighing groaning and weeping as the like hath not beene seen or known in the memory of man.
>
> *Chronicle of England*, 1615

★ Engraving labelled by hand. B.M. MS. Harl. 1440, f. 8.

Anne of Denmark's effigy (Pl. 39 (b)) was probably got up in the queen's own robe, since the wardrobe accounts show a charge for perfuming a robe but not for making one. Underwear was bought.[58]

The body of Queen Mary II, who died in 1694/5, had wrappings and spices costing £250. They included an impregnated cloth called a "perfumed sparadrape". Inside this and also outside, were "crimson and white sawcenetts" (silks—nothing woollen, despite the Act) "and white Ribbon" over all.[59] At last the custom of carrying an effigy was dying out. Hers and Queen Anne's (which still exists) were made and displayed only after the obsequies were all over and therefore do not concern us.

The apparel of the corpse itself continued to take the form of refined grave clothing rather than robes of state. One example is worth quoting. When the young Princess Charlotte, daughter of the Prince Regent, died in giving birth to a stillborn child in 1817, we are told

> The body, after it was embalmed, was inclosed in a number of wrappings after the manner of the Egyptians, and was then inclosed in rich blue velvet tied with white satin riband.
>
> *Gentleman's Magazine*, Vol. 87, p. 432 (1817)

A further paragraph of the same account illustrates the persistence of two other customs.* At Windsor, the day before the funeral,

> The Urn [containing the bowels] was delivered to four yeomen of the guard, who bore it into the Chapel holding it with white napkins. The coffin with the infant was conveyed also by four yeomen, in a correspondent manner.
>
> *Loc. cit.*

(e) Other People of Substance

Before the general use of lead for the bodies of the wealthy, these might be wrapped, like the early kings, in hides. Richard Gough, in his *Sepulchral Monuments . . . of Great Britain* gives some interesting examples of ancient grave-clothes.[60] He states that when the stone coffin of Hugh Lupus (who was created Earl of Chester by William the Conqueror and died in 1101) was opened in Chester in 1724, the body was found to be "wrapped up in gilt leather, and his ancles tied with a string".

For the wealthy, embalming was employed quite early, as for example with Lady Cicely Talmache in 1281, when the chemicals, linen, silk etc. cost

* For use of white napkins under an infant's coffin see Ch. 18.

the equivalent of a hundredweight of wheat.[61] We are not told what clothes the body may have worn. But, like royalty, the rich and distinguished were often displayed after death in fine clothing and at least until the eighteenth century might wear the same in their coffins, unless there was a funeral effigy.

"A gentleman who was upon the spot" describes the opening in 1717 at Southwell of the ancient grave of a "noble Personage". It contained

> the Body of a Man lying in [his] Boots. The leather was . . . to all appearance sound, till on Tryal it tore like London brown paper . . . He was drest in Cloth of Tissue* which plainly showed the Silver by waving it in the sun . . . A wand [staff of office] lay beside him.
>
> Francis Peck, *Desiderata Curiosa* (1732–5), Vol. 1, Bk 7

An interesting glimpse of what already must have been a two-century-old custom is given once more by Machyn (*Diary*, p. 160). He remarks in 1557, about the burial of Robert Rochester, that though created Knight of the Garter, he had died before being installed and "so he was not bered (buried) with the garter". K.G.s were obliged to wear their emblem at all times during life and evidently did so in their graves.

In the early eighteenth century it was still not impossible for even a commoner to lie in state in his coffin wearing particularly elegant attire.

> Last night the corpse of Major Rose, a Jamaican Merchant, was interr'd at St Peters Cornhill from Mercer's Hall in a most pompous manner. The body laid in a lead coffin dressed in the richest linen and lace, and scarlet hose with gold clokes [clocks] after the custom of America.
>
> *London Post or Halfpenny Journal*, 20th–23rd November 1724

Funeral effigies were sometimes used for the aristocracy, at first in special circumstances only. The re-interment of Richard Duke of York in 1466 has been mentioned above. Six years after he was killed at Wakefield, Edward IV wished to honour his father's unsuccessful claim to the throne; but as only the head-less skeleton remained, the role of an effigy was important. Above the coffin in Fotheringay church was set

> an Image Like unto the Prince Living, upp right, in a Surcott, and a Mantle of blewe velvett furred with ermyns . . . and on his Hed a Cappe of Meyntenance,† with an awngell [angel] standing in white holdinge a Crowne over his head in token that he was Kinge of right.
>
> B.M. MS. Egerton 2642, f. 191

* Fabric with metal thread.
† Cap of estate.

Embalming and wrapping in lead became usual in families that could afford it,[62] but near the end of the sixteenth century a reaction set in, especially among women, against the idea of the knife, and other attentions of the embalmers. Frances, Duchess of Richmond and Lennox, ordered that she should be

> presently [immediately] putt up in brann and in lead before I am fully could [cold].[63]

Lady Verney's message to her son in 1639 shows an overstimulated imagination in the same way:

> let me be buried in leade . . . and let no strandger winde me, nor doe not lett me be striptte, but put me a cleene smoke [chemise] over me . . . and lett my face be hid.[64]

Perhaps the decline in trade exacerbated the feelings of the Company of Barber-Surgeons and Surgeons against poachers on their preserves. They succeeded in 1604, in getting a new charter that would prevent their

> science of searinge and embalmeinge being intruded into by Butchers . . . Chaundiers and others.
>
> Bradford, op. cit.

Despite her abhorrence, the Duchess of Richmond and Lennox, when her husband died suddenly in 1624, "caused him to be . . . embalmed". He was then "wrapped up in the best and finest white linnen she had" (James Cleland, *Monuments of Mortalitie*, 1624).

It was the Duke's effigy that lay in state. Commissioners "diligently prepared for the Funeral pomps" at Westminster Abbey, for two whole months. He was Lord Admiral and Lord Steward and worthy of a great funeral. They caused

> the effigie of My Lord . . . to be made and sett up in the best Chamber [of Richmond House] apparelled with his Parliament Robes lying in a Blacke Velvet Bed . . . which they permitted all the people at all times that came to see.
>
> Ibid.

An interesting proof of the way such figures came to symbolize their prototypes is given at the end of Cleland's account of the funeral: "Finally . . . his officers brake their staves *over the Effigie*".

An unusual effigy was the one which played the part of General Monk, Duke of Albemarle, in 1670—at "the layinge in state of his Grace" and at the magnificent funeral accorded him afterwards (Pl. 40). Full details are quoted by Hope (*op. cit.*) from contemporary sources. The effigy had to represent simultaneously a soldier, a duke, a Knight of the Garter and a mere man. Anachronistically it was "in Compleate Armour azured with guilt nailes" and including gauntlets. There was, of course, a sword, on a crimson velvet girdle. Under the armour were "buff-skin skirts" (military style), and an oiled chamois waistcoat and breeches. On top went the General's own ducal robe of crimson velvet, re-furred with ermine, and on the head a cap to match and a ducal coronet. Then there was the "collar" of the Order of the Garter,* the blue velvet gilt-buckled garter itself (under the left knee) and on the feet, gilt spurs. Finally, as a man, it had to be supplied with a lace cravat and cuffs and even linen drawers and "a Perriwigge of Haire to it". An effigy, one might think, to end all effigies! But they remained popular with the nobility for a generation more.

"La Belle Stuart" another and more celebrated Duchess of Richmond (d. 1702), perhaps having liked her own appearance at the coronation of Queen Anne, desired in her will "to have my Effigie as well done in Wax as can bee and set up . . . dressed in my Coronation Robes and Coronet".[65] Her red velvet, ermine-trimmed robe was more effective than the coronet, which was relegated to the back of the head to make room for an ebulliant head-dress of ribbons. She even held a fan.

Finally there still exist the effigies of the nineteen-year-old Duke of Buckingham (d. 1735/6) and of his mother the Duchess (d. 1743), a illegitimate daughter of James II. Both wear their actual coronation robes. According to Horace Walpole, the Duchess supervised the making of her own effigy as well as her son's.[66] She also gave orders about her funeral. To a written instruction for carrying her coronet on a cushion, a note had to be added (presumably by the College of Heralds) "the Coronet cannot be carried, it being on the head of the Effigies".[67] And there it still crowns the last of the long line of representations that were carried at the funerals of the great.

* A richly ornamental chain supporting the enamelled St George.

CHAPTER 13

ORDINARY PEOPLE'S FUNERALS

Among the earliest pictures of burials painted in England are several that occur in the eleventh-century Saxon Pentateuch mentioned above.[1] Here no one wears funeral garb of any kind. In another British Museum MS., as late as *c.* 1350 men and women gathered round a bier are all wearing ordinary clothes in blue and orange colours.[2] But in the Holkham Bible (*c.* 1330) the poor widow of Nain at her son's funeral, though her hood is blue with a red lining, wears it mourning-wise pulled over her face (Fig. 63). This foreshadows the true mourning hood which men wore at funerals for the next three centuries, and women off and on for more than four.

63. Woman at her son's funeral, in a coloured hood but wearing it over the face. (The widow of Nain). *c.* 1330.
After Holkham Bible Picture Book (*B.M. MS. Add. 47682*) *f. 23v. (detail).*

By mid-fifteenth century black, as we have seen, was normal at least with the well-to-do, and where men's funerals were concerned. One Richard Riche, a Mercer and a former Sheriff of the City, in 1463, directed in his will that his wife, three daughters, their husbands (with one servant each), all his grandchildren and all his servants in London "shall be dressed in black cloth on the day of my funeral".[3]

The will of Margaret (d. 1481), widow of John Paston, Esq., confirms the medieval use of white for the funeral torchbearers:

> I will that myn executors shall purveye xii pore meen of my tenantes or other . . . the which I wulle shall be apparailled in white gownes, with Hodes according [to match], to hold xii torches abowte myn herse or bere at such time as I shall be beried.
>
> *Norfolk Archaeology*, Vol. 3, p. 161

During the late fifteenth century, funerals in arms-bearing families began to be conducted by the King's heralds, who added decorum and even glamour to the proceedings and at the same time saw to it that only the arms which the deceased had a right to were displayed. The funeral of Sir J. Shaa, an alderman of London, in 1504, was an early example of a heraldic ceremony for someone not a peer.* By mid-sixteenth century the heralds might be seen at any substantial person's funeral and even at his wife's, provided he was entitled to bear arms. A mere gentleman would sometimes employ them, a Squire or Knight always. With their traditional garb they would parade his "cote-armour" as described on p. 129. This coat would by now be an object painted or worked just for the occasion, but was still of the original tabard shape, like the herald's own. For knights, the targe, helmet with crest and sometimes a sword were carried as well, making up the "hatchments".

The order of the procession, and even the costumes, were laid down by the College of Arms. The schemes varied according to the rank of the defunct but the personnel common to all was arranged in the following order:

> Two conductors
> almsfolk
> friends in black (men)
> clergy
> *bearer of "the penon of his arms"*
> *heralds* with "hatchments"
> COFFIN with bearers and *pall-bearers*
> *chief mourner*
> *other principal mourners*
> women in black
> men and women not in black

Gentlemen's funerals without heralds seem to have followed a similar general pattern.

* Described in College of Arms MS. I 3, f. 63v.

64. Esquires and friends at Sir Phillip Sidney's funeral. Type of mourning hood not worn on head but held on shoulder by its tippet, which may be twisted round neck.
Engr. T. de Bry after Thomas Lant in Funeral Procession of Sir Phillip Sidney, *1588.*

The conductors' function was to make way: hence their invariable black staves. The mourning provided for them, as also for the bearers of the coffin (the underbearers) was of the simplest kind because they were of yeoman class. They just had "black cotes". The almsfolk (earlier "bedesmen"), were allotted, as a form of charity, warm gowns which, as we have seen, were not invariably, black. The true mourning hood worn over the head and with a black mourning gown was always restricted to the chief participants (shown in italics in the above list): namely heralds, bearers of pennons, the four pall-bearers and the principal mourners. These last, if the dead was a commoner, must not be more than five: and at this period and for a long time to come it was customary for

65. Company of Grocers at Sir Phillip Sidney's funeral. Livery hoods
like 15th century chaperons, held by their tippets. 1588.
As for Fig. 64.

a man being deade hee to have only men [principal] mourners at his Buriall
And at a woman's buriall to have only women moreners.

B.M. MS. Egerton 2642, f. 183

This corresponded with the restriction on women's offerings, mentioned
above.

Other gentlemen in black wore gowns, "*with hoodes on there left shoulderes*"[4]
(Fig. 64).

In all hoods the apex was extended into a long tail or liripipe, now con-
fusingly called "tippet" (Pl. 42(a)). Hoods not worn on the head appear from

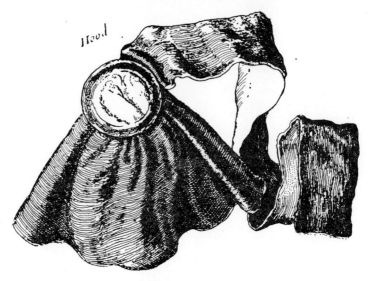

66. Chaperon or hood of the Order of the Garter—carried (or pinned
at the shoulder) by its tippet, like the hoods in Figs. 64 and 73: another
survival. 1672.
Elias Ashmole Institution, Laws and Ceremonies of the Order of the
Garter. *1672.*

drawings to have been vestigial in type, rather like a reduced medieval
chaperon (itself derived from the medieval hood). Like the livery company's
and the Garter Knights' hoods,⋆ it was slung over the shoulder or round the
neck by its tippet (Figs. 64, 65 and cf. 66).

Those most honourable "must have the pre-eminence to goe nearest to
the Cor[p]se",[5] which was not at either end, so that there was a crescendo of
dignity and blackness and then a diminuendo.

A formulary following this plan was laid down, by the middle of the
sixteenth century, specifically for "Knights and Aldermen"[6] (of London).
The three special features of these funerals were connected with charity, with
the livery companies and with the government of the City.

We owe accounts of many such ceremonies in the 1550s and 1560s to
merchant tailor Machyn, whose interest was a vested one since he supplied
all the funeral trappings. His above-mentioned diary shows how many of

⋆ Still called chaperon in Fuller's *Church History* (1655), but called "hood" again by
Ashmole (1672).

Sword Bearer.

Sr Geo : Barnes Lo: Maior .

20

67. Lord Mayor of London; his Sword-bearer with fur hat and
"mourning sword"—at Sir P. Sidney's funeral.
As for Fig. 64.

the aldermen supported not only the aged poor but the "hospitals" or
orphanage schools founded a few years earlier by Edward VI. Thus the
physician Dr Wotton, and Alderman Heardson, who both died in 1555, had
processions headed by "the King's Scollers"[7] and "all the chylderyn" of
Christ's Hospital[8] respectively. The Bluecoat boys were probably already
wearing the uniform familiar to us today. "Master Busse, Skynner", was
followed to the grave, in 1559, by "all other masters of the hospital" bearing
their green staves of office and also by all the Skinners' Company in their
livery.[9]

The funeral of a member of the City Corporation was always attended by
his fellows in a body. At a late Lord Mayor's, in 1556, there were "one
hundred aldermen and gentlemen in black gowns . . . and all the other
aldermen in violet".[10] The violet were state robes such as had been worn for

special occasions since 1419 (and still are). Their use was laid down as follows:

> . . . for the burial of all aldermen, the last love, duty and ceremony one to another: the Aldermen are to wear their violet gownes except such as have (of their friends' allowance) black gownes or mourning.
>
> John Stow, Survey of London, 1598

Some, like Heardson (above) were honoured by the presence of the Lord Mayor with his Swordbearer. The latter had to be supplied with black (ibid.). He would be wearing (as he does today on state occasions) his huge fur cap and he carried the corporation's "mourning sword" (Fig. 67). There is a record of the purchase of this very sword twenty-two years before. It had a black velvet sheath and grip as does its counterpart today.[11]

The funerals of aldermen's and citizens' wives largely conformed to those of their husbands. The Vintners, for example, would turn out in their livery to bury a vintner's wife.[12] "The poor" and "the bearers" (pall-bearers) were often all female.

Ordinary women at this time wore veils ("head-rails"), not mourning hoods (Fig. 47). When in 1561 the wife of the Earl of Arundel's Comptroller was "ded in chyld-bede"

> iiij women dyd bere her and they had cassokes★ nuw and raylles.†
>
> Machyn's Diary, p. 262

Apparently in London in Machyn's day neither the poor nor the mourners wore white gowns at a married woman's funeral, even if she died in childbed.

Machyn lived through both Catholic and Protestant times and occasionally makes a crisp note on the dress and actions of the new-style clergy. At the burial of a lady in 1559[13]

> there was a great company of people, two and two together, and neither priest nor clerk, the new preachers in their gowns like lay-men, neither singing nor saying till they came to the grave: after, took some earth and cast it on the corpse and read a thing . . . and sang *Pater Noster* in English . . .

In a merchant's funeral procession along Cheapside in 1561, "clarkes [clergy] of London" preceded the coffin "with their surplices under their gowns, till they came to Powlles Cherche-yard" where they met the choir

---

★ Loose unwaisted gowns.

† Rail means veil here, not gown or cloak as has been stated elsewhere.

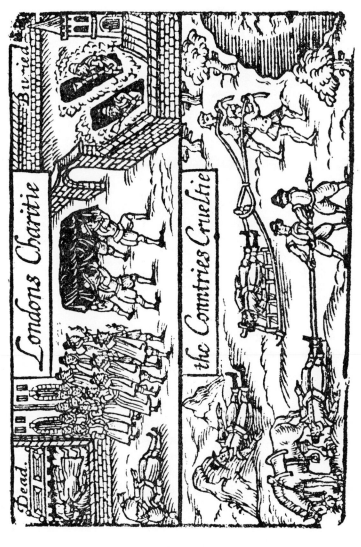

68. Funerals in the plague year of 1641. In London, men mourners have mourning cloaks (under-bearers are without), and carry sprigs (? rosemary). Women have no mourning. In the country, fully dressed corpses are dragged away, one of them by men stripped for work. *Woodcut on title-page of* London's Lamentation *(B.M., Thomason tracts E 166 tract 10).*

A Corpes Bearer

69. (*a*) Corpse-bearer in old-fashioned gown,
(doubtless black) worn perhaps for dignity, and
warmth at night. *Broadsheet "Gryes of London"*.
1655 (B.M. Print Room)

of St Pauls "and then they begane to syng". Before the Reformation there
would be a body of "clerks and priests in surplesyes syngynge" all along the
route.[14]

In the latter part of Elizabeth's reign an innovation was the black "mourning *cloak*", which being eminently practical was to remain in funeral use for
two centuries—although for ordinary wear cloaks went out of fashion *c.*
1670. While more dignified than a coat, the cloak was simpler to make than a
gown and could cover all the clothing without having to fit. Mourning
cloaks were thus mass produced and usually supplied to the mourners of
medium importance. At a funeral in 1604[15] servants of those invited wore
coats, but servants of the household (always ranking higher) wore cloaks:
"strangers" who were only gentlemen had cloaks, but those who were
esquires and knights had gowns.*

* It should be noticed that in some contexts "gown" and "hood" may mean official
garments, not mourning. At the funeral of a civic dignitary at Oxford in 1611 the "gentlemen in gowns" included aldermen, a doctor and a minister. (B.M. MS. Harl. 1368, f. 5).

A Bell Man

69. (*b*) Typical dress of contemporary working
man, for comparison with 69(*a*) (but some
bellmen, who likewise worked at night, also
wore the outmoded gown).
Same Broadsheet.

Except for the introduction of cloaks, an alderman's funeral in 1616[16]
was exactly like those described by Machyn.

All the time there must have been humbler funerals where there was
little or no special attire except for that of the professional corpse-bearer,
who affected a dignified old-fashioned gown. John Weever, looking back
over the past, writes in 1631:

> Now such as could not be interred with all this majestic solemnity, although
> they were of high parentage, for that the charge was very great, were buried
> in the evening, by certain men who had that charge, who were called
> Vespillons.[17]

These, he says, were "clothed all in white",[18] but by day they evidently wore
black (Fig. 69*a*).

"Men of meaner rank" were carried on their own servants' shoulders.[19]

Pepys enriches us with many glimpses of funerals. In 1659 he mentions the shoulder *scarf*, which became typical funeral wear for the next two hundred years. As gowns were gradually given up, cloaks became correct for principal mourners and other people had this scarf instead of a cloak. It was worn diagonally over the left shoulder.

> To Westminster Hall, where Mrs Lane* and the rest of the maids had their white scarfs, having been at the burial of a young bookseller in the Hall.
>
> *Diary*, Vol. 1, p. 2

The scarves here were white because the bookseller was a young woman. Otherwise they would be black.

The giving out of memorial rings (compare mourning rings, pp. 253–5) was now customary. After attending a typical funeral Pepys says:

> I had a very good ring which I did give my wife as soon as I come home.
>
> *Diary*, Vol. 8, p. 261 (1669)

It would seem that these rings were not very precious, as a rule—they were plainly engraved and there were too many of them to have great sentimental value. When Pepys himself died in 1703, one hundred and twenty-three rings were presented, some given to people at the funeral and others sent afterwards. Somewhat invidious distinctions were made—forty-five of the rings were worth 20s., sixteen worth only 10s.,[20] and so on. For Robert Walpole in 1745 there were seventy-two rings.[21] The custom persisted until the end of the eighteenth century.

In the later seventeenth century, as the Verney Memoirs show, carriages began to add to the cost of funerals. Moreover, besides a scarf and ring, "hatbands" began to be given to participants—pieces of black crape or silk to be swathed round the crown and hang behind. (Fig. 70). Gloves were also presented, often of "shammy" leather.

Sir Ralph Verney writes in 1685:

> Sir Richard Pigott was buried very honourably and at considerable charge, with two new Mourning Coaches and a [six horse] Hearse. Wee that bore up the pall had Rings, Scarfs, Hat-bands, Shammee Gloves of the best fashion . . . the rest of the Gentry had Rings and all the Servants Gloves . . . All Sir Richards servants were in mourning.
>
> *Memoirs of the Verney Family 1642–1696*, Vol. 4, p. 327

---

* Mrs Lane occupied one of the stalls in the Hall.

When, in 1688, Sir Ralph's own son "Mun" died, heavily in debt, he advised that Mun be buried "privately in the night time without . . . inviting neighbours with their coaches which is very troublesome". But even so, mourning must be provided for all Mun's staff, down to "Doll the Cooke and Anne the Dayry Mayd".

Walter Calverley, a well-educated landowner with a textile mill was probably typical of many middle class families round about 1700. A dutiful attender of obsequies, from the age of twenty-seven, he averaged a funeral outfit (alamode silk hatband, etc.) once annually for the next ten years. In 1705 for his own sister's funeral he gave gloves to 140 gentlemen as well as gentlemen's men.[22] When his daughter and family lived with him, and in 1744 one of their maids died, he records:

> I buryed her in a handsome manner . . . gave all the women servants gloves.
> *Yorkshire Diaries*, Vol. 1, p. 147

Misson (op. cit., 1698) shows a similar picture of the mourning provided at funerals. He adds that the processions were led by "two men with long staves"—the "conductors" of old, the mutes of the future.

Dudley Ryder (afterwards a Judge) describing his cousin Richard's funeral in 1715 says:

> We were all equally furnished with favours and white gloves excepting . . .
> who were the principal mourners with cloaks, hatbands and black shammy
> gloves.
> *The Diary of Dudley Ryder 1715–1716*, ed. W. Matthews, 1939

"Favours" were ribbon knots, oddly like those that were used at weddings (compare rosemary). White gloves, instead of black were now being given to the less important people, perhaps because more useful afterwards.

As the demand for funeral pomp grew amongst the middle class, the professional undertaker came on the scene and promoted it.* The eighteenth and nineteenth centuries saw a steady advance in the use of funeral trappings until they became essential even for the very poor.

The mute's black mourning staff (later "wand"), was improved by being swathed in crape and underwent an evolution illustrated in Fig. 70 and 71.

---

* The word "undertaker" in this sense seems first to have been used in Queen Anne's reign. The Books of the Ironmongers' Company record that "an undertaker for funerals had . . . buried one Mrs Mason for the Hall" and his contract included supplying gloves, hatbands and rings to all invited.

FUNERAL TICKET.

Hogarth pinx.t   *I. Cook sculp.t*

You are desired to Accompany y.e Corps of   *from*
h   late Dwelling in   *to*
on   *next at.*   *of the Clock in the Evening.*

Perform'd . by Humphrey Drew Undertaker, in King-street Westminster.

Published by Longman, Hurst, Rees, & Orme, July 1.st 1809.

70. Funeral invitation. Mute (on the left) holds a "mourning staff"
moderately draped in black. Pall with escutcheons. Woman mourner
in hood.
Engr. after Hogarth (? drawn c. 1730) published 1808.

Evening funerals were fashionable[23] and an undertaker's bill dated September
1780 includes charges for thirty-two men carrying "branches"* (branched

★ Quoted, Alexander Andrews, *The Eighteenth Century* (1856), p. 50.
Compare: "When Hopkins dies, a thousand lights attend
              The wretch who living saved a candle-end" (Pope).

71. (*Left*) Mute with heavily draped wand, mourning scarf and weeper
in hat: caption includes the words
"Then wet your melancholy eye
With a prime pot of Barclays' double".
(*Right*) Undertaker dignified by an old fashioned wig and dressy neck-
wear. Black gloves.
Print. Guildhall Library, Noble Collection, C22. 83.

candlesticks, as in Pl. 34). There was also a charge for "two beadles attending the corps", with gowns and "silk dressings" (drapes for staves?)

Parson Woodforde (recording 1758–81) received the usual mourning accessories every time he conducted a gentleman's burial service. The gloves were sometimes "grey Beaver", the hatbands often white when the deceased was a woman;[24] but although their mistress's pall-bearers had white scarves, "three servant Maids" at her funeral were "dressed in black Hoods".[25] For women, black hoods were a fashion in the eighteenth century, and naturally people took advantage of this at funerals. (See Pl. 41 and Fig. 70.)

The Parson's own basic dress was always a gown, whether he was officiating or not:

> I met the corpse at my great gate and walked before it in my gown all the way to church.[26]

Of another occasion, when he was not officiating, he remarks that directly the interment was over he pulled off his gown.[27]

Some delicate distinctions in the quality of accessories, made to correspond with social levels, will be noticed in Woodforde's account of burying his father in 1771.[28] Gloves for the pall-bearers and ladies were black shammy, for the Clerk "mock shammy" and for the underbearers, sexton and six women wakers,* only black lamb. Hatbands were "black silk" for the pall-bearers, "black silk, common" for the Clerk and "black crape" for the servant. The latter was fitted out also with a black coat and waistcoat and black buckles (compare buckles for court mourning, p. 256). "Everything I hope was done decently, handsome and well," he says, except that he forgot to invite the gentlemen to "pull off their cloaks" before taking a farewell drink.

Writing at exactly Woodforde's time, F. de la Rochefoucauld[29] describes funerals at social levels just above and just below those familiar to the Parson.

> In the case of a gentleman or a man of some property, which is much the same thing in England, his funeral is magnificent. The whole procession [hearse and carriages] is escorted by thirty or forty outriders on black horses; all of these wear long crepe bands, have their hair unpowdered and are in deepest mourning . . . the funeral of a poor man is as miserable as that of the rich is splendid. Three or four men carry the bier, which is draped with a single black cloth; the bearers themselves are not even in black.

In the *Benenden Letters*, pp. 222–4, are detailed all the expenses of a fine gentleman's funeral in 1785. There are eight hearse-pages with black silk gloves and a new character makes his appearance—the "Feather-man"— wearing the same. The "lid of feathers" was a fascinating feature of eighteenth and nineteenth-century funerals. It was a tray supporting a crowd of waving black ostrich plumes like those on the horses and the hearse. The featherman carried it on his head for two shillings a time. (Fig. 72 shows him in 1865.)

In the nineteenth century, the funeral procession changed little at first, except quantitatively. An undertaker's enormous bill, dated 1824[30] for a mere Miss Martha Harley's funeral in the country, gives many interesting details but no innovations. Ten "horsemen" (in relays), four mutes, twenty-two pages, one "featherman" and two "feather-pages" were all supplied with hat bands, scarves and gloves.

More modest, but still costing over £200, was the funeral of Mrs

* Watchers of the corpse at night.

72. Funeral of Lord Palmerston. Featherman bearing "lid" or "tray" of plumes. Coffin (just removed from hearse, at Abbey door) has typical white-bordered black pall with escutcheons. Mute with large draperies.
Illustrated London News *4 Nov. 1865.*

Wyndham of Salisbury in 1817. The accounts run into four pages of foolscap (now in Devizes Museum) and contain many interesting details.[31]

For mourners, the requirements seem often to have been hired out; for example, for ladies: "scarf and hood (Common 6d. Best 9d.)", for men: "Cloak and Band (ditto)" (J. Turner, *Burial Fees* . . . 1838).

The voluminous "dressing" of a mute's wand was tied in place by "love ribbon" in black or white. His scarf and hatband would still be white for girls' funerals (Pl. 42 (b)).

In the 1830s, while English crape production grew, men's hats were getting taller and taller. Hence the typical Victorian mourner's and mute's chimney-pot topper with massive "weeper" hanging behind nearly to the waist.

For ladies' funeral wear, black hoods, though still seen in *c.* 1840 (Pl. 31), were no longer correct by the time Thackeray was writing *Vanity Fair* in 1846–8. There, a funeral party included Becky Sharp in a neat black bonnet and cloak, and

> Lady Southdown with a large black headpiece of bugles* and feathers which waved on her ladyship's head like an undertaker's tray.
>
> (Edn. 1911, pp. 335–8)

And did not Miss Jenkyns of *Cranford* (1851–3)

> send out for a yard of black crape and employ herself busily trimming her little black silk bonnet for the Captain's funeral?[32]

By 1850, G. J. French was complaining of the "extravagance which has crept into funeral ceremonies". A MS. account-book kept by a Colchester undertaker from 1859–81 gives an idea of the cost of middle-class country funerals in terms of garments supplied to all and sundry (see Appendix 3). The vogue reached its peak in mid-Victorian times, as was beautifully shown by the Exhibition "Death, Heaven and the Victorians" at the Art Gallery, Brighton, 1970. An official estimate reckoned that £4,000,000 a year was spent on "silk scarves and brass nails, feathers for the horses, gin for the mutes and satin for the worms".[33]

However, the whole edifice at last began to topple. In about 1880 a Church of England Burial, Funeral and Mourning Reform Association was founded to encourage "moderation" and "simplicity instead of unnecessary show".[34] The Rev. W. H. Sewell says that by 1882 "a little has been done in respect of hatbands and armlets worn by men but much remains to be done especially for women" *Practical Papers on Funeral Reform*.

Mr Sewell might well have added "especially among the destitute". Edwin Chadwick, writing of the abjectly poor (in 1843), says "nothing can exceed their desire for an imposing funeral".[35] They would "starve to pay the undertaker" and even the parson must receive "a silk scarf of three yards and a half", which he would wear across his surplice. B. Puckle[36] mentions seeing, as late as *c.* 1900, "a drawerful of wide black scarves" which had been presented to a Yorkshire Vicar; and the Rev. J. Vaux corroborates, saying that such scarves used to be stored up by a West Riding parson's wife of his acquaintance till there were enough to make her a dress (*Church Folklore*, p. 125).

* Black tubular beads.

There were some rigid conventions even with manual workers. According to Vaux (*loc. cit.*) some of the poorer folk at Arundel, even in the 1890s, would put on black smocks to bury a friend; and he says that in Derbyshire the inmates of workhouses appeared in black cloaks when acting as bearers— a very ancient survival. Bearers in similar circumstances, shown in Pl. 43, are wearing ordinary clothes, dignified only by a rusty top hat.

Finally it seems worth while to quote from three of Charles Booth's records made in the London slums in 1898—notes which he uses as illustrations of pathetic extravagance.

(*a*) There had been a fire, a mother and eight children were burnt to death and the same day the father died of consumption.

> There were four hearses, . . . four mourning carriages, plumed horses, and mutes on foot with flowing crape bands . . . Handerchiefs with deep black borders were conspicuous in the hands of the mourners. Everybody . . . in their Sunday clothes, washed and dressed for the occasion.[37]

(*b*) "Funerals", said the chaplain, "are still very extravagant . . . especially in flowers . . . Fish and cats-meat dealers and coster-mongers are the people most addicted to showy funerals."[38]

(*c*) A girl was dying. Fellow members of her Burial Club joined together before her death to buy a wreath for the coffin.

> They were exceedingly anxious she should live long enough to see it, which happily she did, and . . . they went with it in a body to her room. She was immensely pleased and touched.[39]

An epilogue to the story of girls' garlands!

The funerals most lacking in ceremony have not been for the poor but for those outside society altogether—some who have never been integrated within it, like the still-born and the unbaptized, and others who have been rejected, like excommunicants, suicides and murderers. All these were denied Christian burial rites, and murderers at one time were not even provided with grave clothes. In the seventeenth century prisoners went to the gallows "wearing a sort of white shirt over their clothes and a cap on their heads", but their garments were all perquisites of the executioner.[40]

The following account, as recent as 1812, describes the treatment meted out to the body of a man who had murdered a Mr and Mrs Marr and then taken his own life. *The Morning Post* for 1st January describes the scene.

As a suicide, the man could not be buried in consecrated ground, and since "it was imagined the ceremony would have a powerful effect on all . . . loose characters" the crossroads at Turnpike Gate near the Tower, was chosen for the sake of publicity.

> The procession included Magistrates on horseback and constables with their appropriate batons . . . and patroles with drawn swords, and many thousands of the populace.

It will be noticed, in what follows, that two precautions were taken to prevent the restless criminal from "walking" (compare p. 124).

The dead prisoner was roped to an inclined platform on a cart, arranged for

> the greatest possible degree of exposure to the face and body . . . on the body was a pair of blue pantaloons and a white shirt with the sleeves tucked up to the elbows, but neither coat nor waistcoat. About the neck was the white handkerchief with which Williams put an end to his existence. There were stockings but no shoes upon the feet.
>
> On the right hand side of the head was fixed . . . the MAUL [heavy mallet] with which the murder was committed . . . [and above was fixed a stake].
>
> [At the grave] the body was pushed out of the cart and *crammed* neck and heels into the hole . . . which was purposely so formed as not to admit of its being laid at length . . . The stake was immediately driven through the body . . . with the identical pin-maul which had been used in murdering the family of MARR.

CHAPTER 14

GRAND FUNERALS—I

(a) General Features

Until the end of the seventeenth century, the funerals of peers and prelates were not unlike those of kings; indeed in the early sixteenth century one and the same heraldic ordinance applied to both, and it uses the words "ytt hath ben accustomed . . ."[1] The styles of mourning and the plan of the procession were like those described on pp. 183–6, but the numbers, especially in the

73. Usher with white rod of office (shorter than a Steward's staff). Mourning gown and hood, its tippet over both shoulders; buff coloured gloves. (Funeral of Lady Lumley, 1578).
B.M. MS. Add. 35324 f. 21 (detail).

sixteenth century, were fantastically swollen, because the many attendant notables brought several servants each, and all the defunct's enormous staff were there as well. There would be his Comptroller, Treasurer, Steward and Chamberlain, all wearing black gowns with hoods on their shoulders and

74. Entombment of Richard Beauchamp, Earl of Warwick, drawn
c. 1485. Bishop in mitre, cope and crossed-over stole, sprinkling holy
water, his crook held by a cleric in fur almuce (amess). Mourners in
hoods with tapers and rosaries.
B.M. MS. Julius E IV art. 6 f. 27.

carrying their white staves of office; similarly ushers with rods. And there
were countless others, from the servants of servants to aristocratic pages, and
from cooks to chaplains. The entire personnel except the humblest and most
distantly connected would be issued with mourning, its design and quality
corresponding with their position. Hoods worn over the face were restricted
to the protagonists, as before, but there were some extra people eligible.

Thus the coffin, when it was borne on a horse-drawn chariot, had an attendant (or two for royalty) sitting or kneeling beside it (Pl. 44). For a Queen these might be two "ladies of the Bedchamber to take care of the body" (who had to be helped down on arrival).[2] Such attendants—and the postilions too, as a rule—wore a mourning hood in this way. So did the executors and the banner-bearers (a feature of this type of funeral); also those holding a canopy over the coffin when it was not in a chariot (Fig. 85, p. 222).

For the wealthiest, almost the whole procession might be mounted on trapped horses, including the ladies. Only the poor folk, conductors, choir (and friars if any) then went on foot. A letter has come down to us from the organizer of the 6th Earl of Shrewsbury's funeral in 1591 in which he declares himself "in some debat whether it were more honourable to have the funeralls perfourmed on horseback from the Mannor, or one [on] fote from the Castle" (Joseph Hunter, *Hallamshire*). Economy and tradition pointed to the Castle, but the trouble was it lay too near the church for a big enough procession on horseback to be ranged in order.

As regards the clergy, the "preacher" would probably be a prelate, often with other prelates, *in pontificalibus* at least when in church (Fig. 74).

75. Bishop with mitre, almuce (grey fur amess) and jewelled gloves: his companion a knight of the garter. Depicted in *c.* 1565–1575. *B.M. MS. Stowe 583 f. 15v.*

Before the Reformation, at a royal funeral, dignitaries of "The King's Chapell . . . in their surplesses and grey Ameses★ singinge" (compare Fig. 75) formed part of the procession, but the almuce was prohibited by the Reformed Church in Elizabeth's reign.

★ For amess see footnote p. 48.

Bishops, after the Reformation, might walk in their non-liturgical dress—
a sleeveless chimere (gown) over their very wide-sleeved surplice, the rochet,
with a black silk scarf (Fig. 76). Other priests or ministers wore gowns, with
academic hoods if entitled.

76. Bishop of London at funeral of Lady Lumley, 1578. Episcopal
sleeveless gown (chimere) over wide-sleeved rochet, black silk scarf
and headgear of academic dignitaries—a square cap over a black
skull-cap with vestigial ties.
B.M. MS. Add. 35324 f. 20v. (detail).

But the clergy's dress varied and Elizabeth's decree that all should wear
square caps was not obeyed at her own funeral. The staff of the royal chapels
on that occasion wore the startling combination of highly colourful copes
with the ordinary tall black hat of their day (Pl. 45).

The academic dignitary's small square cap and separate skull-cap grew
into a typical "mortar board" and was worn thus by bishops in General

Monk's funeral in 1670 (Fig. 77), while other divines in that procession wore hats.

77. Bishop at General Monk's funeral, 1670. Dressed like the Bishop Fig. 76 the square cap now larger, stiffened, lacking ties and provided with a tump (the mortar-board's tassel came in later).

Engr. after Francis Barlow in Francis Sandford . . . Interment of Duke of Albemarle *1670 Pl. 4 (detail).*

The cortège was often flanked (as at middle-class funerals later) by the bearers of torches (Pl. 44) or costly wax tapers. An ordinance of Henry VII's time decrees that there should be at all noble funerals "a certayne of Innocentes clothed all in white, every innocent bering a Taper in his hand".[3] Tapers were less used in the Protestant church, but lay torch-bearers remained, as laid down in a rule for "The Burial of a Prince of the Blood Royall" which reads:

> If he be a Duke xlviii torches are little inowche [few enough] borne with poore men cladde all in blacke.
>
> B.M. MS. Harl. 6079, f. 25v.

The same ordinance lays down that the King at a funeral should wear Garter Robes, not mourning.

> yf the King be in presence, he must . . . wear his robes of blewe, and if he have on his mantell, he must have his hoode layd on his shoulder, and pynned [on] the one shoulder with an owche;* his cap of estate of blewe upon his head, his sceptre in his hande and the Chamberlaine to beare his trayne, and

* Jewelled clasp.

if he weare not his mantell he must have his hoode slyved [wound] about his necke.

The Garter hood is chaperon-shaped, and though it is vestigial, its apex, retains the elongated scarf-like form (as we saw in Fig. 66). This explains the final injunction.

However, the King was rarely seen at a funeral at all. It seems that he could not be a mourner for one of his inferiors and only a woman could be chief mourner at the funeral of his queen. Henry VII did not attend his own wife Elizabeth's funeral. However a king could attend that of a king, which was done by Charles I, as we shall see (p. 228).

To all other grandees and their servants, cloth for mourning was supplied on a strictly protocol basis (see Appendix 4). As the regulations seem to have applied to a whole period of court mourning some of them are dealt with on p. 255. Included is an injunction:

> Be it remembered that none maye weare hoodes under the degree of an Esquire of the King's household but only tippettes of a quarter of a yarde brode . . .
>
> B.M. MS. Harl. 1354, f. 4v.

The tippet here may mean a scarf, like the streamer of a chaperon-type hood without the rest of it (Fig. 66).

The number of principal mourners was scaled to correspond with rank— e.g. earls had 9, dukes 13, kings 15 or 20. The typical mourning gown was, for the chief mourner of whatever rank, distinguished by having an extra long train. As this had to be borne up by someone else, its manipulation on horseback required skill (Pl. 46).

Foreign ambassadors, presumably because they represented royalty, also had extremely long trains (Pl. 47 (a)). To honour Prince Henry in 1612 the Dutch and French ambassadors were each allowed nine yards of black and this would be for a gown only. At Cromwell's funeral the "Holland, Portugal and French ambassadors" each had "his train held up by four gentlemen"[4] (*Heath's Chronicle*).

The parade of a peer's "hatchments" or "trophies" of course formed an essential part of his funeral. As well as his coat of arms, helmet with crest, shield and sword, he sometimes had displayed his gauntlets and knightly gilt spurs and the insignia of his Orders. Always there was his coronet and a "banner of his arms" (to which even knights were not entitled).

If he was the king, or a peer above the rank of baron, there would also be the horseman mentioned on p. 128 who, clad in a gleaming suit of the dead man's armour (helmet excepted) rode into the church to offer his battle-axe or a lance. The horseman would then be unarmed in the vestry to return humbly wearing a mourning gown like the rest,* and the suit of armour was added to the "hatchments". Apparently this custom had died out by 1572, for the immense pageant of Lord Derby's funeral in that year lacked this one splendid episode. On the other hand the helm, shield, etc. have been carried at state funerals of great men right down to that of Sir Winston Churchill in 1965.

It was natural that the officers-of-arms, commonly called the King's heralds,† as custodians of aristocratic traditions, should here play an even more important part than in the funerals of commoners. Half a dozen of them might be present at once. Sir A. Wagner[5] writes that the earliest record of the King's heralds conducting a funeral relates to that of the Earl of Salisbury in 1462/3. Here even Garter King-of-Arms wore a coat of the *Earl's* arms, i.e. a tabard embroidered thus. But after the King's heralds were incorporated by Richard III it was usual for them to officiate wearing their own red velvet or silk tabards, embroidered or painted with golden leopards and fleurs-de-lis. This gorgeous colouring showed up against the jet black of their ground-length mourning gowns and hoods (Pl. 47 (b)).

The reason for the heralds'. "wearing the King's coat of Arms" at a non-royal funeral is given in a mid-sixteenth century manuscript. It was

> to intent [that] the defuncte may be known to all men to have dyed the Kinge's true and faithfull subiecte.
> B.M. MS. Harl. 6064, f. 26v.

An Officer-of-Arms would be supplied with mourning by the defunct's executors. An Elizabethan manuscript on the subject of his "Droites" reads:

> Item for his gowne and hoode 5 yards at 11s. a yard and yf the corps be farre of[f] then hee must have cloth for a Rydyng gowne and hoode . . .
> B.M. MS. Egerton 2642, f. 204

The officer's "blacke gowne and hod" must be "the same as the mourners do

---

* E.g. Henry VII's funeral, 1509 (B.M. MS. Harl. 3504).

† The Officers-of-Arms, or incorporated Heralds of England, under the Earl Marshal, comprise three (originally four) Kings-of-Arms, Garter being the chief, and six Heralds and four Pursuivants.

weare".[6] There was also to be three yards of cloth for his servants.

Heralds attended the funerals of prelates though no hatchments were then carried. In Catholic times

> at the Buriall of a Cardinal or of an Archbishop iiii Heraulds wearing theire Coates of Armes shall beare the fower Banners of the Sayntes in mo[u]rning habittes and theire horses . . . covered all with blacke".
>
> B.M. MS. Harl. 6064, f. 183

The heraldic costume changed little until the 18th century, when gowns and hoods were given up. The tabard then had to be worn over a special black coat or cloak, with the addition of the black shoulder scarf that was revived for Sir Winston Churchill's funeral. A black-draped hat and black gloves were soon added (see Lord Chatham's funeral (Appendix 6)). Breeches were worn even in the nineteenth century, with black stockings (Pl. 48).

For women, strict rules of mourning etiquette were prescribed by Margaret Beaufort, in the reign of her son Henry VII.★ There were even orders for the Queen herself.

For all ranks above knights' wives there were to be (in black) (a) a mantle, (b) a surcoat (this was so old-fashioned that it had to be defined—a garment "made like a close-bodyed gown"),[7] (c) a plain hood without "clokes".†

Except for baronesses, the mantle and surcoat must have a train behind. All surcoats were to have "a traine before". To make walking possible the front train would be "trussed up under the girdle or on the left arm" (see Fig. 78). As regards the mantle—"the greatest estate [rank] the longest traine".

The size of the "tippet at the hood" was another variable—those of the Queen and the King's mother‡ were to lie a good length along her train and have a breadth of "a nayle and an inch" (3¼ inches): those of others get shorter

---

★ College of Arms MS. I 3 f. 52, dates the ordinance "*xxiii*" *H VII* but B.M. MS. Harl. 1776 and other copies give "*viii*" *H VII*.

† On f. 9 in the same MS. we read that in time of mourning "Ladies when they ride wearing mantells" were to "have short clokes and hoods with narrow tippets". The word "cloke", also spelt clocke, cloake, thus seems more likely to mean the closed cape-like shoulder piece generally part of a hood, rather than a decorative clock as has been suggested. Moreover it was to be worn by the lower ranks, not by ladies (except when riding).

‡ Strutt in *Dress and Habits* . . . p. 324 seq., transcribes from Harl. 1354, where "King's mother" is changed to "Queen's mother" (although neither Mary nor Elizabeth, when on the throne, had a mother living).

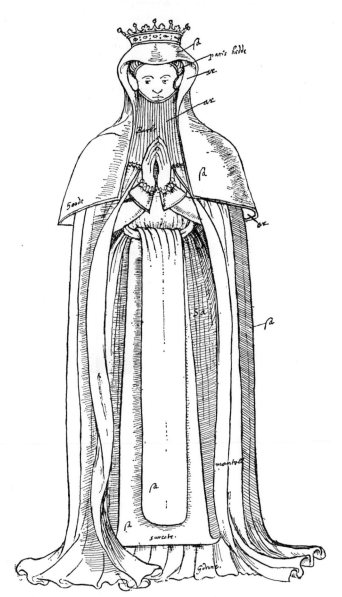

78. "A Countesse in mourninge apparaill". Mantle with train (*sa* for sable); surcote with front train folded over girdle; open mourning hood, black, lined white (*ar* for argent) over Paris head-dress and pleated barbe covering chin (sign of rank). *c.* 1576 but costume established earlier.

B.M. MS. Harl. 6064 f. 91. (Photo.)

and narrower till we reach the Baroness's, which was ¼ yard off the ground and "in breadth the scarce nayle" (2 inches).

Knights' wives and certain gentlewomen of the household, were to have surcoats with "meetly" trains (moderate front trains), no mantles and their tippets "pinned upon there arme".

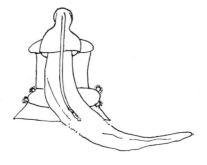

79. Lady chief mourner with long train and long tippet to her hood (sign of rank) *c.* 1576. *After B.M. MS. Harl. 6064 ff. 96v and 97 (detail).*

All other gentlewomen were quite differently dressed. They wore only a slop ("a mourning cassock not open before") and* the antiquated over-garment called a coat-hardy. Their hoods must have clokes and their comparatively short tippets must be pinned to the side of the hood. "Chamberers" must have "noe manner of tippettes" at all.

80. Female mourner ("gentlewoman?") in hood fastened under chin (most of her companions have entirely closed hoods as in Fig. 95(a)). She rides in Anne of Cleves' funeral, 1557.
After B.M. MS. Add. 35324 f. 8v.

Requirements of fine broad cloth for funeral wear were assessed, as with men, according to rank (6 to 16 yards). The lists show that a peeress, poor

* A later version of the ordinance (B.M. MS. Egerton 2642, f. 209v.) reads *or* instead of *and*.

creature must have worn a slop★ and a kirtle as well as the voluminous surcoat and mantle. Her allowance also provided for a barbe, a "mantlelet" and a head-dress consisting of a band, the frontlet, and a coverchief (one on and three in the wash).[8]

Everyone was to wear the white linen barbe or wimple covering the front of the neck. There was even a rule as to "the maner of wearinge of barbes". Only peeresses might cover the chin: others, down to the level of knights' wives,

> to weare yt under theire throtes; and other gentleweomen beneath the throte goyll.
>
> B.M. MS. Harl. 1354, f. 12

It is interesting to find that these elaborate regulations were still in force after half a century, as witness the contemporary account of Queen Mary's funeral in 1558.[9] The ladies' costumes were as follows.

Top Peeresses (riding horses "trapped to the pasturne") wore black mantles with "their Barbes above their chynes"; other peeresses had "a mantle with [only] a small Trayne, their Barbes on their chyne"; and finally there were mere gentlewomen in a "Gowne without a Trayne and their Barbes under their Chynes". Chamberers, simply "in black", brought up the rear.

With changing fashions, beginning probably about 1500, there was a slight revision as to head-dresses and fortunately some herald in *c.* 1575 made a drawing to illustrate how a mourning countess should then be dressed[10] (Fig. 78). He copied out some of the old rules that still applied and added:

> Every of these estates peeresses in tyme of mourning are also to weare paris heddes.
>
> B.M. MS. Harl. 6064, f. 91v.

The Paris head was apparently a variety of the "French hood" fashionable in Queen Mary's day, not a hood, but a close fitting cap with a little curtain hanging behind (well shown in Pl. 49). For mourning and funerals it was white. The term "Paris head" is used as early as 1503 (see p. 214).

The barbe, already an anachronism, underwent a curious evolution, or devolution, during the course of the century. In the later 1570s it became a sort of bib just below the neck and by the time of Queen Elizabeth's death it

---

★ "Sloppes", the word used in this context in Harl. 1534 f. 12v, is clearly a scribe's error, the plural word being common usage for a man's loose breeches.

extended down to the waist. Freeing the neck gave room for larger and larger ruffs. Compare Pls. 49 and 51.

In the second half of the sixteenth century a principal lady mourner, and sometimes only she, continued to wear an open mourning hood. This had a very long tippet and was lined, tippet and all, with white lawn.

The whole costume changed radically at the turn of the century and will be described in connection with Queen Elizabeth's funeral.

The chief mourner's train-bearer was more humbly dressed than herself and was nearly always a woman. However a late Elizabethan ruling on noblewomen's funerals reads:

> A gentleman with his habitt of Dowle,* haveinge his hoode over his hed must Leade the chieff morener and a man also to beare her Trayne.
> B.M. MS. Egerton 2642, f. 205

A lady Mayoress in 1614 did indeed have her train "borne by an officer".[11]

By the end of the seventeenth century women's wear at noble funerals was different from their ordinary mourning only in the use of accessories that have already been dealt with, such as scarves—until we reach the nineteenth century. Then the important mourners would don for the funeral a black crape veil like a widow's.

(b) Historical Examples—Medieval Times to 1600

From the many contemporary records of opulent funerals we will now review chronologically some facts of costume interest that have not already been given.

The boom in heraldic funerals, and therefore the period richest in records, was almost exactly coeval with the Tudors. But Edward IV's funeral in 1483 is an earlier one that is particularly well documented.

An eye witness says "the corps wt. the personage [effigy] was accompanied by a long procession including the iiii orders of friars" (who would wear the habits of their rule). There were offered at the Mass, the King's "riche embroidered cote of armes which Garter King of Armes hyld wt. as grete reverence as he coude . . . a rich swerde which had been sent from the Pope and a basenet [helmet] wt. a riche crowne of gold . . ." Finally the horseman offered "the axe . . . the polle† downward".[12]

---

* Mourning (cf. dolorous).
† Poll, meaning head. MS. Egerton 2642, f. 188, wrongly reads "Pomell".

Henry Percy, Earl of Northumberland, whom "the Vulgar . . . tumul-
tuously murthered" in 1489, had a funeral which was emulated for a long
time to come and cost about £1,000 (something like a year's income). The
accounts[13] show, among other interesting charges:

> Item for forty poor Men for the bering of Torches on Horseback . . .
> eighteen Myles at 2s. a Man . . . 4 l. [and a gown each].

The ordinances given on p. 206 were being followed, at least in part:

> Item for twenty-four Gownes with Hods for Lords and knyghts [each five
> yards at 10s.] . . . 60 l.
> Item for sixty gownes with Typets for Squyers and gentlemen [each four
> yards at 6s. 8d.] . . . 80 l.

81. Mounted herald in royal tabard (worn
typically) at funeral of a Knight of the Garter.
He bears the dead man's sword, point downward. *c.* 1578.
After B.M. MS. Add. 35324 f. 2 (detail).

No less than 576 gowns were charged for altogether.

In the opinion of the Crown the aristocracy was getting a bit above itself.
Henry VII fined the Earl of Oxford £10,000 for the excessive size of his
retinue.[14] But even so at the Earl's funeral 900 gowns were presented.[15]

There were always the eccentrics who worried about the evils or the
expense of all this pomp. In 1538 the fourth Earl of Shrewsbury's will enjoined that only twenty-five poor men, torch bearers, and not more than one
hundred servants should have gowns.[16]

The Duke of Suffolk went so far as to will in 1544 "that no black gowns or coats be given at my funeral except to my own servants and torch-bearers".[17] On the whole, however, there was a crescendo of pomp. In 1556 the Earl of Sussex (Knight of the Garter and Captain of Queen Mary's forces) had a funeral with a huge cavalcade of horsemen which was recorded in drawings, probably by an officer-of-arms.[18]

There were herald outriders (as well as the other officers-of-arms). All show the style of mourning hood that was fashionable—the tippet hanging down to the knee and, as though its origin from a liripipe and its mournful meaning were equally forgotten, ending in an ornamental tassel (cf. Fig. 82). The new Earl, chief mourner, has an identical hood and gown—oddly enough no train.

82. Funeral of a Duchess. Lady chief mourner in open hood, barbe and trained mantle. Her woman train-bearer in closed hood. Her male escort and a lady mourner show tasselled tippets. *c.* 1580. *After B.M. M.S. Add 35324 f. 4*

Meanwhile a number of splendid royal funerals had taken place.

Elizabeth of York's in 1503, exceptionally beautiful and interesting, has already been mentioned. A few more extracts from the transcription[19] are worth giving. Watching beside the coffin for several nights were:

> Ladies . . . in such most sadd and simplest Clothing that they had, on their heads thredden kierchiefs hanging on their shoulders and close under their chins and this daily until their slopps, mantells, hoodes and paris [headdress] were made.

After the horse-drawn hearse, there were fifteen ladies and the Queen's five sisters, some in carriages, others mounted. There were viii palfreys saddled, traped and emparelled with black velvett for the viii ladies of honour . . . in their slopps and mantles every horse led with a man affoote without hood in a demy [short] black gowne.

A hundred of the King's servants wore hoods over their heads and even some of the foreigners such as twenty four Venetians, bore torches,

> and as for surplus of strangers [who] had no torches [such] as Esterlings, Portingalls . . . Lukeners even they rode all in black.

In the previous year came the death of Prince Arthur (whose christening and burial we have mentioned), only months after his marriage at the age of fifteen to Catherine of Aragon. He died at Ludlow Castle and the funeral procession, which was beautifully described by a participant,[20] took two days to reach the burial place, Worcester Cathedral. When it set out "it was the foulest cold windye and rainey Day and the worst Waye that I have ever seene: they were fain to take oxen to draw the Charre [chariot]". The Earl of Surrey as principal mourner wore "sloppe, Mantill of Blacke" and his "morenynge Hoode over his Hed".

At Worcester they were met by

> The Vicar General of that See, with a good number of Secular Canons in grey ameys with rich copys [copes]. And other Curates, secular Priests, Clerks and Children in Surplisses in great Number and I suppose all the Torches of the Towne.

At the final service every ceremony was observed, mounted man-of-arms with battleaxe included.

In all this, the Prince's father and his ill-fated bride, are never mentioned at all—the principal mourner could be neither a king nor a woman.

When Henry VII died at Richmond in 1509, his body and effigy were carried first to St Paul's and then to his Chapel at Westminster with a mounted procession.

An account[21] opens with the words:

> First there came rydinge through the Cittie, the Swordbearer of London . . . to sett the Crafts in their order . . . The Maior and his brethren* with many

---

* We learn from B.M. MS Harl. 1979, f. 31 (in connection with Henry VIII's funeral), "that the King's Council allowed to the Lord Mayor and Aldermen . . . and their servants . . . black livery, one hundred and four gowns according to the president [precedent] at the interment of Henry VII."

commoners, all clothed in black, met with the corps at London Bridge . . .
the stretes were set with long torches.

After the chariot and the chief mourners (nine Knights of the Garter)
there followed a cavalcade which in later funerals would have come in front.
It was unique in several ways.

> ix of the Kyng's Henchmen ridinge on goodlie coursers trapped in Black
> Velvett . . . the foremost did bear three Capps of Maintenances wch iii
> Popes had sent the Kynge. The next iii Henchmen did beare iii rich swordes,
> the Pointes downward, the seaventh a Target of the Armes of England other-
> wise called a Shield crowned, the eighth an Helmet with a Lyon of Golde [the
> crest] and the ixth bare a Speare covered with Black Velvett.
>
> B.M. MS. Harl. 3504, f. 253

This is a rich example of the carrying of ceremonial attire and equipment
towards the grave. The coat of arms is also mentioned, but only in connection with the offertory.

Henry VIII gave Catherine of Aragon, in 1536, a funeral that was respectful, though it was described as: "the Interment of Lady Catherine . . . late
weif of the . . . Prince Arthur".[22]

It affords a good example of the way the chariot was manned. On each
end "upon" the coffin, which bore the effigy, "must knele a gentleman
huissher [usher] all the waye. On the fore horse and the thill [tiller] horse ii
charet men in black cotes with hodes uppon their heddes . . . every horse
to have iiii scutchions [shields embroidered on their trappings] of Prince
Arthur's armes and hers".

Jane Seymour's funeral, a year later, was interesting in two respects. First,
although she survived the birth of her son by only twelve days,[23] she was not
deemed to have died in childbed, so there were no garlanded girls. Secondly,
on the way from Hampton Court to Windsor the poor men, who had their
torches lit as they passed through each village (spares being carried in carts),
were wearing black gowns "with the queen's badge on their shoulders".

Henry VIII's own funeral (1547) was conducted magnificently "to the
great admiration" of the "innumerable People . . . very desirous to see the
sights".* Nearly the whole procession from Westminster Palace to Windsor

---

* Quotations here are from the splendid account in College of Arms MS. I 11 ff. 92–105v.
(which is transcribed with slight inaccuracies, by Strype in *Ecclesiastical Memorials,* Vol. 2,
Appendix p. A).

went on horseback, headed by two Porters with black staves "to stay, that neither Cart, Horse nor Man should . . . cumber them in the passage". The standard of the Lion was "born by Lord Winsor hooded and trapped . . . and on each side of him went a Sergeant-at-Armes with his Mace". Every imaginable dignitary of Church and State was there, including "Ambassadors of divers kingdoms . . . accompanied with such of the Lords as could best entertain them and understand their language". Garter himself carried the King's "rich Coat of Arms curiously embroidered". The chariot's seven hooded horsemen carried aloft bright banneroles and their horses, each led by a man in mourning, were trapped in velvet down to the pastern. Thirteen principal mourners were followed by the chamberlain with his traditional staff. The stay for the night at Syon monastery involved much reorganization and no little changing of costume. The City Aldermen in black made a lane leading to the chapel and the gorgeous effigy of the King was placed in the vestry. Six bishops *in pontificalibus* conducted the coffin to its lighted "hearse" or canopy and the hatchments were laid upon it—

> and so rested awhile until the Lords had shifted themselves . . . the mourners were then honourably brought to the church, every Man in a long gown with their Hoods on their shoulders save only the [principal] Mourners, and Officers-at-Arms, which had them on their heads.

After the Dirge everyone repaired to his lodging where, doubtless disrobing again, "they had chear abundantly". But by 7 a.m. all were on horseback again. At Eton they were met by the Provost, the Bishop of Carlisle

> . . . and al the Fellowes and Masters . . . in their best ornaments and copes; and by all the young children scollers of the colledge [Eton] in ther whyt surpleces bare-headed, holding in there one Hands Tapers, and in th'other Books, saying the seven psalms.

At Windsor the coffin, with its pall, was laid under a still more splendid "hearse", erected over the burial vault, and the effigy laid upon it. After they had "shifted themselves of their riding apparel" for another Dirge, the thirteen mourners were ranged round the coffin, shrouded in their black, under the many candles of the hearse, and surrounded by banners and all the officers-of-arms in their brilliant tabards.

As we have seen, women played little or no part in a great man's funeral but we are told that on this occasion "in the Queen's Closet above, the Queen

stood . . . to see the Divine Service and the royal order of the funeralls"⋆.
The chief mourner was Henry Grey, Marquis of Dorset† whose "train was
borne after him by the Vice Chamberlain".

Next day while most of the company breakfasted after attending two
Masses,

> al the Knights of the Garter there present came in their Mantles of their
> Order [blue velvet, with badge and a train] to their Oblations, as they are
> bound to do by their Religion.‡ That don they went into the vestry and put
> off their mantles.

Followed the Requiem Mass and offering of the hatchments and then, as
usual, a pole-axe was handed to the Bishop at the Quire door by a man
at arms on horseback.

At last the effigy was brought with reverence into the Vestry, the vault
uncovered and the coffin lowered "with the help of sixteen tal Yeomen of the
Guard". This guard, founded by the dead King's father, retained their pri-
vilege of bearing royal coffins to the grave for at least three centuries. Finally
five staves and four rods were broken by their holders "to shivers upon their
heads" and thrown into the vault.

One element in all these ceremonies is conspicuous by its absence; there
could be no gorgeous presents from His Holiness the Pope.

The funeral of Anne of Cleves[24] divorced Queen Dowager, falling in
Queen Mary's reign (1556), received full catholic rites at Westminster Abbey.
The choir and grey amesses (canons) of St Paul's and thirty Benedictine
monks with the Westminster School boys in their cassock-like long gowns all
joined the cortège on the eve of the burial and "proceaded over the fyldes
by Charing Crosse".

The Queen's own "Fayre white palfrey with a syde saddle" was led in the
procession (her "horse of estate", not one to be offered). See Pl. 44. The chief
mourner, "the old Duchess of Norfolk in a black gown of velvet" had her
train stretched out between her horse and the bearer's behind. Ladies wore
"paris heads" under their hoods, servants the same without hoods.

It is interesting that each of the chief mourner's two gentleman "assistants",
who escorted her at the offering, like certain others "executing a charge" (i.e.
a ceremonious duty), wore his mourning hood over his head "during the

⋆ The plural was often used for funeral.
† Father of Lady Jane Grey.
‡ St George's, Windsor, is the chapel of the Order of the Garter.

tyme of that chardge" but otherwise "put it off or had it on his shoulder".
It was a highly symbolic object.

Of Queen Mary's funeral (1558), one of the long contemporary accounts
is transcribed in Leland's *Collectanea*.[25] An interesting detail is the use of the
bishop's crook. Like the hood-on-head it was used in the active performance of
a duty. In the Catholic practice of using incense over the corpse at the church
door, it was only the bishop actually doing this, not the four others present,
who had his crook borne before him. A feature that was to disappear was the
carrying of white banners of saints by the four heralds around the bier.★

The ladies' traditional dresses have been discussed (p. 211). After the
Requiem the chief mourner, her train borne up, laid seven palls "on the feate
of the corse [coffin]". She was followed by the "Embassator for King
Philippe"—the dead queen's husband did not attend in person.

Machyn[26] tells us that when all was over, souvenir hunters tore down pieces
of the funeral hangings from all round the church.

For much of Elizabeth's reign noblemen's funerals were almost as elaborate
as those of the sovereign. One of the most famous is that of the Earl of Derby,
Privy Councillor and Knight of the Garter, in 1572.[27] It took six weeks to
organize and there were some nine hundred participants (who are listed,
with their costumes, in Appendix 5). Nearly everyone was mounted, mostly
on trapped horses, and all three kings-of-arms were there. It is unusual that
the royal herald who carried the helm wore Lord Derby's coat of arms
instead of the Queen's.

The chief mourner, being the young Lord, had "the mourning robes of an
earl", i.e. black gown, sloppe and mantle. We are told that at the offertory
he stood beside the vicar to "receave the honourable hatchments of his
father, which were offered up by the other eight mourners unto him"—an
implication, clearer than usual, that the hatchments now symbolized the heir's
inheritance, blessed by the church. The standard and banner were offered at
the end, and again it is significant that "the esquires that bare them, as soone
as they had offered them, put of(f) their hoods".

The chief officers of the household, after shattering their staves at the graveside, received before the funeral feast "their offices and [new] staves agayne
of the new Earle their lord and master".

A fine description of a baroness's funeral dated 1578 is given by some

★ The last Abbot of Westminster participated. It was the last Requiem Mass held at the
Abbey except for the Emperor Charles V's a few days later.

captioned paintings (now at the British Museum),[28] illustrating that of Lady Lumley, wife of the book collector and herself a scholar. The yeomen, who might almost have been dipped bodily into black ink, nevertheless show that mourning, unless of the "closest" followed the fashions of the day, for they are cross-gartered and wear white ruffs. Even the poor women have elaborately wired out white veils (Pl. 50). Likewise the gentlemen's gowns have fashionable sleeves and their headgear is the square cap of the period (Fig. 73).

83. Mourning robes of a peer—hood, caped mantle with train. (Lord Zouche with banner of Chester in Queen Elizabeth's funeral).
c. 1603.
After William Camden (?) B.M. MS. Add. 5408 f. 33.

The women mourners's costume illustrates the bib-like substitute for the barbe described on p. 211. The chief mourner (Pl. 49) still wears the antiquated mourning surcoat with front train looped over its girdle.

J. G. Nichols transcribes some formularies, probably of about this date, for the respective funerals of nearly all ranks of men and women.[29] These show clearly how the mourning cloak for men, when it came in soon after Lord Derby's funeral, became a symbol of middling status at the ceremony. Some of the yeomen are promoted to cloaks instead of coats and gentlemen walking furthest from the bier are demoted from gowns to cloaks.

From now on there can be detected a slight decline in the opulence of funerals other than those of the State.[30] When the heads of a family died in quick succession the effect of such extravagance was crippling. After the third Earl of Rutland's funeral his agent writes to the new earl in December 1587:

> your debt to the woollen draper for the funeral black of my late Lord is 898 l. 8s. 6d.
>
> MSS. of the Duke of Rutland (R.H.M.C.), Vol. 1, p. 232

84. Sir Phillip Sidney's funeral.
(*a*) Conductors with their usual (black) staves, now in mourning cloaks.

(*b*) "Steward of his house" with white staff of office and deep mourning.
Engr. T. de Bry after Thomas Lant in Funeral Procession of Sir Phillip Sidney. *1588.*

85. Effigy of Mary Queen of Scots on her bier wearing ermined robes and a crown. The men bearing pall, canopy and banners have (like the lady mourners) hoods with exaggerated tippets and tassels. 1587. *After B.M. MS. Add. 35324 f. 16 (detail).*

The fourth Earl was himself to die less than three months later, aged thirty-six, when his heir was only a lad at Cambridge. The executors were then advised by Lord Burghley that

> Blackes should be provided for the widow, her sons and daughters and also for the gentlemen and yeomen that are ordinarily in the house, but there should be no charge for the retainers.

Ibid., p. 241

In the event, sixteen gentlemen retainers crept in, at three and a half yards for each cloak, and even then the agent had to "allow some cloaks over to supply wants". But he expressed the view that the allowance was "meaner than has been at any funeral for many years" (ibid., p. 243).

Not only in families stricken by early deaths were economies attempted, for the heralds' charges were becoming extortionate. In 1591 Lord Shrewsbury was warned by his agent not to accept the estimate submitted by the heralds for conducting his father's funeral. It compared unfavourably even with the charges for Lord Derby's; moreover the heralds

> In grosse . . . gott xx or xxx li at the E[arl] of Rutland's funeralls which might have been saved and in the Sco. Q. funerall 150 li.
>
> Joseph Hunter, *Hallamshire*, edn 1869, p. 98

86. Gentlewomen in white head-dresses at Mary Queen of Scots' funeral, 1587. *B.M. MS. Add. 35324 f.16v (detail).*

The funeral of Mary Queen of Scots (1587), which we have mentioned earlier, must indeed have been expensive. Disinterred at Fotheringay 6 months after death she was carried to Peterborough with "achievements of honour" (sword and all) and a huge procession. Among the ten peers present was the same Earl of Rutland whose death a few months later is mentioned above. Queen Elizabeth commissioned him to attend the funeral, with his countess and a suite of twenty-one, all provided with blacks from the Queen's Wardrobe.[31] It must have been one of the last funerals where the principal lady mourners, like the men, still had tippeted hoods, and the chief one, "the old Countess of Bedford"[32] wore a surcoat with her mantle.[33]

87. Sir Robert Sidney, chief mourner at his brother's funeral, wearing
train, in contrast to other principal mourners.
Engr. T. de Bry after T. Lant Funeral Procession of Sir Phillip Sidney.
1588.

The ladyes had parris heads and barbes.
The gentlewomen had whyte hoaddes.*

The Scottish ladies-in-waiting declined to wear the English style head-
dresses which Elizabeth offered to have made for them and appeared in what
they had worn at the dead Queen's original burial.[34]

In recognition of the Queen's royal blood two yeomen of the guard were
on duty wearing black cloaks over their brilliant uniform.[35]

In the same year (1587) a state funeral took place which rivalled even those
of royalty. Sir Phillip Sidney, killed in action, was laid to rest in an atmosphere
of hero-worship. We are indebted to the then Windsor herald, Thomas Lant,
for making captioned drawings of some two hundred figures in the procession.†

We do not propose to deal with military dress at funerals—a large subject

* Ibid. "Hoaddes" doubtless means "Headdes"—head-dresses, probably veils.

† Engraved by de Bry and published 1588. Lant was "a gentleman servant" of Sir Phillip
and must have walked in the procession himself.

88. Sir Phillip Sidney's spurs and gauntlets borne at his funeral by officers-at-arms (though pursuivants, they wear their tabards herald-wise).
As for Fig. 87.

in itself—but it is worth noting that "Citizens of London practised in Armes about three hundred" marched three by three wearing "black cassokins", and carrying reversed Halberdes or Pikes, etc. The most distinguished friends are in mourning gowns and hoods, for example Sir Francis Drake; and except for "Doctors" and "Preachers" all have their sword-tips projecting from beneath. Lesser folk, even yeomen, have long black cloaks.

Seven grandees from Holland, and the Mayor and Swordbearer (Fig. 67, p. 187) are all mounted, and wear long mantles. They are followed by the aldermen, riding in their purple; finally come 120 "Cittizens called the Company of Grocers in theyr livery" (Fig. 65, p. 185).

Five heralds in single file parade with Sir Phillip's hatchments, gauntlets and gilt spurs "the dignitye of his knighthood".

CHAPTER 15

GRAND FUNERALS—II

Historical Examples from 1600 to 1900

As might be expected, Queen Elizabeth's funeral in 1603, though not on horseback, was bigger and better than any before it and is very well documented. At the British Museum, besides a long roll of sketches believed to be by William Camden himself,[1] there is an extensive series of larger, somewhat crude but detailed paintings in full colour.[2] These were probably done a little later, but correspond well and are very fully captioned.

Only special features will be noted here. The servants, in vast numbers, were very grandly dressed. The humblest had black cloaks nearly down to the ground and these included numerous youths called "children of the almondry, scullery, scalding house" etc. and scores of "gromes" such as those of the woodyard and the "Laundrie", wine-porters and the maker of spice bags. All these wore swords and many had gloves. Heads of departments such as "clarks" of the "dyett", stable, wardrobe, etc. had long gowns and hoods on the shoulder. Grooms of the chamber and servants of Ambassadors are shown by Camden with black sword-scabbards on black belts,—the earliest examples we have seen of mourning in this form.

Banners were borne by Lords, who wore peers' robes with their hoods (Fig. 83). Sir Robert Cecil (Principal Secretary) and Sir Walter Raleigh (Captain of the Guard) are shown in identical mourning garb (Fig. 89). Others display various official costumes of the Law, Church, etc. Sir Thomas Egerton, Lord Keeper, carries the magnificently emblazoned red purse.

Specially interesting are the female participants. There were 266 poor women, who are shown in ground-length black gowns and elbow-length veils. The chief mourner, is a Marchioness, whose mantle-train needed two countesses to bear it up. She and the other sixteen principal mourners have broken away almost completely from the old rules (Pl. 51). Instead of surcoats they have dresses with fashionable farthingales. Their black head-dresses—scarcely "hoods" any longer—are combined with their mantles into one extraordinary structure, wired out in a huge arch so as to leave the head

(a)   (b)

89. At Queen Elizabeth's funeral, 1603.
(a) Sir Walter Raleigh; (b) Sir Robert Cecil, both with mourning
gowns and hoods held by the tippet.
(a) *After William Camden (?) B.M. MS. Add. 2408 f. 38v (detail).*
(b) *After B.M. MS. Add. 35324 f. 35 (detail).*

and the ruff free. Something like this was the mode in Antwerp in 1598★ and an arched head-dress hanging to the elbows is sometimes seen on English monuments of the seventeenth century. The barbe is replaced by a larger than ever white pleated front, like an oblong stomacher.

Maids-of-honour differ in having no mantles or barbes and their black head-dresses are not lined with white.

In the life-like effigy of the Queen herself, lying on the bier with her sceptre and orb, the fashion of the day shows only in her ruff. Without farthingale, her gown and ermined mantle lie in straight folds.

James I's funeral was on similar lines to Elizabeth's, but some interesting points of difference are on record.[3] Such of the King's servants as were at Theobalds, Hertfordshire, where he died, rode before the six-horse carriage,

> all the footmen in black suites and velvet cappes . . . The guard on Horse-back carried torches round the Body [and its effigy] bare-headed.

★ Illustrated in C. Vecelli's *Habiti Antichi e Moderni*, Venice, 1598.

There were one hundred Earl-Marshal's men "with batons, to keep order". The same enormous royal retinue attended, with the interesting addition of a "groom of the otterhounds" and a "Master of the Tennys play".

Charles I was chief mourner and had his train borne by five Lords. But when he went up to the altar to offer in his own name, in accordance with tradition his train was not borne. However, such was its enormous weight that

> two gentlemen of his Bedchamber did followe behind him to lift it sometymes for ease.

A peer's funeral of this period is worth noting, that of the Earl of Shropshire, K.G., who was buried at Sheffield, in 1616. The Archbishop of York himself walked in the procession with "his gentleman usher before him (bare headed)" and, like all the earls and viscounts, he had his train borne. No hatchments were carried in the procession, only a black velvet cushion (perhaps to represent the Garter insignia). (Compare Fig. 91 (c).) This seems evidence of a real decline in the popularity of the heralds as masters of ceremonies, a decline borne out by the tenor of a petition which they submitted to the Archbishop of Canterbury at about this time.[4] It related to the growing popularity of nocturnal funerals. The heralds deplored this, ostensibly on the grounds (among other things) that the use of candlelight "may seeme to draw neere unto Popery". The real reason came out at the end of the document— the heralds were losing employment, their records became incomplete and upstart families took advantage of their absence in a disgraceful way:

> Manie in the dark doe presume without warrant to bury the dead either with new invented ensignes of gentry [coats of arms] or with such as rightly belong to other men.★

A system of fines was instituted in 1618 directed against any (truly or pretendedly) armigerous family who conducted a funeral in the absence of heralds.[5]

Though on the wane, magnificent funerals did however continue through the seventeenth century, for example at the Duke of Richmond's in 1624 there walked to the Abbey "one thousand men in mourning". (Cleland)

A conflict between the claims of loyalty and economy is expressed in a letter by the Countess of Sussex in 1643. Her husband's burial

★ Compare Steele's satire below.

will cost me a great dell of mony but i must not be falinge in my last sarvis to him.

She resolved not to spend all that the Heralds suggested but would be content to have them carry an assortment of trophies (not unlike that in Fig. 90).

a great flage banner of arms and a crone [coronet] helmett and sworde and spures.

Memoirs of the Verney Family, Vol. 1, p. 268

People could be mortally hurt if not invited to a funeral and this of course tended to keep up the cost. A propos of General Ireton's funeral in 1652 we read

Colonel Hutchinson was . . . one of the nearest kinsmen he had, but Cromwell passed him by and neither sent him mourning, nor particular invitation to the funeral . . . but such was the flattery of many pitiful lords . . . that they put themselves into deep mourning.

Lucy Hutchinson, *Memoirs of the Life of Colonel Hutchinson*,
10th Edn. (1880), pp. 359–60

The Colonel in offended protest, appeared that day in his usual "scarlet cloak very richly laced" and thereby drew an apology from the Protector.

The Restoration did not save the private heraldic funeral from extinction. By 1671 John Gibbon, Bluemantle Pursuivant was writing

It was my hard hap to become a member of the Heralds' Office when the Ceremony of Funerals (as accompanied with Officers of Arms) began to be in the wane . . . in eleven years time I have had but five Turns.

Apart from State funerals, after 1691, there were apparently only three more that were attended by heralds, all in the eighteenth century.

At about the same time mourning gowns, and for men mourning hoods too, came to an end; thus even the artistocratic funeral was at long last deprived of its medieval appearance.

As the heralds' business with the eminent diminished, they became more obliging to the middle classes (if we may believe Richard Steele). A bereaved family in *The Funeral*, 1701 (Act I, Sc. i), sent to the Heralds "for a coat of arms for Alderman Gathergrease for display at his burial". A herald "promised to invent one".

Turning to seventeenth-century state funerals, there are three where costume is worth a comment. Cromwell's in 1658 was military in style and cost £60,000.

90. Funeral of Robert Earl of Essex, 1646. Use of mourning gowns and hoods now declining: here even penon-bearers wear cloaks instead. The Earl's helmet, sword and gauntlets on coffin; another helmet and his coat of arms carried by bare-headed heralds. Note escutcheons of his arms displayed on the coat and on the hearse.

Broadsheet, dated 1646, in B.M. Thomason tracts (699.f. 10/89).

The streets . . . were guarded by souldiers in new Red coats and Black buttons with their ensignes wrapt in Cypres [black silk].

James Heath's *Chronicle* . . . 2nd Edn., 1676

This wearing of a bright uniform contrasts with earlier days (for Henry VIII, all the guard was in black):[6] however black gowns and hoods were given to the veterans known as "poor Knights of Windsor".

Several pieces of the "Protector's arms" were carried by eight officers of the Army—not by the heralds, who only "attended them".[7]

Even Cromwell's obsequies were put in the shade by those of the venerated General Monk, Duke of Albemarle in 1670. At the command of Charles II, these were recorded by Francis Sandford, with a splendid series of drawings by Francis Barlow and others.[8]

Even if we ignore the armed forces, there remain some noteworthy costumes. The poor men are still in foot-length gowns but now have hats, not hoods. The mourning gowns and long-tippetted hoods of the chief characters have not changed in the least and look more anachronistic than ever: nearly all the other men follow the new fashions, wearing buttoned coats that reach to mid-thigh with wide hats and long hair or wigs. However the mourners were allowed to wear "their hatts upon their heads untill they came within sight of Whitehall".[9]

Servants still have swords; those of upper servants and gentry hang from ornate wide baldricks. "His Grace's Watermen" show their brass badge of livery (Fig. 91 (c), p. 233 and (b), p. 232).

Knights of the Garter and peers are robed, wear the collars of their Orders and are marshalled by their usher, Black Rod. One of his Majesty's ushers carries "the Carpitt and cushion" with nothing on them, for the Duke's coronet adorns his splendid effigy (Fig. 91 (c) and Pl. 40).

Charles II's funeral need not detain us. As Evelyn says, he was "obscurely buried because of dying in a different religion than that of his people".[10]

A propos of the funeral of the young Queen Mary II in 1695 (witnessed and well described by Celia Fiennes,[11]) Macaulay says

> both Houses with their maces followed the hearse, the Lords robed in scarlet and ermine, the Commons in long black mantles . . . On the gorgeous coffin of purple and gold were laid the crown and sceptre of the realm . . . No preceding monarch had ever been attended to the grave by a Parliament, for till then Parliament had always expired with the Sovereign.[12]

(a)   (b)

91. At funeral of General Monk, 1670.
(a) Almsmen in mourning gowns, with walking sticks suggesting
infirmity; (b) two of the Duke's watermen in typical dress of their
calling, wearing his badge.

The black mantles were a royal gift to the Members of Parliament.

The last two non-royal heraldic funerals were those of the Dukes of
Buckingham (1735/6) and of Kingston (1773). The haughty Duchess of
Buckingham★ and the bigamous "Kitty Crocodile", the former Miss Elizabeth Chudleigh, who posed as the Duchess of Kingston, saw to it that their
husbands should have full heraldic honours. At Buckingham's funeral, Garter
himself attended "completely habited" and this time he was carrying his
ancient silver sceptre of office, with its enamelled St George's Cross and royal
arms.

Mourning gowns and hoods being a thing of the past, we find the eleven
principal mourners in cloaks "with trains suitable to their degrees".[13]

In the eighteenth century, evening funerals were again fashionable, per-

★ His and her effigies are discussed on p. 181.

91. (*c*) Cushion symbolizing the Duke's coronet; usher with fashionable
baldrick for his sword.
Engravings in Francis Sandford . . . the Interment of George, Duke
of Albemarle . . . *1670.*

formed without the heralds and, as they scornfully said, lit only by a lanthorn,
a torch and a two penny link.[14] They now had another cause for complaint.
From the Duke of Gloucester's death in 1700, until George III's in 1820, royal
funerals were all "private". This meant that attendant heralds had to supply
their own black and had nothing to carry.[15] Apart from this, love of ceremony tended to defeat the object of the change.

Queen Caroline's interment in 1737 was conducted in the darkness of a
December evening, but the clergy wore copes and carried tapers and there
was a huge attendance of dignitaries.* However, perhaps to emphasize in-
formality, the programme expressly stated that the Lords Archbishop would

* The *Gentleman's Magazine* gives an account (Vol. 7, p. 764) which is not wholly in
agreement with the threepenny programme published at the same time (B.M. 816 m. 4. 9).

have "no train borne" and "the Lord Chancellor with the Purse, no train borne and no mace carried before him".

Princess Amelia, the chief of seventeen mourners, did have her train borne in the traditional manner by two Duchesses. She was preceded by "Gentleman Usher of the Black Rod" with his rod "reversed" (like a weapon, upside down). All the ladies wore "long veils of Black Crape"—a new substitute for the small black hood that was usual.

An interesting detail regarding precedence is that below the Dukes and the "Bishops in their rochets" went "Knight of the Garter, not a peer, the Right Honourable Sir Robert Walpole in his collar of the Order". Walpole at this time was head of the Government but not yet Earl of Orford.

Horace Walpole, his son, found George II's funeral in 1760, "private" though it was, an "absolutely noble sight".[16] It too was an evening affair and along the route every seventh man of the foot guards bore a torch. Mounted officers of the horse guards had "crape sashes" (shoulder scarves) and drawn sabres. Drums were muffled.

The chief mourner was the King's son, the elderly Duke of Cumberland, whose train was borne in the cortège by the Duke of Newcastle and another Duke. But thereby hangs a tale, as Horace Walpole recounts (loc. cit.). In the crush in Henry VII's chapel

> all solemnity and decorum ceased; . . . The Duke of Cumberland . . . had a dark brown adonis [long bushy wig] and a cloak of black cloth with a train of five yards . . . sinking with heat [he] felt himself weighed down, and turning round found it was the Duke of Newcastle standing upon his train to avoid the chill of the marble.

In the Georgian period, as the heralds waned, the undertakers waxed. By the end of it, their feathers and wands almost entirely replaced the hatchments and banners of old. But tradition in state funerals died hard, as witness that of Lord Chatham (the Elder Pitt) in 1778. An extract from a contemporary account, mentioning many of the costumes, is given in Appendix 6.

It was still quite customary for a Duke, or even an Earl, to have his coronet on its cushion borne by a bareheaded attendant riding a horse in rich mourning caparison. This was done for the Duke of Northumberland, conveyed from his home at Charing Cross to the Abbey, as late as 1817. His was a remarkably old-world funeral, for the "trophies" were carried as well—this time by some of the thirty-six horsemen in mourning, distinguished from the rest by their black silk scarves. The cavalcade was seen off by

> Six beadles belonging to St Martin's Parish in their coats and hats of office, with silk hat bands, and poles covered with black, similar to mutes.
>
> *Observer*, 1817

The magnificent state funerals accorded to Nelson (1806) and Wellington (1852) put the remaining royal funerals in the shade. Details of naval and military mourning being beyond our scope, suffice it to mention a few of the more picturesque features of Nelson's obsequies.[17] They began with a beautiful procession of barges, with trumpeters and flags, from Greenwich to London. The central barge was adorned with black velvet and plumes and at the head of the coffin stood Clarencieux King-of-Arms bearing the Viscount's coronet. In front of this went another barge with all his trophies—from surcoat to spurs—in the hands of heralds.

At Whitehall steps the coffin was carried by eight seamen of H.M.S. *Victory* wearing their blue uniform blouses and trousers, and long bands of crape in their sailor hats.*

The procession on the following day from the Admiralty to St Paul's was a fascinating spectacle of half modernized medievalism—as the programme, reproduced in Appendix 7 will show. Knights' collars, trophies, feudal badges, staves of office, royal tabards, all were present. There was even the traditional number of mourners for a viscount (seven). The chief of these, Admiral Sir Peter Parker, wore a long mourning cloak over his uniform and had a train-bearer to hold it up, as he would have done in the middle ages.

The officers-of-arms are now alas, shut up in coaches and wearing hats, but the last acts of the drama again reflect ancient custom. The heralds place the trophies beside the grave and Garter himself casts into it Nelson's three chief officers' broken staves.

During most of Queen Victoria's reign, dress for the grander funerals, developed on much the same lines as for others.

For women the special feature was the crape veil. For the Duchess of Cambridge in 1889, Queen Victoria herself and all the ladies had black bonnets surmounted by these shrouding veils. The chief lady mourner's

---

* Contrary to popular belief, the black neckerchief had been used by sailors *before* the death of Nelson.

92. Funeral of Prince Albert ("private"). Undertakers' batons and
top hats with weepers. Escutcheons on hearse and hammer-cloth.
Illustrated London News. *1861.*

traditional train was seen at Princess Sophia's funeral in 1844, and this was one of its last appearances.

> The chief mourner was the Countess of Gainsborough veiled, her train borne by Miss Waldegrave, veiled.
>
> *Illustrated London News*, Vol. 5, p. 379

However, the convention that the chief mourner at a woman's funeral should necessarily be a woman had long since weakened. When Queen Elizabeth of Bohemia was buried at Westminster Abbey in 1661, the chief mourner was her son Prince Rupert, his train borne by a page.[18] And for Princess Charlotte (the Regent's daughter) at Windsor in 1817 it was her husband Prince Leopold, his train borne by a baron and a knight.[19]

For men (other than chief mourners) the correct wear was service uniform for those entitled to it, now with a crape arm band instead of a black cloak; others wore black frock coats with crape accessories. Till near the end of the century it was crape with everything. Swathes of it were wound round even the Watermen's hats and round the very bearskins of the guardsmen (Fig. 93).

Lord Palmerston's (1865) was one of the last state funerals with costume pageantry (despite his wish for it to be private). Member of the hereditary peerage though he was, no trophies were borne, but the coronet on a cushion did feature (Fig. 94) and the scutcheons on the hammercloth of the hearse represented the glamour of heraldry. Indeed they struck one of the *Illustrated London News* reporters as "too glaring for the vehicle of death", though otherwise he saw only "propriety and good taste in all the arrangements".*

The young Prince of Wales was "in mourning dress with the Star and ribbon of the Garter". Though the Queen was not present her Royal State coach was in the procession with six horses, "the drivers and outriders wearing black silk scarves over their scarlet liveries".†

The ten pall-bearers, of whom Gladstone was one, had hat-weepers and immensely wide shoulder scarves down to their calves; but it is noteworthy that by now the other mourners are without these.

Remarkably enough (as mentioned earlier), the very ancient custom of making a gift of apparel to the corpse was observed:

---

* Quotations here are all from *Illustrated London News*, Vol. 47, pp. 429–47 (4th November 1865).

† At the Queen's own death the same scarlet was seen, but an arm band replaced the now extinct scarf.

93. Bearskins, on the right, draped in crape. (Funeral of Princess Sophia
of Gloucester, 1844).
Illustrated London News, *Vol. 5, p. 381 (detail). 1844.*

TRANSEPT OF WESTMINSTER ABBEY.

94. Lord Palmerston's funeral in 1865, "simple" compared with the past but: "If we are to discard symbolism altogether, why retain those meritricious heraldic emblazonments on the pall, and that coronet of crimson and ermine which, we know perfectly well, the dead Viscount never wore in the whole course of his life".

Illustrated London News *Vol. 47, Picture p. 436/7 (detail); comment p. 435.*

The coffin was lowered into the vault; the mourners, drawing jewelled rings from their fingers, cast them in—a fond token of affection for the dead.

When Gladstone's own state funeral took place it was already 1898. The vogue for simplicity that had set in was probably further encouraged by the anxiety he expressed that his funeral should be modest. Gone were the feathermen and all the scarves and weepers. The pall-bearers, of whom the Prince of Wales was again one, were led by the Earl Marshal (head of the College of Heralds) bearing his jewelled rod. But they all simply wore frock coats and black gloves, and carried plain top hats (Pl. 52).

It was nearly two centuries since John Gay wrote his satire, but at last people had come to agree with him.

> Why is the Herse with 'scutcheons blazon'd round
> And with the nodding Plume of Ostrich crown'd?
> No, the Dead know it not, nor profit gain:
> It only serves to prove the living vain.
> How short is Life! how frail is human **Trust**!
> Is all this pomp for laying Dust to Dust?
>
> *Trivia*, Book 3, p. 53 (1716)

CHAPTER 16

MOURNING

The present chapter deals with mourning as distinct from funeral wear.

(a) Before 1700

There is evidence that before black was adopted in the fourteenth century, some sombre garment would be superimposed on otherwise ordinary dress. Around the tomb of Sir Roger de Kerdeston at Reepham in Norfolk, dating *c.* 1338, his parents and children are represented as mourning figures of the kind called "weepers",* carved and painted. Stothard describes their colours and says "some have black cloaks over coloured garments, one has black hosen, another is clad in brown" (*Monumental Effigies*, edn 1876).

Planché[1] states that the earliest record of full black being used for mourning in England was when Edward III put his court into black for John II of France in 1364.

Chaucer, in *c.* 1387, in the *Knight's Tale*[2] has Palamon at Arcite's funeral

> With flotery berd, and ruggy asshy heres
> In clothes blake y-dropped al with teres

and some time later Palamon was still mourning ". . . in his blake clothes".[3]

But at first there was inconsistency. Chaucer himself makes Cresyde wear "widewes habit large, of Samite brown" in line 109 of *Troilus and Cresyd* and "widewe's habite blak" in line 169.[4]

The weepers on the tomb of the Richard Beauchamp, Earl of Warwick, at Warwick, made in 1453, are actually referred to as "mourners" in the contract of the craftsman who made them.[5] Some have rosaries, but they represent "Lords and Ladyes in divers vestures", not bedesmen. Their headgear indicates mourning, for the lord shown in Pl. 53 (a) pulls a hood right over his face and some of the ladies, wearing a head-dress fashionable in their day, have exaggerated it so as actually to cover their eyes as we saw in Fig. 51 (Pl. 53 (b)).

* Figures surrounding tombs at first represented mourning relatives or bedesmen. In the late sixteenth century these weepers were replaced by kneeling children.

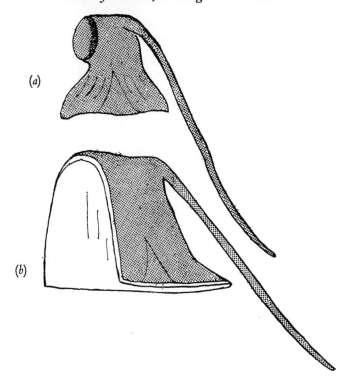

(a)

(b)

95. "Ladys Mourning Attire". Black tippetted hoods, (a) closed type, (b) open type, lined with white. (cf. Fig. 80). Early 17th century. *After College of Arms MS. Vincent 151 f. 394.*

Court mourning ("dolorous dowle") was ordered at the death of Henry V[6] and some time in the fifteenth century there must have been a form of conventional court mourning even for women. The edicts for ladies "in time of mourning" made by the King's mother in the reign of Henry VII (mentioned on p. 208 in connection with funerals) are called already "Ordinances and *reformacions* of apparel".[7] She is clearly referring to a former fashion—perhaps the peak that was clung to by widows—when she says that ladies' apparel must

> be made of the fashion and largenes as they were used when they were [wore] beakes except now the tipet to be instead of the beakes and . . . the beakes be in no manner of wise used, for [because of] the deformitie of the same.[8]

Some further details of these ordinances are given under "Court Mourning" on pp. 255–6.

In the seventeenth century mourning not only at Court but in the family was strictly observed and is well illustrated in "The Aston Death Scene" painted in 1635 (Pl. 54). Sir Thomas Aston stands beside his dead wife. The figure at the foot of the bed is meant to show what she would have looked like when alive, but is in mourning herself. The husband is in deep black except for shirt and collar. His small son Thomas, being too young for breeches, wears a doublet and skirt, also all black, like the hat he carries.

Sir Ralph Verney's wife died in 1650. A year later he was still in mourning and when abroad in 1651 with his 14-year-old son Edmund ("Mun", mentioned also on p. 193) he ordered the following apparel to be sent to him:

> Black cloath Doublets (new and old)
> Black Breeches and Cloake,
> Black Cloath Cape for a Cloake and 2 other peeces of Black Cloath
> Black Hats and Hat bands
> Old Blake Tafety Garters and new Black ribbon roses*
>   and several peeces of extra crape . . .
> 2 Black Taffety night-cloathes with the
> Black night capps and
> Black comb and brush and
> 2 Black sweet-baggs†
> Slippers of Black Velvet
> 1 Great Fustian Dressing Wastcoate
> Black paper
>
> *The Verney Memoirs*, Vol. 3, p. 37

In 1686, 16th February, another young Edmund Verney, at Trinity College Oxford, receives news of his brother's death, and the father writes five days later, sending him £5,

> to Buy you a black cloth sute. And I have a new black Beaver Hatt for you wch I will send you next Thursday in a little deale Box, with a black crape Hat-band, Black mourning gloves and stockings and shoe Buckles, and 3 Payres of black Buttons for wrist and neck: And I have also sent you a new

---

* Decorative shoe rosettes as in Pl. 54.
† Small silk bag filled with spices as cosmetic—Halliwell, *Dictionary of Archaic Words*.

ffrench cordebeck Hatt* to save yr Beaver. The Box is to Keepe yr Beaver in—no Body useth Hat cases now.

Ibid., Vol. 4, p. 375

When Pepys's mother died in March 1667 (her last words being "God bless my poor Sam"), he set to work to provide mourning apparel not only for his family, himself and his wife, but also for his attendants and domestics:

> On March 31st (Lord's Day). Up, and my tailor's boy brings my mourning clothes home, and my wife hers and Barker's [her woman] but they go not to church this morning; I to church, and with my mourning very handsome, and new periwigg, make a great show.

The Diary of Samuel Pepys

(b) Eighteenth-century Full Mourning

For the first mourning, all black with occasional touches of white for women, was essential. Men's suits were usually of black cloth.

> Making a suit of mourning cloathes . . . of fine black shalloon.† (1764)
> Essex Record Office, D/D By. A23

For women, black silk or bombazine was generally worn and in the 1790s black satin and velvet were fashionable. The use of the (more matt) crape came gradually. The *Lady's Magazine* for 1797 gives the following description of a mourning outfit.

> Black velvet turban ornamented with white bugle bandeau . . . three black craped feathers placed behind each other on the top of the head; petticoat and Roman corset [bodice] of black satin . . . Plaiting of white lace round the neck, and a string of black beads loose over the shoulders. Black ear-rings, gloves and shoes . . .

Parson Woodforde shows us what his niece wore for mourning in 1789.

> Briton . . . brought all our mourning home, viz. a Black Bombazine Gown and coat [petticoat] for Nancy with long sleeves and also a black stuff German Great Coat for her to wear in common.

In important households the whole of the domestic staff was usually put into mourning with the family, the upper women servants in bombazine,

---

* Imitating beaver, cheaper.
† A light woollen material.

the lower in bombazet. Mrs Delany, who was abroad, wrote to her sister on 13th October 1747, about mourning for their mother, who had died two months before.

> I suppose my brother will mourn the old mourning, I shall as I am such a distance; I have put my own maid and housekeeper into mourning and D.D. [her husband] has put his own servant out of livery into mourning though it isn't now a general fashion, but as it is a mark of respect D.D. thought it right to do so, and we are now of a time of life to indulge the dictates of the heart more than the reigning fashions.
>
> *Autobiography and Correspondence of . . . Mrs Delany*, edn 1861

On 20th October she wrote again about her own mourning for Mr Dewes, brother to her sister's husband.

> I think black bombazine will do very well in a sack [i.e. a sack-back gown]. I have a [bombazine] manteau* and petticoat, which I wear when in full dress; at home a dark grey poplin; and abroad, undrest casual, a dark grey un-watered tabby: I shall make no more dark things; . . . after 3 months black silk is worn with love hood and black glazed gloves for 3 months more.
>
> Ibid.

The following letter describes the etiquette of mourning for a gentleman:

March 14—1780, London:
My dear George . . .
    Mr. Beauclerk dyed last Friday . . . We put on our mourning next Sunday the 19th. It is six weeks mourning for you, a month black buckles [of breeches and shoes] and sword [scabbard] and a fortnight colour'd sword and buckles; you must mourn for him tho' abroad, as an Uncle is very near, and in France it will be well known.
    Henry, Elizabeth and George 1734–80 (Pembroke Papers), ed. by
        Lord Herbert, edn 1950

(c) Eighteenth-century Second Mourning

Second mourning was costume adopted for a period between deep mourning and the return to normal wear. Clothes were less uniformly black and made of less sombre materials.

The wearing of second mourning was a custom already established by the

---

* The manteau or mantua was a loose gown with a train, open in front showing the petticoat, i.e. skirt.

end of the seventeenth century (earlier at Court). The *London Gazette* of 1693 advertises: "A dark grey second-Mourning surtout coat [i.e. an overcoat]."

In the eighteenth century grey was usual for men but for women there seems to have been much more licence. In 1724 Mrs Pendarves, who had lost her father in December 1723, wrote to her sister:

> I will answer Mrs. Carter's question about her mourning to you.
> I think her in the right in buying a white satin to top her black . . . but that she can only wear as a nightgown negligée and if she was in town she would wear only mourning when she is dressed, but in the country that will not be minded, white gloves coloured fan and coloured shoes and edging as she pleases and black or white short apron and girdle which [-ever] she likes best.
>
> *Autobiography and Correspondence of . . . Mrs Delany*, edn 1861

The following statement occurs in the same Mrs Delany's autobiography:

> My mama must not wear black handkerchiefs [neck wear] with her second mourning

and in 1727 she wrote:

> Undrest people wear all sorts of second mourning unless they go to Court; then they must wear black silk or black velvet.
>
> op. cit.

The second mourning described in a letter by Lady Elizabeth Noel, written in 1760, was exceptionally gay; she was, however, on her way with friends to watch the races:

> We are in mourning, Mamma in her white sprigged lily-of-the-valley negligé, the blond [lace] morning cap from Tunbridge which was very becoming, treble blond ruffles, a very handsome white spotted satin cloak . . .

Two of the girls also wore only white, but one was in blue. On reaching the racecourse they saw their brother on horseback

> very handsome . . . in a second mourning frock* and a silver laced† hat.
>
> From *Some Letters and Records of the Noel Family*,
> compiled by E. F. Noel

* Coat with turn-down collar.
† Braided.

A letter from Anne Noel in 1793 describes slightly more sombre clothes for half mourning for young women at the

> Dandelion breakfast, the two eldest in second mourning, black silk, and little white hats, the youngest of the two without powder . . . fine young women and seem not to have imbibed any of the follies of fashion.
>
> Ibid.

Less frequent are descriptions of men's second mourning. In 1738 Elizabeth Purefoy wrote to her London agent:

> Pray send some patterns of cloath of a fashionable colour for second mourning for my son [Henry] and let mee know if they wear coat, wastcoat, and Breetches all alike or wear black wastcoat and breeches . . . My nephew Leonard Porter is dead, so we mourn somewhat longer on that account.

Thirteen years later Henry Purefoy had to go into second mourning again. He wrote to his tailor:

> July 7. 1751.
> I desire you will come over here as soon as may be to take measure on mee for a suitt of second mourning and to bring patterns of Cloath with you . . . Pray let the patterns be fine fast cloath. The grey Breetches you made mee are too shallow in the Seatt and must be let out, so desire you will bring with you a naill of grey cloath the same to the pattern enclosed to enlarge them.

Having to provide second mourning was costly and obviously a nuisance to some folk. Fanny Burney's friend Mrs Rishton denied herself a pleasure to save such an expense. She wrote in 1773

> [Mr] Rishton, who is rather more exact about dress than I am . . . wanted me to buy a suit of mignionet linnen fringed for second mourning—but my economy prevailed over that and as he was unwilling I should appear else, I gave up the dear Fischer. [Concert][9]

Fringed linen was always a second mourning symbol and the mignionette was a synonym for dainty.

(d) Nineteenth Century

The etiquette for mourning in the nineteenth century was rigid and fashion laid down many rules: consequently advertisements on the subject abound. Here are some examples. Jay's London General Mourning Warehouse, founded in 1841, was ready to supply mourning attire of every description, even for bathing dresses.

> Ladies . . . are particularly invited to a trial of the new Corbeau silks and Velvets introduced at this house . . . more durable . . . the colour very superior, unaffected by the strongest acids and even sea water . . .
>
> Advertisement, *Illustrated London News*, 1844

For another advertisement, 1872, see Appendix 10. At Jay's again in 1889:

> Costumes, Mantles, Bonnets, Caps, Fichus, Dinner Dresses . . . Jet Ornaments, Gloves and Handkerchiefs are here to be found in every tasteful guise. The etiquette of Mourning is continually changing in certain matters of detail . . . [The necessary] guide is to be found here, from the length of a widow's veil to the texture of a ball dress.
>
> *Illustrated London News*, 1889

The mourning section of Peter Robinson, known as "Black Peter Robinson" had "Black Brussels Net Dresses . . . White Tarlaton Dresses . . . full-trimmed skirts with fashionably made tablier* and Sash" (*Illustrated London News*, 1874).

Modified mourning could be obtained in the "Mitigated Affliction Department". Here again there were rules. "The mourning worn after the first twelve months, while the crape was gradually lessened, was called second mourning (Fig. 97b). Ordinary mourning was the third stage when crape was completely discarded. This was followed by half-mourning, white, grey or lilac trimmed with black. Black and white were deeper mourning than black and grey" (Anne Buck).[10]

Queen Victoria gave the following advice to her daughter, the Crown Princess of Prussia, about attire at the forthcoming wedding of the Prince of Wales in March 1863, fifteen months after her father's death.

> One more word. I think decidedly none of you ought to be in colours at the wedding but in grey and silver or lilac and silver, or grey, or lilac and gold and so on but not merely gold and white; it is the first occasion of any of you children appearing in public and as all, when in England, will not wear colours next year [1863] I think it ought not to be.[11]

The following advertisements speak for themselves.

> Black! Black! Black! Samuel Osmond & Co. Dyers . . . beg to acquaint Ladies they continue to dye every article of Dress Black, for mourning, on Wednesdays in each week and finish the same in a few days.
>
> *Illustrated London News*, 1847

* Apron design to front of skirt.

"MITIGATED

96. *Mourner:* 'Look here, I shan't wear 'em at the ground. Couldn't
you stand a pair of slate colour?'

Undertaker: 'Very sorry, Sir, but we never do anything inmiti-
gated.' "

Charles Keane in Punch, *1879.*

Half-Mourning Costume of a woollen velvet; violet ground striped with
thick lines of grey, white and black, sleeves of violet looking-glass velvet;
the consoling influence of such a costume could not fail to be great.

Advertisement by Pontings, 1892

Mourning garments were often stored away ready for next time. In August
1803 Lady Caroline (wife of the later Lord Wharncliffe) in mourning for the
grandfather wrote:

I have seen Mrs. Kelly dearest Mama and she says you have no bombazine
gown, she says you finished your *best here* last year. All your mourning things

are together but she thinks there is a black silk handkerchief and a crape veil in a small drawer in the Wardrobe . . .
The First Lady Wharncliffe and Her Family 1779–1856, Vol. 1, pp. 93, 94

Then in September, when grieving for the death of a young cousin, she wrote:

> There is some rich handsome brown and black mixture which I think beats the olive and black . . . of course over bombazeen, with black crape and black gloves, . . . there can be no impropriety in wearing one's coloured pelisse as one cannot be expected to make up such ruinous articles for every mourning.
> Ibid., Vol. 1, p. 99

The expense of mourning is again shown in Jane Austen's letter to her sister in 1808 when they had to go into mourning for their brother's wife.

> I shall send you such of your mourning as I think most likely to be useful . . . I am to be in bombazeen and crape, according to what we are told is universal *here* . . . My mourning however will not impoverish me, for by having my velvet pelisse fresh lined and made up, I am sure I shall have no occasion this winter for anything new of that sort . . . My bonnet . . . is to be silk covered with crape.
> *The Letters of Jane Austen* (1775–1817). Selected by
R. Brimley Johnson (1926), pp. 73, 74

Deepest mourning for girls in 1864 is shown in Pl. 55. Surtees gives an amusing description of a countryman's mourning in *Mr. Facy Romford's Hounds*, 1865.

> Facy . . . arrayed himself immediately after his porridge breakfast in a glossy suit of black that he had long kept in lavender to be ready for his uncle, he craped his Sunday hat deeply and drawing on a pair of new black kid gloves, took his way across the fields.

By the 1880s, as with funerals, the conventions for mourning were easing. In 1884 Mrs John Sherwood wrote:

> A mourning dress does protect a woman while in deepest grief against untimely gayety of a passing stranger . . . Behind a black veil she can hide herself as she goes out for business or recreation, fearless of any intrusion. The black veil on the other hand is most unhealthy; it harms the eyes and it injures the skin . . . Ladies are beginning to wear a small black gauze veil over the face and are in the habit of throwing the heavy crape veil back over the hat . . .

97. (*a*) Widow in full mourning, long veil and "dress of crape or crape
cloth over a black lining".
(*b*) "Dress for second mourning. Cashmere with . . . crape trimming."
From Ladies Treasury, *Nov. 1890, reproduced in article by Anne Buck in*
High Victorian, (*V. & A. 1968*). *Photographs kindly lent by Miss Buck.*

The question of black gloves is one which troubles all who are obliged to
wear mourning through the heat of summer. The black kid glove is pain-
fully warm and smutty, disfiguring the hand and soiling the handkerchief
and face. The Swedish kid glove is now much more in vogue, and the silk
glove is made with neatness and with such a number of buttons that it is
quite stylish and much cooler and more agreeable.

Manners and Social Usages

In 1875 the National Funeral and Mourning Reform Association was founded.* It was being realized that the long hours working on black materials often in a poor light, by the women employed, was very damaging to their health. A short cut appeared for men. In 1878 "a mourning crape arm-band, previously Naval, is now worn by civilians" (*The Tailor and Cutter*). The width of this arm-band was regulated by the relationship to the deceased. Three to four inches was usual and it was worn round the left upper arm, by men only. As for women, this note appeared in *The Graphic* of 1892. It was indeed a sign of the times.

> There has been a decided stand against wearing crape for some years past, but the Princess of Wales gave it the *coup de grâce* by dispensing with it during her mourning for the Duke of Clarence.

(e) Mourning Accessories

Mourning accessories consisted of handkerchiefs, weepers, fans, parasols, umbrellas, aprons, pin-cushions and jewellery.

Mrs J. Sherwood remarks on mourning handkerchiefs:

> The fashion of wearing handkerchiefs which are made with a two inch square of white cambric and a four inch border of black, may well be deprecated.
>
> Op. cit.

Weepers, in the sense of white linen or muslin cuffs, were fashionable and worn by both sexes. As mentioned on p. 147 they are part of a Q.C.'s mourning to this day.

> Mourners clap bits of muslin on their sleeves and these are called weepers.
> Oliver Goldsmith, *The Citizen of the World*, 1762

Horace Walpole refers to them in a letter written in 1746 to Sir Horace Mann about the trial of the Scottish rebel lords. Walpole was at the trial and was very much moved by the spectacle.

> I had armed myself with all the resolution I could . . . and was assisted by the sight of the Marquis of Lothian in weepers for his son who fell at Culloden.
> *Horace Walpole's Letters*, edn 1926, p. 339

A nineteenth-century example occurs in John Strange Winter's *Mrs. Bob*: "Mrs Antrobus wore very deep and very wide weepers" (1889).

* This Society was reinforced a few years later by that mentioned on p. 198.

In the eighteenth century black mourning fans were sometimes added to mourning accessories for women.

> For black gloves, fans and girdles for all the women servants . . . (1721).
> Kent Record Office, *Earl of Thanet Accounts*

The nineteenth century produced crape-trimmed and other black mourning parasols, umbrellas and even walking sticks (Pl. 56).

Mourning aprons in Victorian times were generally ornamental and bibless. Two that are still in a private collection are of black silk trimmed with black cord, crape and bugles. One is large with jet ornaments, the other is small, rounded (of the kind called "fig leaves") and trimmed with white lace—half mourning?

Mourning pin-cushions also appeared in the nineteenth century, decorated with suitable designs. On the death of Queen Caroline (George IV's wife) in 1821, pin-cushions of cream velvet with the queen's portrait painted in the centre, surrounded with roses and leaves, were hawked about the City of London on the day of her funeral and bought as souvenirs.

Mourning jewellery consisted of rings, brooches, lockets, pins, necklaces and ear-rings. The rings were the most important, and were often designed before death and left to friends and relations in the will of the deceased. They were usually decorated with symbolic figures and surrounded by an appropriate inscription. Lady Jane Grey's sister, Catherine, who died in 1568, gave her husband a memorial ring engraved with a death's head and inscribed "While I live yours".

In the seventeenth century mourning rings are often mentioned. In 1616 Shakespeare's will states that for wife and daughter rings were to be inscribed "Love my memory". The following is from the will of Anne Lady Newdigate of Arbury, who died in 1637:

> Item my Will and desire is to have a fewe playne gould Rings made of tenne or twelve shillings price with a pansie being my ffather's Crest, engraven on the outside and two letters for my name enamelled with blacke on either side the pansie and an inscription within to be lattyn these wordes followinge *Death is the beginninge of life*; and to be delivered unto soe manie of my friends as a memorie of my love as I heare nominate.
> *Gossip from a Muniment Room, Being Passages in the Lives of Anne &*
> *Mary Fytton 1574–1618*, ed. by Lady Newdigate-Newdegate 1897

William Jones in *Finger-Ring Lore* (1877) describes as follows some rings commemorating famous people.

Isaac Walton added a codicil to his will (1683) for the distribution of memorial rings; some were to have the motto "A friend's farewell I.W. obiit", those for his wife, son and daughter the motto "Love my memory I.W. obiit", and that for the Bishop of Winchester "A mite for a millian I.W. Obiit".

Memorial rings, Charles I.

98. See text. *William Jones F.S.A.* Finger-Ring Lore (*1877*) *p. 366.*

Some memorial rings for royalty were still in existence, for example two in memory of Charles I, both in gold set with diamonds (Fig. 98). The example (b) was engraved "C.R. January 30 1649 Martyr". A memorial ring for Queen Anne was decorated with a coffin containing her hair and crowned with initials A.R., the hoop being enamelled black with the inscription "Anna Regina Felix" in gold.

The contents of a box lost out of a waggon between Stamford and London in 1702 are interesting.

> 3 Hair Rings, 6 with a Death's Head, about 2 penny weight apiece the Posie [motto] Prepared be, to follow me; 3 other mourning rings with W.C. ob 18 Dec. 1702; 1 Ennamelled Ring . . .
> Quoted by John Ashton in *Social Life in the Reign of Queen Anne*, 1882

The meaning of "hair ring" is well shown in the romantic letter written by James Power to his betrothed, Julia Woodforde, in 1818. About to sail for Sierra Leone (to take up a post offered him by Zachary Macaulay, the historian's father), he had a premonition that he would die there of a fever—as indeed he did, in the following year.

> I purchased yesterday a Diamond Mourning Ring, I will place a brade of your hair and mine in it. On the inside I will inscribe "James T. Power, died — ". . . if this should be my fate shortly you will . . . get it [the date]

fill'd up and I have no doubt you will regard the ring with affection and wear it on my account.

Woodforde Papers and Diaries, ed. D. H. Woodforde (1932), p. 197

Other articles of mourning jewellery in the eighteenth and nineteenth centuries were brooches and lockets.

The lockets might have locks of hair mounted on mother-of-pearl and framed with gold or pinchbeck, with a portrait of the deceased in water colour, or in the nineteenth century, in cameo, on the opposite surface.

Mrs John Sherwood in 1884 writes (op. cit.):

> Diamond ornaments set in black enamel are allowed even in the deepest mourning, and also pearls set in black. The initials of the deceased, in black brilliants or pearls, are now set in lockets and sleeve-buttons or pins.

Then she makes the firm statement that (apart from commemorative jewellery): "Gold ornaments are never worn in mourning."

In Tennyson's poem "The Flight" (1885) we have the description of a mourning locket, worn by a girl whose lover, Edwin, was drowned and whose hateful father intends her for another.

> Hate, that would pluck from this true breast, the locket that I wear,
> The precious crystal into which I braided Edwin's hair!
> The love that keeps this heart alive beats on it night and day—
> One golden curl, his golden gift before he past away.

The nineteenth century added jet jewellery of all kinds to mourning accessories. These included even hair-combs. Many have survived and a quantity of excellent specimens were recently exhibited at the "Death, Heaven and the Victorians" exhibition at the Brighton Art Gallery, 1970.

(f) Court Mourning

As has been indicated already, strict rules were formulated for court mourning as early as the fifteenth century.

The King's mother's ordinances of Henry VII's reign quoted above (pp. 208 and 242) seem to have applied to a whole period of court mourning. Thus any time when riding great ladies were to have mantles and hoods "with narrowe tippetes to be bounde about there heades and as soon as they come to the Courte they to lay away there hoodes".[12]

There are even notes on half-mourning. For example "after the first quarter of a year" the Queen, the King's mother and duchesses might have their mantles lined with black satin or with ermine and

> after the first month none to weare hoodes in the presence of their betters but when they labour or ryde.
>
> B.M. MS. Harl. 1354, f. 12v.*

It is not surprising to read, in a manuscript of somewhat later date, that this elaborate protocol

> hath been and is much abused, by every mean and common Woman, to the great wrong and dishonour of Persons of Quality.
>
> College of Arms MS. I. 3, p. 52

In the eighteenth century the etiquette for Court mourning was again very complex and was regulated, as now, entirely by decrees issued through the Lord Chamberlain's office on each occasion.

It was deepest of course at the death of the sovereign himself. The "Orders" given out when George II died in 1760 will serve as an example. It will be noticed that the dull finish of shammy leather is required, even for shoes: and that "Norwich crape" (an inferior but English kind) is promoted (cf. p. 149).

> The *Ladies* to wear black bombazine, plain muslin or long lawn linnen, *crape hoods* shamoy shoes and gloves, and *crape fans*.
>
> Undress: Dark Norwich crape . . .
>
> The *men* to wear black cloth, without buttons on sleeves and pockets, plain muslin or long lawn cravats and *weepers*, shamoy shoes and gloves, crape *hatbands* and *black swords* and *buckles* [for breeches and shoes].
>
> Undress: dark grey frocks.[13] [loose coats with turn-down collars]

Three months after the King's death "Second Mourning" was announced. For ladies' full dress, black silk replaced the bombazine and all the accessories were to be white including "white necklaces and ear-rings".

Men's linen was now "fringed or plain"; gloves and shoes are not mentioned. "Undress" for both sexes may be grey (or white for ladies).[14]

Ten years earlier the rules at the death of Frederick, Prince of Wales, were the same, except for expressly mentioning that diamonds were forbidden.

---

* This version is worded slightly differently from the original and was evidently written in the reign of Mary or Elizabeth, since where the word "King" occurred it is generally changed to "Queen". This is the version quoted by Joseph Strutt in *Dress and Habits of the People of England 1796–9*.

So strictly was sombreness imposed that at the death of Princess Caroline in 1758 William Talbot, a gentleman usher at court, wrote

> the King even took notice of the ladies having put flounces on their bombazine, and they were stripped off.
> *Williamson Letters 1748–1765* (ed. F. Manning), 1954

When it came to foreign personages, the regulations varied in the subtlest way with the eminence of the deceased and with the court's favour towards them. For the Queen of Prussia in 1810 full mourning was so respectful as to be the same as second mourning for our own king; then after three weeks ladies' dresses and men's waistcoats could be variegated with silver or gold, white ribbons were allowed and swords could be "coloured".[15]

The royal houses of Europe being numerous, the court was constantly being plunged into mourning. A lady-in-waiting, the Hon. Mrs McDonnel, writes in 1766

> Dear Jack, next Sunday we put off Black gloves for Prince Frederick [fifteen year old brother of George III] . . . King of Denmark and Dauphin still to be mourned for.[16]

The repercussions of all this mourning on the textile trade are the subject of a protest in the *Universal Spectator* in 1731. Several deaths in quick succession had ruined their season and the writer extols the court's practice "in the last reign" of "changing the stuffs and appendages of Mourning every fortnight or three weeks" for the sake of the trade.

> Thus the mourning for Prince George of Denmark was white anserine* with Black Lace.

In this way the lace trade had been compensated for loss of sales in the fashionable gold and silver braid. At a Select Committee on the silk industry in 1766, three witnesses maintained that mourning was one of the factors responsible for its depression.[17]

The making of black materials did not fully compensate, although in 1713 it was stated that

> There had been at least £300,000 worth of black silks for hoods and scarves yearly made here . . . at Spittlefields [as well as those of the Royal Lustring Company].[18]

---

* A material like bombazine and probably a mixture of silk with wool or worsted.

Despite the suggestion voiced above, at Princess Charlotte's death in 1817 the orders were exactly the same as for her great-great-grandfather, George II.

By the time the Prince Consort died, in 1861, ladies' hoods were out, at last. Men and women still had to wear "plain linen" and the ladies "crape fans"; but for everybody's black shoes and gloves, chamois was no longer demanded. For dresses, instead of bombazine it was to be black wool trimmed with true crape (now made in England).

For "second mourning" (after a fortnight) ladies could have black silk with black "feathers and ornaments", the men "black court dress". For the last three weeks white accessories and a variety of jewellery were allowed for the ladies. Mourning lasted altogether for three months.

The feelings underlying private, as distinct from court, mourning are beautifully dealt with by Queen Victoria in a letter to her daughter (see Appendix 8).

(g) Public Mourning

Public mourning was decreed through the Earl Marshal on specially important deaths, for example, those of the monarch and his immediate family. Then "everybody that thinks themselves anybody wears deep mourning" (*Williamson Letters*, p. 28).

At George II's death the decree went out

> it is expected that all persons do put themselves into deepest mourning (long cloaks only excepted).
>
> *Gentleman's Magazine*, Vol. 30, p. 488 (1760)

The result, says Mrs Delany, was

> nothing else talked of. 1500 yards of crape sold at one shop, they say.[19]

Elizabeth Montagu, three weeks after the death, wrote

> I found that a Scotch Countess had bought all the black cloth . . . ribbons and fans at Darlington before the poor shopkeepers knew of the King's death . . . to sell them at a higher price in town.[20]

William Talbot, at court on the same occasion, advises his parson brother on a fine point for his wife's benefit.

> Women's black silk cloaks and hats must be trimmed with crape, not with love ribbon.
>
> *Williamson Letters*, p. 28

Evidently some people went beyond the orders and even had black cloaks.

Exactly what was expected was spelt out when the King's mother, Princess Augusta, died in 1772—three phases of "public mourning". Mrs Philip Powys's diary tells us: twelve weeks in crape and bombazine with broad-hemmed linen (weepers?), a fortnight black silk with fringed linen and a fortnight "colour'd ribbons, white and silver". "Undressed" a lady could wear grey, but not in the first phase.[21] The same Mrs Powys went into the milder mourning prescribed for the king's brother in 1790 by wearing "black silk with love-ribbons" (ibid.).

Mrs Delany shows what a sacrifice it meant thus to keep up with the court—this time for Princess Caroline in 1758.

> About mourning . . . broad hemmed muslin or white crape that looks like old flannel 7s. a yard and won't wash; Turkey gauze is also worn; which is thick and white but is extravagant as it does not wash, dirties in two days and costs 5s. a yard; the mourning will be worn six months.[22]

William Talbot, two years later, is firm about the cheap gauze:

> You desired three yards of gauze. It is not the thing. Muslin is the wear.
> *Williamson Letters*

Public mourning was a status symbol to which almost everyone seems to have aspired in the eighteenth century. In the *Universal Spectator's* article mentioned above (in 1731) it was even necessary to urge that

> Women of inferior Rank, such as Tradesmen's wives behind the Compter should make no Alteration in their Dress since it cannot arise . . . but from a meer Affectation of the *Mode* at St James's.

It was not only for English royalty that the public mourned, though there were twelve occasions for this in 60 years.[23] In 1797, Theresa Park wrote:

> I can tell you but little about fashions, everybody is as black as coals from head to foot for the old King of Prussia. The heads [women's] are quite flat and tied up in handkerchiefs, hardly showing any hair, than which nothing can be more ugly and unbecoming.
> *The Early Married Life of Maria Josepha, Lady Stanley,*
> ed. Jane H. Adeane, 1899

As early as 1711 the *Spectator* had shown what it all meant to an impecunious Man of Fashion (let alone the fashion trade). He was very much put to it to bear the Mortality of Princes. He made a new black suit upon the Death of the King of Spain, he turned it for the King of *Portugal* and he now keeps his Chamber while it is scouring for the Emperor. He is a good Oeconomist in his Extravagance and makes only a fresh Button upon his iron-grey Suit for any Potentate of small Territories; . . . the true Mourners are the Mercers, Silkmen, Lacemen and Milliners.

Public mourning continued through the nineteenth century. Much genuine sorrow was felt at the loss of Princess Charlotte and her still-born infant in 1817.

> Never was a mourning so universal . . . All persons of respectable condition were clothed in entire suits of deep mourning;* even domesticks very generally wore black; and even those whose circumstances would not allow the greater expense, assumed at least a crape or riband or some other indication of their sympathy.
>
> *Gentleman's Magazine*, Vol. 87 (1817), p. 454

There was some decline in such observances towards the end of the century, but many will remember the public mourning devoutly practised as late as 1910 when King Edward VII died. A lady of our acquaintance recalls that although they were small children and living abroad, she and her brother had black ribbons put into their hats on that occasion. A German lady was overheard to remark "Look at that—what a patriotic people the English are!"

---

* A description of an elaborate dress for this occasion, given in the *Ipswich Journal* (1718), is quoted in C.W. and P. Cunnington, *Handbook of English Costume in the Nineteenth Century*.

WIDOWS' WEEDS

(a) Special Features

The mourning apparel of widows was considered, from earliest times, to be of the utmost importance and the dictates of convention became very exacting. The very terms "weeds", which in Chaucer's day signified garments of any sort, was transferred to the mourning garments worn by widows only.

> Let her there provide her mourning weeds
> And mourn for ever her owne widdow-hood.
> *The Lamentable Tragedie of Locrine*, V. i. 24 (1595)

Even the period of mourning has been called "weeds".

> There were no entertainments . . . during the year of her weeds.
> W. M. Thackeray, *Pendennis*, 1849

On the whole, widows being mourners *par excellence*, tended modestly to wear the fashions of a bygone day. Two items specifically indicating widowhood have been worn, in addition to their black or white mourning attire. One was the barbe, a garment carried over from the earlier fourteenth century, when any woman might have worn it under the name of wimple. It continued with modifications into the late sixteenth century.

The barbe was initially a piece of linen or muslin covering the front of the neck, ears, part of the bosom and sometimes even the chin. It was fastened on the top of the head under the head-dress proper. At first the barbe was plain, but later it was finely pleated down the front. The head-dress over it might be a simple medieval-type of "veil" (Fig. 99), or else a more fashionable style: for example, Lady Margaret Beaufort wore with her barbe the gable-shaped head-dress of her day (Pl. 57 (b)).

The hair was generally covered, like a nun's, and this might be done with the help of a forehead cloth as well as of the wimple. There might also be an inner "veil", (Pl. 57(a) and Fig. 99.)

Widows' barbes probably followed the changes referred to on p. 211 to allow for the wearing of ruffs.

The other item signifying widowhood from the sixteenth century on, was the peak. This was a flap projecting from the widow's mourning hood or other head-dress. The peak of a head-dress fell over the forehead and was probably derived from the hood's "beake" to which the same Margaret Beaufort objected (see p. 242). Palsgrave in 1530 speaks of the "peake of a ladyes mourning heed [head-dress], biquoquet" and Cotgrave in 1611, gives "*Biquoquet,* the peake of a Ladies mourning hood" (Pl. 58).

99. Widow's head-dress of a Duchess, 1399. Pleated barbe over the chin, veil or coverchief over head and shoulders and an inner pleated veil underneath.
Brass of Alianore de Bohun, Duchess of Gloucester, Westminster Abbey.

In the early seventeenth century, the peak could be represented by an exaggerated dip in the front of an arched head-dress; later by a black triangle under a veil (Pl. 59).

In 1706 Addison mentions the veil:

Widow Trusty why so Fine?
Why dost thou thus in Colours shine?
Thou should'st thy husband's death bewail
In Sable vesture, Peak and Veil.

Rosamond III, iv

From late seventeenth century to *c.* 1730, the combination "Bandore and Peak" was used. This consisted of a black hood pointed in front, worn with a black veil flowing behind, secured by the bandore (bandeau) across the forehead.

100. Mary Queen of Scots as widow aged 36. A black dress replaces her earlier white. White yoke and ruffs, white transparent rail (veil) hanging from the "Mary Stuart" head-dress to full length, and wired out.

After a painting, artist unknown. National Portrait Gallery.

The Buxom Widdow with Bandore and Peak
Her Conscience as black as her Cloathing.
        Thomas D'Urfey, *Pills to Purge Melancholy*, Vol. 2, p. 11 (1719)

(b) General Attire before 1800
Black, in the correct materials, was the rule, but there were occasional exceptions. Some widows followed the French fashion and dressed in white. Mary Queen of Scots (aged 16) wore white on the death of her first husband's father, Henry II of France. When she arrived in Scotland in 1561, she was still

dressed in white mourning and became known as "The White Queen". In 1567 she also mourned for Darnley in white, but later in life she was nearly always in black with a white head-dress, as in the painting (1578) at the National Portrait Gallery.

Carola Oman gives an interesting account of the widowhood of Elizabeth, Queen of Bohemia (daughter of James I). When her husband died in 1632, she was "petrified with grief" and lay in a bedroom hung with black serge for eight days.[1] She then assumed her widow's costume.

"Honthorst painted her always arrayed in mourning robes of white satin shrouded by a voluminous black veil secured to her head by a small crown." After the period of deep mourning had expired, she dressed in the fashion of her day, but never in colours. Her costume was always a "plain black or pure white gown of silk, satin or wool with bertha [i.e. deep falling collar] and cuffs, of point lace." The "bertha" encircled a low décolletage which was disapproved of by her Dutch ministers; they asked her chaplain to stop her from wearing such low necked gowns!

In the sixteenth and seventeenth centuries widows continued wearing black clothes for three or four years or even longer and often retained their heavy black veils for the rest of their lives. In Plate 30 (b) we saw a portrait of Henrietta Maria, widow of Charles I in *c.* 1649 (about a year after his death). She is in black, relieved by a white neckerchief and cuffs, and one red bow. On her head she has a black lace veil in the form of what was then called a shadow. This seems to take the place of a peak.

In a letter of *c.* 1679–80 a Mrs Venables, writing to her aunt who had been widowed for about two years, advises her not to wear a "white bando" (bandore and peak) as this was correct only for

> the first three quarters but to wear a cap and cornet* and white hood and a black hood hanging behind, all of crape. If that mantua† fitted you pray send me word. I did not buy the best crape in hopes you would alter your mind and have another Mantu of something else.
>
> Lady Newton, *Lyme Letters* (1660–1760)

But the aunt was disinclined to discard any of her crape.

In Richard Steele's *The Funeral*, 1701, the black garments worn by all are emphasized, as is the widow's train. In Act V, Sc. i, the widow exclaims:

---

* A cap with a peak. Some sort of peak seems therefore to have been essential.

† A loose gown with a train.

But to my Dress—How solemnly magnificent is Black—And the Train—I wonder how Widows came to wear such long Tails!

In 1761 Mrs Elizabeth Montagu[2] gives the following advice to a friend:

> The fashionable dress for a widow is a gown with two broad plaits in the back [the sack-backed gown] a short cuff which comes a little below the elbow, round double ruffles [frills] very shallow. The dress weed [best dress] is made of silk . . . [with] a black silk long apron, black handkerchief,* black hood . . . or a sack may be worn with a short train, no flounce or ornament of any sort . . . Many women of condition wear merely a common crape.

When the self-styled Duchess of Kingston† was tried for bigamy in 1776, her widow's weeds were described by Hannah More who was present:

> The prisoner was dressed in deep mourning; a black hood on her head, her hair modestly dressed and powdered; a black silk sacque with crape trimmings; black gauze deep ruffles [on sleeves] and black gloves . . . there was nothing white but her face and had it not been for that, she would have looked like a bale of bombazine.
>
> Wm. Roberts, *Memoirs of the Life and Correspondence of Hannah More*, 3rd Edn, Vol. 1 (1835)

(c) Nineteenth-century Attire

Though widows' attire often kept up with the fashions in cut and style all through this century, convention dictated what was correct for them to wear as regards materials and duskiness.

A mourning dress worn by Queen Victoria in 1862 (a year after Prince Albert's death) is preserved in the London Museum. The dress is of black silk, but is very heavily trimmed with black crape, the skirt being almost completely covered with it. This was typical for deep mourning.

The indoor cap, the outdoor bonnet with veil, and to a lesser extent weepers, were characteristic of the nineteenth-century widow's costume. In 1801 Susan Sibbald described her grandmother's head-wear:

> She had on what it was the fashion for all Widows to wear then, a small plain close-fitting white cambric cap, with a very narrow border, crimped

---

* Neckwear, not a pocket handkerchief.

† The Duke had died in 1773 (see p. 232).

each side of the face and plain across the forehead; above it a small black silk hood, with a narrow lace border. No hair seen, so that it must have been particularly unbecoming.

The Memoirs of Susan Sibbald (1783–1812), ed. Francis P. Hett

This custom of showing no hair is reminiscent of the nun-like head-dress of earlier times. Indoors widows always wore caps, although these went completely out of fashion in the 1880s. They were usually of white muslin trimmed in front with ruched white crape, and by the mid-century, a long white streamer hung down behind (see Pl. 60). In 1884 Mrs J. Sherwood wrote

> Some widows even have the cap made of black *crêpe lisse*, but it is generally of white . . . Her [Queen Victoria's] widow's cap has never been laid aside, and with her long veil of white falling down her back, when she appears at court, it makes the most becoming dress that she has ever worn.
>
> *Manners and Social Usages*

Out of doors a black veil was indispensable. It was worn with whatever headgear was fashionable at the time, but usually this would be a bonnet (Pl. 56).

Dickens in 1834–5 describes a widow

> dressed in deep mourning . . . her face was shrouded by a thick black veil.
>
> *Sketches by Boz,* "The Black Veil"

Mrs J. Sherwood (op. cit.) states:

> . . . it is deemed almost a sin for a woman to go into the street, to drive, or to walk, for two years, without a deep crape veil over her face.

However, to judge by an advertisement of Jay's (Fig. 97 (a)) it was permissible to let the veil hang behind, at least in the 1890s.

Mrs Sherwood also tells us that

> Mourning bonnets are worn rather larger than ordinary bonnets. In England they are still made of the old-fashioned cottage shape, and are very useful in carrying the heavy veil and in shading the face. The Queen has always worn this style of bonnet.

Weepers, in the sense of cuffs (Fig. 101), were often worn by widows both in the eighteenth and nineteenth centuries. Thackeray mentions them in *Bluebeard's Ghost* (1843).

101. Empress Frederick of Germany, daughter of Queen Victoria, just widowed
in 1888. Deep weeper cuffs; very long black veil with widow's peak.
Black dress trimmed with white.
Reproduced in Richard Davey A History of Mourning. *1889.*

There is not a widow in all the country who went to such an expense for
black bombazine. She had her beautiful hair confined in crimped caps and
her weepers came over her elbows.

In the nineteenth century the term was also used for a widow's veil.

She [Mrs Glegg] resolved that she would have scarcely any weeper on her bonnet.

George Eliot, *The Mill on the Floss*, 1860

In *Middlemarch*, 1871–2, a lady's maid remarks to her widowed mistress:

If anybody was to marry me flattering himself I should wear these hijeous weepers two years for him, he'd be deceived by his own vanity, that's all.

The rules dictating the period during which a widow had to remain in mourning were strict and complex. Deep mourning was required for a year and a day, after which the widow "slighted her mourning". For the next six months she might change paramatta for black silk, still trimmed with crape. After eighteen months, crape was omitted and after two years half mourning began, which was usually black and white.

Mrs Sherwood had some comments to make on this subject:

The discarding of mourning should be effected by gradations. It shocks persons of good taste to see a light-hearted young widow jump into colours, as if she had been counting the hours. If black is to be dispensed with, let its retirement be slowly and gracefully marked by quiet costumes.

Loc. cit.

The battle between a Victorian widow's vanity and her sense of decorum was ridiculed in *c.* 1890 as follows.

The widow who considers with seriousness whether she will best express her sense of loss by a Marie Stuart cap* or an Alsation bow of tarlatan, is already half consoled, and will return in a month for another which will express "mitigated" grief by various lightsome pleatings . . . She will . . . express her appreciation of the solace a good dinner affords by donning a cap of tulle to eat it in. The black dress will soon . . . require a dainty frilled fichu of tulle to make it endurable. She will ere long, bestring herself with jet beads that will take the place of the tears that have ceased to flow . . . and the day when gray, and violet [are] permissible, is one characterised by a sober but genuine joy . . .

For deepest mourning some interesting details are revealed.

If she lift her skirts from the mud, she must show by her frilled black silk petticoat and plain black stockings her grief has penetrated to her innermost

* A widow's cap, once again with a dip over the forehead.

sanctuaries. If she put up her parasol, it is at once evident that she would deem it wrong even to shelter from the sun beneath anything less emotional than black chiffon arranged in puffs . . . Even the brooch that fastens the dress, and the chain that retains the watch, must do their duty in the livery of woe.

Mrs F. Douglas, *The Gentlewoman's Book of Dress, c.* 1890

CHILDREN—FUNERALS AND MOURNING

(a) Grave-clothes and Funerals of Children

Infants have generally had grave-clothes like the simplest used for adults. An undertaker's advertisement of 1838 offers, for example, winding sheets of uniform type in lengths from 6 feet 3 inches down to only 20 inches.[1]

An exception obtained in the pre-Reformation and Catholic churches for infants dying within a month of birth. These had to be buried in the chrisom cloth* used at their baptism wound round with swaddling bands (Fig. 102). Westminster Abbey Register records: "The Princess Ann's chrisome bur. 22 Oct. 1687." This was the second of the many infant losses suffered by the future Queen.

The leading feature of child burials has long been the use of white adjuncts. Even today a white coffin is usual. The disobedient little Augusta, in Mrs (Butt) Sherwood's† *The Fairchild Family* (1818) had a white velvet pall; and in real life two years earlier the remains of the baby Duke of St Albans left Portman Square in

> a hearse drawn by six horses . . . and was preceded by a splendid plume of white feathers.
>
> *Morning Herald,* 1816

Again, white bands were used for handling the coffin. Christina Hole notes: "In Cheshire up to the middle of the last century, a child's coffin was carried by women dressed all in white who supported it by white napkins slung through the handles."[2] Another example of white napkins will illustrate, at the same time, the traditional denial of religious rites to the still-born. The *Morning Herald* reports the burial in 1817 of an infant born to the Duchess of Cumberland, daughter-in-law of George III. It was given a royal attendance and buried at the Abbey, but

---

* Cf. p. 41. Hence the "christom child" to which Falstaff, in dying, was compared Henry V, II, iii, 9).

† Mrs Sherwood *née* M. M. Butt.

(a) (b)

Benedict Lee, Chrysome,
c. 1520, Chesham Bois,
Bucks.ꟼ

102.(a) Infant buried in its chrisom cloth, turned up at the bottom and
fastened by swaddling bands. Monumental brass, Chesham church,
Bucks. *c.* 1520.
Herbert Haines Manual of Monumental Brasses . . . British Isles
1861, Vol. 1.
(b) Infant buried in its chrisom cloth and swaddled with the end
free. Incised slab, Croxwell, Derbyshire. 16th or 17th century.
After J. Cox Parish Registers of England *1910. Fig. p. 63.*

the funeral was very private . . . of course without any church service, as
the infant was still born . . . The Yeomen of the Guard in their royal uniforms were in readiness to receive the corpse and they carried it on white
napkins.

A royal child's grave-clothes might be quite elaborate. The body was often
embalmed and beautifully dressed. Among the infants lost to Anne of Denmark and James I, before they came to the English throne, was one aged
twenty months in 1599. Accounts record the embalming of "Ladie Margaret",
and the purchase for the body (and for a pall?) of 10 quarters of wool, 6 of
lining, 6 of crimson taffeta @ £8 the ell and 8 ells of florence ribbons.[3]

Much later (1808), Mrs (Butt) Sherwood, who was an officer's wife in
India, describes her own 2-year-old child in death:

> My precious baby . . . was laid out on the sofa . . . The fair corpse wore a
> delicate holland cap, with a white rose, and a frill round his neck, but other-
> wise dressed as he had been in life. Flowers were scattered over the infant
> corpse.
>
> *Life of Mrs. Sherwood*, ed. Sophia Kelly (1854), p. 327

For people attending children's funerals the accessories were frequently
white. A political cartoon of 1766 (Pl. 61) shows mourners wearing white
shoulder scarves at what is supposed to be the burial of a baby.

At the death of a 3-year-old child in 1811, its nurse wrote to the mother,
Lady Stanley,

> I find it is not customary to give mourning for so young a child [i.e. to
> present it to friends for the funeral] . . . but all who attend will be in black
> with white hat-bands and gloves.
>
> *The Early Married Life of Maria Josepha Lady Stanley*,
> ed. Jane Adeane, 1899

As late as 1875 a Colchester undertaker was supplying for an infant's
funeral four sets of hatbands and gloves in white as well as one set in black
(? for himself).[4] The white accessories that a mute would use at a child's or
young girl's funeral are shown in Plate 42.

(b) Children at Funerals and in Mourning

To us it seems astonishing how much the children of the past themselves
attended funerals, and they have "gone into mourning" almost like grown-
ups.

That they should not miss the obsequies of their parents is vividly shown
by the fact that when in 1575 a woman was buried a month after giving birth
to quadruplets, the four baby survivors were "borne to church after hir";[5]
and again in 1817: three of a family were burnt to death in Bermondsey and
at the funeral

> the infant that was saved alive, carried in the arms of a nurse, followed as
> chief mourner.
>
> *Morning Herald*, 1st July 1817

But it was not only their parents' funerals that children might have to
attend. At that of Catherine Parr (one-time widow of Henry VIII) in 1548,
the chief mourner was none other than Lady Jane Grey at the tender age of

eleven.* "Her trayne [was] borne uppe by a yonge Lady"[6] and this was probably another child.

The young Earl of Rutland, whose death in 1587 we have mentioned, left
small children for whom full black mourning was ordered:

> for the two little ladies two yards each and the three young gentlemen, each
> one a cloak of a yard and a half. Item for each of the young gentlemen, hose
> and doublet of black bombazine.
>
> *MSS. of the Duke of Rutland*, Vol. 1, p. 243

Mary Villiers, daughter of the Duke of Buckingham, was a widow at the
age of about 12 and was dressed as such. Dorothea Townsend re-tells, in *The
Life . . . of Endymion Porter*, a charming story about her at this time, "on
the chance that it may be true."[7] Fostered at the royal palace, Mary had the
run of the king's orchard, and one day (*c.* 1635)

> her ladyship scrambled up into a tree, but there her black dress and fluttering
> veil attracted the king's attention and made him think some strange bird had
> alighted.

In 1641 little "Mun" Verney, aged only 5, because he had lost his grandmother, was denied a blue figured satin coat. His godmother writes:

> I entendede a cote to my godsone this Easter, and now I know he is in
> mourninge therefore have sent him a porringer to ete his breakfast in.
>
> *Memoirs of the Verney Family*, Vol. 2, p. 2

"Mun" would have been dressed like little Thomas Aston mourning his
mother in 1635, to be seen in Pl. 54. (The dead infant whose birth took away
her life is mourned for by means of black velvet on his cradle.)

When "Mun" himself died in 1688, his "little Jacob Hughes about nine
years old, taken out of charity" was duly put into mourning. The baby and
three toddlers left behind by Mrs John Verney when she died at the age of 21
in 1686 were all enveloped in black crape (ibid., Vol. 4, pp. 420, 422).

Hogarth (Pl. 41) shows that in 1731 even a very small and unconcerned
little boy could be made to wear a mourning cloak and a black weeper in his
hat for a funeral. (Apparently he was only spared the gloves.)

For little girls in the eighteenth and nineteenth centuries, mourning, when
not at its deepest, took the form of a white dress and black ribbons. In 1785

---

* Who was to meet her own horrible end only six years later.

Sophy Curzon's *great grandfather* had died. Her adoptive mother was re-minded, by an aunt:

> I see Lord Portmore is dead. As Sophy is past six should she not have a black knot [hair ribbon] and sash?
>
> *The Noels and the Milbankes,* ed. Malcolm Elwin, p. 273 (1967)

103. Widow at graveside and her little girl, wearing exactly similar black dresses and bonnets. Widow wears weeper cuffs. *c.* 1815–20. *Hand coloured print.*

In this same year a teenage girl, Charlotte Jerningham (afterwards a lady-in-waiting to Queen Adelaide) showed considerable interest in the mourning she wore for her grandmother. She sketched herself in the schoolroom in Paris, wearing a black dress and neckerchief and a black ribbon in her mob-cap.[8] Her mother wrote to her

> Your brothers . . . look very pretty in their black coats and I am sure by the description you give me of your mourning *you* must look charmingly. If you do not like to wear your black Linnen at present, keep it for second mourning or at Christmas. You shall have a Black silk and it will be better to wear that only on Sundays, and the Linen every day.
>
> *The Jerningham Letters,* 1780–1843, ed. Egerton Castle (1896), p. 23

Children must also take notice of public mourning. In 1780 Elizabeth

Ham, as a small girl at school, "wore a black sash and a black ribbon on my bonnet, as mourning for the Duke of Clarence, brother to George III" (*Elizabeth Ham by herself* . . ., 1945).

The whole of Eton College mourned for George III in 1820, when their blue or red jackets were replaced by black for good and all. Hence the Eton suit of today.

All through the nineteenth century, the involvement of even tiny children in mourning continues. Mrs (Butt) Sherwood did not lament her lost children by herself. When her 2-year-old died in 1808, she spent the funeral day at home with "Lucy":

> I remember . . . occupying myself in trimming her [Lucy's] cap with bows of narrow black love-ribbon, and tying a black love-sash round her waist.[9]

Lucy was three months old! When Lucy herself died in the following year Mrs Sherwood put her two adopted daughters, aged about 2 and 4, into similar caps.[10] Pl. 62 shows how such little girls would have looked in their best frocks.

The authoress's own experiences bore fruit in the vivid descriptions of forlorn occasions that she gives us in her novels. The Fairchild children, aged about 6 to 9, were desired to attend their play-fellow Augusta's funeral. On arrival at her house they were met by a footman in black, who took them into the hall, "where white gloves and scarves were given to them".[11]

Again in her *Lady of the Manor* (1825) we meet with a little marquis, ten months old, still in mourning for his mother who died at his birth:

> He was dressed in white, having a sash of black love* and a small straw hat on his head with a plume of ostrich feathers.

For Queen Victoria's views on babies' mourning, see Appendix 8.

A very small boy in *c.* 1840 is seen at his father's funeral in Pl. 31. Like the boy in Hogarth's picture, he wears a cloak and trailing weeper, but now a top hat and black trousers. The Bath Museum of Costume has a half-mourning tunic for a boy of the same age, made of white duck with black braid trimming all over it (1880s).

Children had to comply with rules as to depth of mourning and girls had to follow the fashions as well. The Mrs John Sherwood who wrote on etiquette says that children who have lost a parent must dress like widows,

---

* Love-ribbon.

i.e. in "black woollen stuffs and crape for one year, and then lighten it with black silk, trimmed with crape".[12]

In the Gallery of English Costume, Manchester, there is a black silk dress for a teenage girl which is already lavishly trimmed with crape, though dating as early as *c.* 1830. By the 1860s a little girl of 6 or 8, mourning her mother would indeed look rather like a widow (Fig. 104). Emerging, later, she might

104. Little girl aged 5 in mourning for her mother. Crape ruchings, black bonnet and boots. 1864.
From a photograph, authors' collection.

have black silk. (The same Gallery has two black silk dresses for children aged only 2 to 6, dating in the 1860s). Finally for half mourning she would have an elegancy like the one of her period to be seen in the London Museum —a white muslin dress with black net round the low neck and a broad black lace-edged silk sash. In the 1880s in full mourning she would have a bustle like her mother's and everything black except for a white lining to her bonnet.[13]

The slight let-up that ensued after this is reflected in our Pl. 60, where a child of 1890, who has just been bereaved of her father, actually wears a white dress. But even in 1898, as Mr Gladstone's coffin was lowered into its grave in Westminster Abbey, there stood beside it a little boy in an Eton suit and an even smaller grand-daughter in black from head to foot except for a white yoke to her dress (Pl. 63).

Throughout the whole of our period it has been customary at important funerals, perhaps partly for the decorative effect, to line up a number of children in uniform dress. At first they were "innocentes all clothed in white" with tapers—perhaps choir boys and others. Certainly the children of charitable foundations were for a long time the mainstay, and we have seen the part they played in Tudor civic funerals in the City of London (Merchant Taylors', Christ's Hospital, etc.) The actual words "Charity Children" are used in the *Illustrated London News* in connection with Princess Sophia's funeral escort in 1844. The "King's scollers" were roped in, from their nearness to the Abbey, to assist at many great funerals, for example at Lord Palmerston's. Eton boys, being near Windsor, wore surplices and held tapers when Henry VIII was buried there, and Harrow boys in caps and gowns were stationed on the route of Queen Adelaide's procession in 1849.

One Mr Tuke of Rotherham, in 1810, having presumably no benefactor's claim on the youngsters, left in his will (according to the *Morning Post* of 15th August) "To every child that attended his funeral one penny each".

Finally children, until quite recent times, might be appointed as the actual bearers of an infant's coffin. Pl. 64 shows a procession of such little girls carrying the coffin with white napkins. They wear white dresses in token of the dead child's innocence and black ribbons for their grief. The picture decorates an early Victorian broadsheet, with a hymn, *The Tolling Bell*, ending with the words

> Then when the solemn bell I hear,
> If saved from guilt, I need not fear;
> Nor would the thought distressing be,
> "Perhaps it next may toll for me".

Anon

*   *   *

There have been birth chimes and wedding peels, and now the bell tolls for death. And on this note we near the end of our book.

In tracing, through some thousand years, the history of costume worn for the ever recurring events of births, marriages and deaths, it has been obvious that many influences were at work with ever changing balance of effect. Perhaps it may be worth while to summarize these briefly.

Throughout the years mere utility had constantly to yield to other tendencies. In earlier times one of the strongest of these was fear, both of natural and supernatural forces and this affected the clothing of infants, that of the dead and even of mourners.

Other factors were social, involving the wish to express or induce emotions, ideas and religious feeling. Hence symbolic colours and expressive forms, as in the use of white for purity and the long train for grandeur.

Since an essential in ceremony is faithfulness to the past, we find not only antiquated styles of dress, but functionless vestiges.

A large factor making for splendour of costume at funerals and weddings was not merely love of spectacle, but—only too obviously—social competition and vested interests.

Finally, diametrically opposed to the influence of the past, and ultimately wiping out each relic in its turn, was the persistent power of fashion. The white christening cap gave place at one time to a baby's feathered hat, and the mourning hood eventually yielded to a top hat and weeper. An Elizabethan woman ousted half her barbe in favour of a ruff, and in the 1860s, for the sake of a crinoline dress, a girl would forgo the time-honoured bridal train.

Only when the need to escape the real world was most urgently felt, would the claims of fashion be defeated altogether. Perhaps Colley Cibber was right when he wrote:

One had as good be out of the World as out of Fashion.

Love's Last Shift, 1696

THE "CHRISTENING PALM" AND A SEVENTEENTH CENTURY CHRISTENING SET

'The "palm" or "pall" was not in use only for the baptism of an infant, but, certainly as late as forty years ago, the wrapper (often of fine muslin and lace) was so called in which the child was brought down to see company. The christening palm, like the christening robe, was therefore only a better kind of an article in daily use. I have in my possession some christening garments provided about the end of the seventeenth century, consisting of:

1. A lined, white figured satin cap.
2. A lined white satin cap, embroidered with sprays in gold coloured silk.
3. A white satin palm, embroidered to match. Size 44 in. by 34 in.
4. A pair of deep cuffs, white satin, similarly embroidered, trimmed with lace, evidently intended to be worn by the bearer of the infant.
5. A pair of linen gloves or mittens for the baby, trimmed with narrow lace, the back of the fingers lined with coloured figured silk.
6. A palm, 54 in. by 48 in., of rich stiff yellow silk, lined with white satin.

According to the Sarum use, yellow was the altar colour for confessors' festivals. May not this yellow pall have been considered specially suitable at the child's being first openly pledged to "confess the faith of Christ crucified"?'

Beaminster, C. E. K., *Notes and Queries* (1875), 5th Ser., Vol. 4, p. 139

BRIDE'S ATTIRE AT A
MIDDLE-CLASS PROVINCIAL WEDDING IN 1850*

Devizes Miss M. Coward April 1850
    To M. and J. Bull
    Millinery and Dress Rooms
    Saint John Street

		£	s.	d.
Making Bridal Dress			6.	0.
13yds. figured Silk	7/4	4.	15.	4.
Irish [linen]			1.	1.
6¾ lining	7		3.	11¼.
¼ corded do.	9		1.	8¼.
⅞ sarsnet [silk]	2/-		1.	10¾.
Whalebone 4½ Braid 6				10½.
1½ Wide Fringe	5/-		7.	6.
2¼ Narrow do.	2/6		5.	7½.
Galloon,† Tape Cord Hooks			1.	8.
Honiton Sleeves	6/6		6.	6.
Making Dress Body [Bodice]			3.	6.
Irish			1.	2.
¼ Lining	7			1¾.
Whalebone				4½.
Galloon, Tape, Cord, Hooks			1.	4.
Edging				9.
Making Lace Sleeves			1.	0.
5/16 Net	2/-			7½.
⅝ Insertion	2/-		1.	3.
1yd. Lace	3/4		3.	4.
¾ do.	3/10		2.	10½.
Glace‡ Mantle		3.	13.	6.
1 Bridal Favour	2/6		2.	6.
2 do.	2/-		4.	0.

   * Extract from a tradesman's account (in manuscript) reproduced by kind permission of the owner, Miss Doris Homan.

   † A woollen or thread kind of tape used for edging.

   ‡ A plain taffeta with a lustrous surface.

Lace Chemisette§	4/0		4.	0.
Honiton do.	14/6		14.	6.
Scarf Shawl	63/–	3.	3.	0.
Honiton Veil	30/–	1.	10.	0.
Lace Scarf	28/–	1.	8.	0.
Lace Bonnet	32/6	1.	12.	6.

§ Fill-in to front of low cut dress.

EXTRACT FROM THE ACCOUNT BOOK OF G. RICKWORD, UNDERTAKER, COLCHESTER

Funeral of Mrs Jackson, Dedham, 1st May 1863.

2 best crape hatbands and scarves	14s.	1	8	0
14 best silk hatbands and scarves	28/6	19	19	0
4 best hatbands for Self, plumber, mason and assistant	10/6	2	2	0
15 silk hatbands for 8 Bearers, 4 Coachmen, 1 Horseman, Church Clerk and Sexton	7s.	5	5	0
4 crape hatbands for servants	4/3		17	0
4 pair of Kidd gloves for [?]	2/9		11	0
18 pair of dents* best Kidd gloves	4s.	3	12	0
[2] pair of black Kidd gloves for Clerk and Sexton	[2/9]		5	6
13 pair of gloves for Bearers, Coachmen, etc.			13	0

* I.e. made by Messrs Dent & Co.

ALLOWANCES OF MOURNING AT STATE FUNERALS

Liveryes for Noblemen att Interymentes, every man
accordyng to his eastat [rank]★

[Ordinances originally *temp.* Henry VII, re-issued at different times in the sixteenth century]

	For Himself			No. of his servants to be supplied
	Garments	Yards required	Price per yard	
Duke	gown, sloppe,† mantle	16	10s.	18
Archbishop	gown, sloppe, mantle	16	10s.	18
Marquis	gown, sloppe, mantle	16	9s.	14–16‡
Earl	gown, sloppe, mantle	14–16	8s.	12
Viscount	gown and mantle	8–12		10
Baron or Banneret being Knight of the Garter	gown and hood	6–8		8
Knight	[the same?]	5–6	6s. 8d.	4
Esquires of royal household	as a knight	0–6		3
All other esquires and gentlemen	gown and tippet	0–5	5s.	2–3

★ Four MSS. collated: Bodleian MS. Ashmole 837 (ed. F. Furnivall); Harl. 1354 (ed. J. Strutt); B.M. MSS. Egerton 2642 and Harl. 1440. A few misreadings occur in the two printed versions.

† Sloppe = probably, as for women, "a mourning cassocke not open before" (see p. 210).

‡ Where there is a range of quantities, the lower figures occur in the later MSS.

FUNERAL CAVALCADE OF THE RT HON. THE EARL OF DERBY, IN 1572*

Note—Those with mourning hood "over the face" are shown in CAPITALS.
Those with hood "over the shoulder" *in italics.*
All who wore hoods also had black gowns.

No. of Men		Category and Order of Proceeding	Costume Notes
On Foot	2	Yeomen conductors	[Black Coats]. Black staves
	100	Poor men	Gowns [of coarse cloth]
	40	Choir and singing men	Surplices
	1	STANDARD-BEARER (an Esquire)	
Horse-back	80	*Gentlemen* on comely geldings	
	2	*Secretaries*	
	50	*Esquires and knights*	
	2	Chaplains of the defunct	"Hoods . . . according to their degrees"
	1	*Preacher* (Dean of Chester)	Doctor's hood
	3	*Steward, Treasurer and Comptroller*	White staves of office
	1	BANNER-BEARER (an Esquire)	
	1	HERALD bearing Helm and Crest	Coat-of-arms of defunct [Tabard]
	1	HERALD (a King-of-Arms) bearing Shield	Coat-of-arms of England [Tabard]
	1	HERALD (a King-of-Arms) bearing Sword	Coat-of-arms of England [Tabard]
	1	HERALD (a King-of-Arms) bearing Coat [Tabard]	Coat-of-arms of England [Tabard]

> **CHARIOT**
> 4 BOYS (PAGES) riding the 4 horses
> 1 USHER on the fore-seat
> 4 ESQUIRES†
> 6 BANNEROLL-BEARERS

No. of Men		Category and Order of Proceeding	Costume Notes
Horse-back	1	CHIEF MOURNER, the new Earl	Mourning robes of an earl
	1	His train-bearer	Bare-headed
	2	USHERS, one each side of the Earl	White rods of office
	1	GENTLEMAN OF THE HORSE leading Horse of Estate	
	8	ASSISTANT MOURNERS (Principal)	
	1	Yeoman	Black coat, bare-headed
	2	*Sons of chief mourner* (grandsons of the defunct)	
On Foot	2	Gentlemen to lead their [the grandsons'] horses	
	2	Yeomen ushers	White rods
	500	Yeomen of the defunct‡	[Black coats as for other yeomen?]
	all	Servants of gentlemen attending	
	certain	Yeomen to whiffle the procession all the way	Black coats, black staves

* Summary of the account transcribed in J. G. Nichols, *Manners and Expences* . . . (1797), pp. 65–71.

† These four probably acted as the pall-bearers when the chariot was at rest. Besides these, there were twelve bearers, not listed above, who carried the coffin into the church "8 gentlemen, 4 yeomen in gownes, theire hoods on theire heads" (ibid., p. 69).

‡ There were usually yeomen and gentlemen servants in the *fore* part of the procession. After the introduction of mourning cloaks some of the yeomen were upgraded to cloaks (from coats) and some of the gentlemen were downgraded to cloaks (from gowns).

FUNERAL OF WILLIAM PITT, 1ST EARL OF CHATHAM*
IN 1778

The funeral was "solemnized at Public Expence". The Members of Parliament assembled in their respective Houses and the rest of the procession in rooms adjoining.

> Cloaks, Scarves, Hatbands and Gloves were sent for from the [Royal] Wardrobe and distributed under the Direction of the Officers of Arms.

The Procession included:

> The High Constable of Westminster in his usual dress with a black Silk Scarf, Hatband and Gloves and his Silver Staff.
>
> Twelve Almsmen of Westminster in their Gowns. [The gown being a survival from the sixteenth century.]
>
> A Messenger of the College of Arms in a black Cloth Cloak with a Badge of the Arms of the College on the shoulder, a black Cap on his Head, and in his Hand his staff tipped with silver and furled with black Sarsnet [silk].
>
> Six Conductors in black Cloth Cloaks and Caps and long black staves.
>
> Poor men in black Serge Cloaks with Badges of the Crest of the deceased on the shoulder [Cf. Henry VIII's funeral]; black Caps on their Heads and long black Staves . . . in number 70 equal to the years of the age of the deceased Earl.
>
> Rouge Croix, Pursuivant, in his Majesties' Coat of Arms [tabard] over a black Cloth Cloak; black silk Scarf, Hatband and Gloves.
>
> . . .
>
> Servants of the Relations of the Deceased two and two in Mourning with Crape Hatbands.
>
> Servants of the Deceased in the same.
>
> Officers of the Wardrobe in Mourning—black Silk Scarves, Hatbands and Gloves.
>
> A great number of Gentlemen and Esquires in Mourning with Swords.
>
> Several Physicians in Mourning.
>
> Divines in clerical Habits
>
> . . .
>
> Knights . . . in the Collars of their Orders.

The "Trophies" were paraded:

> Helm and Crest borne by   . . . Somerset Herald
> Targe and Sword borne by   . . . Windsor Herald

* From the account in College of Arms MS. I 4.

Surcoat borne by   . . . Richmond Herald
Coronet on a black [cushion]

The chief mourner was the Earl's second son, William ("to us the Younger Pitt") since

> at the request of the family the usual attendance of an Earl as chief mourner was waived because the present Earl was on military duty at Gibraltar.

After the funeral

> The Comptroller, Stewards and Treasurer of the deceased broke their Staves and delivered the Pieces to Clarence [King of Arms] who threw them into the grave.

FUNERAL OF LORD NELSON, 1806*

Part of the Procession Programme

From the ADMIRALTY to ST. PAUL'S.

On Thursday the 9th Day of January, not later than nine o'Clock in the Morning, the Nobility and Gentry, *in Mourning, without Weepers,* and with *Mourning Swords*; the Knights of the several Orders *wearing their respective Collars*; the Naval Officers (who have no particular Duties assigned to them in the Solemnity) and the Military Officers in *their full Uniforms, with Crape round their Arms and Hats,* will pass through the Gates at Constitution Hill and the Stable Yard into Saint James's Park; where the Carriages will be duly marshalled in a Line of Procession.

The ORDER will be as follows, viz.

Marshals Men, on foot, to clear the Way.

Messenger of the College of Arms, *in a Mourning Cloak with a Badge of the College on his Shoulder, his Staff tipped with Silver, and furled with Sarsnet.*

Six Conductors, *in Mourning Cloaks, with Black Staves headed with Viscounts Coronets.*

Forty-eight Pensioners from Greenwich Hospital. Two and Two, in *Mourning Cloaks, with Badges of the Crests of the Deceased on the Shoulders, and Black Staves in their Hands.*

Forty-eight Seaman of His Majesty's Ship THE VICTORY, Two and Two, *in their ordinary Dress, with Black Neck Handkerchiefs† and Stockings, and Crape in their Hats.*

Watermen of the Deceased, *in Black Coats, with their Badges.*

Drums and Fifes.

Drum Major.

Trumpets.

Serjeant Trumpeter.

Rouge Croix Pursuivant of Arms (alone, in a Mourning Coach), in *close Mourning, with his Tabard over his Cloak, Black Silk Scarf, Hatband and Gloves.*

* From J. S. Clarke and John McArthur, *The Life of Admiral Lord Nelson* (1809), Vol. 5, Pl. 206 (italics ours).

† See p. 235, footnote.

QUEEN VICTORIA ON MOURNING

As might be expected, Queen Victoria held firm views on the subject of mourning. The following are extracts from her letters to her eldest daughter, lately married to Frederick, Crown Prince of Prussia.*

(a) Court and Private Mourning

The Duchess of Orleans, a relative of Prince Albert's, had died on 18th May 1858.

Buckingham Palace,
June 6, 1858.

About the mourning. I wish to say a word as I feel strongly upon the subject; and as my daughter and Princess Royal you always remain, you must not separate yourself from us. You should explain to Fritz that there is a difference here between court mourning and private mouring. Court mournings are short and worn here for all Crowned Heads and Sovereigns, etc. who are no relations—but private mourning we wear as long as we like; and this private mourning no earthly being can prevent you from wearing in your own home and when you do not appear at Fêtes. When you do then you can take it off. I must ask that you should respect our customs and feelings in this respect—and no one can prevent it, dear. Poor Aunt Hélène was not a near relation of yours—but a fortnight you ought to have worn it. Here we wear it a month on account of respect for her memory and relationship to Papa—and our very near and numerous relationship with the Orleans family who are in this country. You cannot ignore your relations (on our side) and therefore you ought to mourn (in a less degree, as you are not living with us, than we do—as you are a degree further off) for your own relations—in private as you would naturally do, leaving it off at Fêtes if it is wished—and you should explain this fully and openly to the Prince as a very strong feeling of mine—and I am sure he would not object. For those who are not yours but Fritz' and the Prussian families' relations that is another thing, you would naturally mourn as they do. This is a long story but I wish it to be set right.

(b) Infants in Mourning

When the Crown Princess's first baby was 5 months old, its great-grandmother (of Weimar) died. Queen Victoria wrote:

* *Dearest Child—Letters between Queen Victoria and the Princess Royal, 1858–1861*, ed. Roger Fulford, 1964.

July 6, 1859.

I think it quite wrong that the nursery [i.e. the staff of the nursery at the Prussian Court] are not in mourning, at any rate I should make them wear grey or white or drab—and baby wear white and lilac, but not colours. That I think shocking. Well of course with your German relations you must I suppose do what is custom but you must promise me that if I should die your child or children and those around you should mourn; this really must be, for I have such strong feelings on this subject.

In 1860, the Queen put even her youngest child, aged three, into mourning for its mother's half-sister's husband.

Darling Beatrice looks lovely in her black silk and crepe dress.

CRAPE

Since crape features so largely in mourning attire a brief account of its qualities and manufacture will be given. The quotations are from Professor D. C. Coleman's *Courtaulds* (Oxford University Press, 1969, pp. 29, 88, 89), by kind permission of the author, the firm and the publisher.

> Because public display of mourning was royally determined, silk, the most expensive and exclusive of fabrics, long the mark of high rank, was the fabric for the occasion. And the technical equivalent of the transference from lustrous, gleaming display to funereal darkness was retention of the gum, high throw, black dye, and certain methods of manufacture and finish which crape makers surrounded in industrial mystery.

The presence of gum in the thread reduces the glossiness of silk. For mourning, therefore, the gum natural to raw silk was retained, or, if removed by other processes, was replaced by other gums. "Throw" is the technical term for twist. Silk thread used for crape was extra highly twisted.

The special methods of manufacture consisted first in embossing on the material a visible "figure", a pattern of ridges running more or less at right angles to the warp threads (this can be done without damage only after stretching it sideways so that the warp threads are relatively slack); secondly by allowing the material to "crimp" so as to increase the dullness of the texture (Pl. 36).

> The path by which the eighteenth-century efforts to imitate the "Italian . . . crapes" were finally transformed into the techniques of nineteenth-century English crape makers is hard to trace . . . however, a fair amount of evidence on this subject survives in the Courtauld archives.★
>
> The lengths of undyed crape gauze went from the looms first to be "biased" or "angled" . . . the gauze was first . . . pulled sideways so as to lay the weft thread askew to the warp. The distorted gauze was then passed through the rollers of a crimping machine. This, like the biasing machine, was power driven. It consisted essentially of two rolls which could be run together under controlled pressure; the upper of brass, capable of being heated internally, and on the surface of which was engraved a "figure" . . .; and the lower of compressed paper. The latter was "worked in" so that the figure was transferred in reverse on to its surface. When the crape was between the two rolls, under heavy pressure and with the brass roll heated to 275°–

★ E.R.O. D/F 3/2/28, 33–38, 40–90, 110–15.

300°F., the figure was embossed upon it . . . After crimping, the bias was pulled out . . .

. . . the next major procedure was to allow the gauze to assume the curl or crimp which would follow from its being made of highly thrown yarn. This was done by steeping the gauze in a liquid at temperatures sufficiently high to cause the twist to unwreathe and thus the entire fabric substantially to contract. In this way the figure was set and the crape made to assume the peculiar craped and crimped quality which apparently made it desirable. What was used in the early days for this "wetting" process is unknown, but after 1848 the gauzes were steeped in a strong extract of valonia.*

. . . mourning crapes had not only to be dyed black but also to receive the final process: dressing. For black dyeing in the early years sundry vegetable dyes were used . . . By the time the silk had emerged from the dye-house it had lost much of the hardness given to it by its natural gum. It might even begin to look bright and soft, which would never do for the authentic mourning crape: the dull stiffness appropriate to this funereal trimming had to be put into it. This was done by passing the crape through a dress into which had been boiled up a variety of glutinous ingredients.

* Valonia: the name given to the acorns or acorn cups of *Quercus aegilops* and the related *quercus vallonea*, types of oak growing especially in the Mediterranean area. It contains much tannin.

ADVERTISEMENT OF MOURNING WEAR, 1872

From Walford, E. *County Families*

MOURNING.

Messrs. JAY have always at command experienced Dressmakers and Milliners, who act as travellers, so that in the event of immediate Mourning being required, or any other sudden emergency for dress, one can be despatched to any part of the kingdom on receipt of letter or telegram, without any expense whatever to the purchaser. All articles are marked in plain figures, and charges are the same as if the goods were bought for ready money at the Warehouse in Regent Street.

Messrs. JAY, anxious to remove an impression which they find has gained undue circulation, that none but the richest materials in Made-up Skirts, Mantles, and Millinery are sold at their Establishment, deem it a duty to themselves and the public to assure all Families who have not yet dealt at JAY's Mourning Warehouse, that they sell an excellent Family Mourning Dress, full length, for the small sum of One Guinea and a-half. Good Wearing Materials are cut from the piece, and at more than an equivalent for the price, which is from 1s. per yard upwards.

JAY'S,

THE LONDON GENERAL MOURNING WAREHOUSE,

247, 249, & 251 REGENT STREET.

MESSRS. JAY,

Having adopted a fixed tariff, publish the following epitome of their charges for

DRESSMAKING.

Making Dress, with Plain Skirt	10/6
Making Dress, with Tucks of Crape or Fancy Trimmings	from 14/6
Making Bodice and Mounting Skirt into Band	7/6
Making Widow's Bodice do. do.	8/–
Mounting Skirt into Band, with Alpaca Pocket	1/6
Mounting do. do. with Black Silk Pocket	2/6
Mounting do. do. without Pocket	1/–
Silk Body Lining	5/6
Silk Sleeve Lining	3/6
Silk Low Body and Sleeve Lining	5/6
Lawn Body Lining	1/6
Sleeve Lining	1/–
Silk Facing	–10½
Petersham Ribbon for Banding	–/8
Petersham Waistband, Covered Crape and Rosette	2/6
Making Garibaldi	6/–
Making Low Bodies	6/–
Sundries	1/6

Tucker, Braid, and Trimmings extra.

REFERENCES
not given in the text

CHAPTER I Births

1 *Children on Brasses,* 1970.
2 Leland, *Collectanea,* Vol. 4, 249.
3 *Everyman's History of the Prayer Book,* 1912.
4 T. D. Whitaker *History and Antiquities of the Deanery of Craven,* 3rd edn., 1878.
5 *The Life of William Hutton* . . . by himself 3rd edn., 1841.

CHAPTER II The Baby

1 In Joseph Mayer's *Library of National Antiquities,* Vol. 1 (1857).
2 Ibid.
3 *Domestic Medicine* (1769), p. 14.
4 *A Treatise on the Physical and Medical Treatment of Children.*
5 *Babies and How to take care of them.*
6 Ed. P. Hett, 1926.
7 In *Yorkshire Diaries* (Surtees Soc., 1886).

CHAPTER III The Christening

1 *Memorials of St. Dunstan,* ed. W. Stubbs, 1874.
2 John Stow, *Chronicles of England,* ed. E. Howe, 1631.
3 *The Household Books of Lord William Howard of Naworth Castle* (Surtees Soc.),
   1877.
4 *Pageant of the Earl of Warwick* (with facsimile of the B.M. MS. Cot. Jul. E IV,
   ed. Viscount Dillon and W. St. J. Hope, 1914).
5 *Early Married Life of Maria Josepha, Lady Stanley,* ed. Jane Adeane, 1899.
6 *Illustrated London News* (1843), p. 402.

CHAPTER VII Grand Wedding

1 B.M. MS. Roy. 14 C. VII, f. 225v.
2 B.M. MS. Cot. Nero D 1, f. 6v.
3 Hall's *Chronicle* . . . (1548–50), Edn. 1809.
4 *Court and Private Life in the Time of Queen Charlotte* . . . ed. Mrs V. D.
   Broughton, 1887.

CHAPTER IX The Wedding Ring

1   *Diaries of a Duchess . . . 1716–1776*, ed. J. Greig, 1926.
2   *Blundell's Diary and Letter Book, 1702–1728*, ed. Margaret Blundell, 1952.
3   William Jones, *Finger-Ring Lore . . .*, 1877.

CHAPTER X Costume and Death Customs

1   Gutch and Peacock, *Lincolnshire County Folk Lore* (1908), p. 240.
2   *Funeral Customs* (1926), p. 37.
3   E. Lewis Thomas Baker, *Law Relating to Burials* (edn. 1898), p. 41.
4   *Ancient Funeral Monuments*, 1767.
5   Charles Payne in *Jour. Gypsy Lore Soc.*, 3rd Ser., Vol. 36, p. 78 (1957).
6   Radford, *Encyclopaedia of Superstitions*, ed. Christina Hole (1961), p. 74.
7   B.M. MS. Vesp. c XIV, f. 181.
8   Leland, *Collectanea*, Vol. 5, p. 308.
9   College of Arms MS. I 4, f. 6.
10   W. H. St J. Hope in *Archaeologia*, Vol. 60, p. 525.
11   Rev. J. Stevenson (trans. and ed.), *Church Historians of England*, Vol. I, p. 784. Hair itself has always had symbolic significance as a *pars pro toto* of the body.
12   *De exequiis regalibus* in *Liber Regalis*, Westminster Abbey; also in B.M. MS. Egerton 2642, f. 181.
13   Sir Joseph Ayloffe in *Archaeologia*, Vol. 3, p. 384.
14   *Folklore*, Vol. 72, p. 489 (1961).
15   *Jour. Gypsy Lore Soc.*, 3rd Ser., Vol. 36, p. 78 (1957).
16   *Gentleman's Magazine*, Vol. 76, p. 91.
17   *Notes and Queries*, Vol. 9, p. 536.
18   Funeral of the Earl of Salisbury, 1462/3 (B.M. MS. Egerton 2642, f. 195v).
19   Funeral of 5th Earl of Shrewsbury, 1560. (J. Hunter, *Hallamshire* p. 77.)
20   *Archaeologia*, Vol. 28, p. 145.
21   F. Sandford, *Genealogical History of the Kings of England . . .*
22   B.M. MS. Harl. 6079, f. 23v.
23   B.M. MS. Egerton 2642, f. 195v.
24   *Antiquarian Repertory*, Vol. 4, 654 et seq., and College of Arms MS. I 11.
25   Various MSS. One at College of Arms transcribed in *Excerpta Historica*, p. 307 seq.: also Machyn's *Diary*.
26   Leland, *Collectanea*, Vol. 5, p. 315.
27   B.M. MS. Harl. 1354.
28   B.M. MS. Add. 35324, ff. 4–5v.
29   B.M. MSS. Add. 5408 and 35324, f. 36v.

30 Thos. Fuller, *Church History* . . . (edn. 1868), p. 567.
31 *Memoires,* trans. Ozell, 1719.
32 Bodleian MS. Ashmole 837, art. vi, f. 134.
33 Leland, *Collectanea,* Vol. 5, p. 310.
34 *Funeral Procession of Sir Phillip Sidney,* engraved by de Bry after Thos. Lant (1588), p. 16.
35 Evelyn's *Diary* entry for 26th May 1703.
36 MS. copy in The Noble Collection, Guildhall Box 22, 82/83.
37 *Archaeologia,* Vol. 26, pp. 337–9 (1836).
38 B.M. MS. Egerton 2642, f. 196. (Italics ours.)
39 *Antiquarian Repertory,* Vol. 4, p. 662.
40 B.M. MS. Harl. 1368, f. 28v.
41 Quoted by W. H. St J. Hope in *Archaeologia,* Vol. 60.
42 College of Arms MS. I 11, ff. 92–105.
43 *Archaeologia,* Vol. 16, pp. 22–8.
44 B.M. MS. Harl. 3504.
45 B.M. MS. Egerton 2642, f. 204v.
46 *Funeral Customs,* 1926.
47 Ibid.
48 Radford, *Encyclopaedia of Superstitions,* ed. Christina Hole, 1961.
49 R. Davey, *A History of Mourning.*
50 *A Description of England* . . . by . . . Jorevin de Rocheford (trans.) in *Antiquarian Repertory,* Vol. 4, p. 585.
51 B. Picart (ed.), *Ceremonies and Religious Customs* (English trans. 1737), Vol. 2, pp. 106, 108.
52 Shakespeare, *Hamlet* V, i (1594).
53 B. Puckle, op. cit.
54 Vol. 17, pp. 264, 265.
55 Vol. 4, p. 664.
56 Crichton Porteous, *The Ancient Customs of Derbyshire,* p. 2 (illus.).
57 *Church Folklore* (1894), p. 127.
58 B.M. MS. Arundel 26, f. 29v.
59 *Morning Post,* 1810.
60 Charles Bradford, *Heart Burial,* 1933.
61 J. Nichols, *A Collection of Wills* . . . (1780), p. 251 (Latin).
62 *Diary,* pp. 109, 199.
63 B.M. MS. Arundel, 26, f. 29v.

CHAPTER XI Characteristics of Funeral and Mourning Wear

1 *Antiquarian Repertory*, Vol. 4, p. 660.
2 *Archaeologia*, Vol. 66, pp. 197–231.
3 *Chronique de la Traison et Mort de Richart deux*, trans. Williams (Eng. Hist. Soc., 1846).
4 *The Life of Mrs. Sherwood*, ed. Sophia Kelly, 1854.
5 Misson, *Memoires*, 1698.
6 J. Nichols, *Progresses . . . of Q. Elizabeth*, Vol. 2.
7 *Diary of Rev. John Ward*, ed. C. Severn, 1839.
8 Lady Charlotte Campbell, *Diary of the Times of George IV* (1838) Vol. 3, p. 101.
9 Vol. 36, p. 253.
10 Letter dated 1747, in *Mrs. Delany's Autobiography . . .* Vol. 1, p. 478.
11 *MSS. of the Duke of Rutland*, Vol. 1, p. 243.
12 R. R. Steele, *Tudor and Stuart Proclamations . . .* (1910), Vol. 1, item 1334.
13 Quoted in John Ashton's *Social Life in the Reign of Queen Anne* (1882), p. 50.
14 *London Gazette*, 26th October.
15 Natalie Rothstein, *The Silk Industry in London, 1702–1766*, 1961 (unpub. thesis, M.A. History, Univ. of London).
16 B.M. MS. Add. 6310, f. 34v. (Newspaper cutting.)
17 C. Titman, *Dress and Insignia Worn at Court*, 2nd edn., 1937.
18 R. Davey, *History of Mourning*.
19 *Antiquarian Repertory*, Vol. 4, p. 662.
20 J. Nichols, *Manners and Expences . . .*, p. 69.
21 *Leaven of the Pharisees*, E.E.T.S., orig. ser. 74, p. 4.
22 W. Hargreaves-Mawdsley, *Academical Dress in Europe* (1963), pp. 104, 136.
23 *London Journal*, 1762–3, edn., 1950.
24 Vol. 6, p. 78.
25 R. Hertz, *Death and the Right Hand*, 1909.
26 B.M. MS. Egerton 2642, f. 191. (This account misdates the event.)

CHAPTER XII Grave Clothes and Funeral Effigies

1 *Dress and Habits of the People of England* (1796), Vol. 1.
2 B.M. MS. Nero C IV.
3 B.M. MS. Roy. 2 B VII.
4 Middleton MSS. (Hist. MSS. Com. 1911), p. 473 (Willoughby Accounts).
5 Wm. Kellaway, *Trans. London Middx. Archaeol. Soc.* (1956), Vol. 18 (1), p. 8.
6 *Lyme Letters . . .* ed. Lady Newton (1925), p. 98.
7 *Memoires*, trans. Ozell, 1719.

8   Wm. Egerton, *Faithful Memoirs of the Life of Mrs. Anne Oldfield*, 1731.

9   1, line 246.

10 Anonymous. First pub. 1699. Ed. by R. Straus (from the edn. of 1747), 1927.

11 J. Turner, *Burial Fees for Undertakers*.

12 H. Dittrick, "Devices to Prevent Premature Burial" in *J. Hist. Med.*, Vol. 3, pp. 161–71 (1948).

13 *Practical Papers on Funeral Reform* (Paper II).

14 Rolls series, 28 i. 301, 302 (quoted by W. H. St J. Hope, op. cit. below (1893)).

15 *Archaeologia*, Vol. 9, p. 10.

16 Trans. by J. Stevenson in *Church Historians*, Vol. 1, pp. 781–5.

17 B.M. MS. Roy. 2 B VII, f. 298v.

18 *Vita Sancti Thomae,* quoted by W. H. St J. Hope, "On the tomb of an archbishop recently opened", in *Vetusta Monumenta*, Vol. 7 (1893).

19 W. H. St J. Hope, ibid.

20 George Tyack, *Historic Dress of the Clergy* [1897], p. 113.

21 *Testamenta Eboracensia* IV (Surtees Soc. 53), p. 319 (1868).

22 B.M. MS. Harl. 6064, f. 83v. Episcopal gloves, being of perishable linen, were missing from the graves described above.

23 *Diary.* The more detailed account in College of Arms MS. I 11, f. 121 v, mentions no effigy.

24 *Vetusta Monumenta*, Vol. 4, with Pl. 19.

25 *Archaeologia*, Vol. 52, p. 257.

26 Henry Keepe, *Monumenta Westmonasteriensia* (1683), Vol. 2, Appendix.

27 H. Haines, *A Manual of Monumental Brasses* (1861), p. lxxiv.

28 *Archaeologia*, Vol. 3, pp. 276–431.

29 Westminster Abbey Library.

30 Rymer's *Foedera*, Vol. 8, p. 75.

31 F. Sandford, *Genealogical History* . . ., p. 202 (quoting Walsingham).

32 *Chronique de . . . Richart deux* . . ., trans. Williams, 1846.

33 Wardrobe Accounts of Thos. Ousefleet, quoted by Hope (op. cit.). There was also a "German coverchief" which may have been a face-cloth.

34 Stow's *Chronicle*, pp. 362, 363.

35 Thomas Walsingham's *Chronicle* (Rolls series Vol. 28, i) ii, 345/6, quoted in translation by W. H. St J. Hope in "Funeral Effigies of the Kings and Queens" . . . *Archaeologia*, Vol. 60, p. 535.

36 *Archaeologia,* Vol. 1 (edn. 1777), p. 365 seq.

37 Ibid.

38 College of Arms MS. I 14, f. 67, quoted by Hope, op. cit.

39 Transcribed fairly accurately by Strype in *Eccles: Memorials*, Vol. 2, Appendix, p. 9.

40 *Diary*, p. 39.
41 F. Peck, *Desiderata Curiosa*, Bk. 6, p. 8.
42 Hope, loc. cit.
43 *Genealogical History*, p. 530 (1677).
44 P.R.O. Ld. Chamb. Rec. Ser. I, Vol. 557.
45 Wagner, Sir A. *Heralds of England* (1967) p. 114.
46 *Chronicle* . . . (2nd edn. 1675), p. 408.
47 Heath's *Chronicle*, p. 412.
48 Sir J. Ayloffe in *Archaeologia*, Vol. 3, p. 390.
49 Issue Roll Easter 17 R. II.
50 R. P. Howgrave-Graham in *Archaeologia*, Vol. 98, pp. 159–69 (1961).
51 Hope in *Archaeologia*, Vol. 60, p. 550.
52 P.R.O. Ld. Chamb. Rec. Ser. I, Vol. 550.
53 *Antiquarian Repertory*, Vol. 4, p. 654 seq.
54 *Archaeologia*, Vol. 16, p. 24.
55 John Strype, *Ecclesiastical Memorials*, Vol. 2.
56 College of Arms MS. I 14, f. 123v.
57 P.R.O. Ld. Chamb. Rec., Ser. 1, Vol. 554.
58 Ibid.
59 B.M. MS. Add. 5751, ff. 50, 51
60 (1786) Vol. 1, p. xlix seq.
61 Sir J. Callum, *History of Hanstead*, Suffolk.
62 MSS. of the Duke of Rutland (R.H.M.C.), Vol. 4, p. 340.
63 Quoted L. Stone, *Crisis of the Aristocracy* (1955), p. 579.
64 *Memoirs of the Verney Family* (1892–7), Vol. 2, pp. 18, 19.
65 L. E. Tanner and B. E. Nevinson in *Archaeologia*, Vol. 85, p. 176 (1935) (Quotation and Illustration).
66 *Letters,* ed. Toynbee, Vol. 1, p. 331.
67 Tanner and Nevinson, op. cit., p. 180.

CHAPTER XIII Ordinary People's Funeral

1 B.M. MS. Claudius B. IV.
2 B.M. MS. Roy. 6 E VII, f. 145v.
3 Sir N. Nicolas *Vetusta Testamenta*, Vol. 1, p. 299.
4 B.M. MS. Harl. 6064, f. 101.
5 Bodleian MS. Ashmole 837, f. 133.
6 B.M. MS. Harl. 6064, f. 101. Another version, transcribed in the Preface to Machyn's *Diary* (ed. J. G. Nichols, 1848) is less satisfactory. However, the preface gives some useful information on funerals of the period.

7 B.M. MS. Harl. 6064.

8 Machyn's *Diary*, p. 224.

9 Ibid., p. 99.

10 Machyn's *Diary*, pp. 111–12.

11 Raymond Smith, *Ceremonials of the City of London*, edn. 1962.

12 Machyn's *Diary*, p. 234.

13 *Diary*, p. 193. Spelling modernized in this quotation.

14 Sir W. Roche's funeral, 1523. Ibid., Preface, p. xxi.

15 That of "Reade of Codesbrook" (B.M. MS. 6067, f. 30).

16 B.M. MS. Harl. 1368, f. 27.

17 *Antient Funeral Monuments* (edn. 1767), Ch. III, p. xii (first pub. 1631).

18 Ibid., Ch. IV, 12.

19 Ibid., Ch. III, p. xii.

20 Pepys's *Diary*, Vol. 1, pp. lxii–lxvi.

21 J. F. Hayward, *Connoisseur Period Guide . . ., 1714–60*.

22 *Yorkshire Diaries*, Vol. 1, p. 105.

23 *Gentleman's Magazine*, Vol. 83, p. 33.

24 *Parson Woodforde's Diary*, Vol. 3, p. 160 (1789).

25 Ibid., Vol. 2, p. 86 (1783).

26 Ibid., Vol. 3, p. 8.

27 Ibid., Vol. 4, p. 25 (1793).

28 Ibid., Vol. 1, p. 109.

29 *A Frenchman in England*, 1789. Trans. S. C. Roberts, 1933.

30 Reproduced in facsimile in B. Puckle, *Funeral Customs*, 1926, pp. 273–5.

31 Partly transcribed by C. W. Pugh in *Wilts. Archaeol. and Nat. Hist. Mag.*, Vol. 46 (1934).

32 Mrs Gaskell, *Cranford*, edn. 1911, p. 28.

33 G. M. Young (ed.), *Early Victorian England* (1934), pp. 121–2.

34 A. Singleton, Pamphlet on *The Objects of the . . . Association*, 1888.

35 *Supplementary Report . . . on interment in towns* (1843), p. 49.

36 Op. cit., p. 87.

37 *Life and Labour of the People of London*, Ser. 3, Vol. 2, p. 245 (1902).

38 Ibid., Vol. 1, p. 249.

39 Ibid., Vol. 2.

40 Contemporary account quoted in C. R. N. Routh, *They Saw it Happen 1485–1688* (1956).

CHAPTER XIV Grand Funerals I

1 B.M. MS. Egerton 2642, f. 204, and other MSS.

2 College of Arms MS. I 4, f. 85 (Mary II's funeral, 1695).

3   B.M. MS. Julius B. XII, f. 7v. and 8.
4   James Heath, *A Chronicle of the Civil Wars*, Pt III, p. 412.
5   *Heralds of England*, 1967.
6   B.M. MS. Harl. 6064, f. 183v.
7   This and the ensuing extracts are from the version Harl. 1776, ff. 7v–9v.
8   B.M. MS. Harl. 1354, f. 31v.
9   Leland, *Collectanea*, edn. 1770, Vol. 5, p. 317.
10 B.M. MS. Harl. 6064, f. 92. Strutt (ibid.) dates and reproduces this imperfectly.
11 B.M. MS. Harl. 1368, f. 18v.
12 *Archaeologia*, Vol. 1 (3rd edn.), pp. 375–81.
13 F. Peck, *Desiderata Curiosa*, Vol. 2, Bk. VII, p. 10.
14 J. R. Green, *Short History of the English People* (edn. Dent, 1934, p. 286).
15 Puckle, op. cit.
16 J. Hunter, *Hallamshire* (edn. 1869), p. 74.
17 *Testamenta Vetusta*, ed. N. Nicolas.
18 B.M. MS. Add. 35324, ff. 24–25v.
19 *Antiquarian Repertory*, Vol. 4, p. 654 seq.
20 Transcribed in Leland's *Collectanea,* but more accurately in *Antiquarian Repertory*, Vol. 2.
21 The full account in Leland's *Collectanea* (Vol. 4, pp. 303–9), is from B.M. MS. Harl. 3504, ff. 252v.–253. He does not point out that the date given for the funeral in the original, "1485", is incorrect.
22 *Archaeologia*, Vol. 16, pp. 22–8.
23 Strype, *Ecclesiastical Memorials*, Vol. 2.
24 Four accounts collated here: (i) Machyn's diary, p. 145; (ii) a MS. of the College of Arms transcribed in S. Bentley's *Excerpta Historica*, pp. 303–13; (iii) B.M. MS. Egerton 2642, ff. 200, 201; (iv) Drawings in B.M. MS. 35324, ff. 8, 8v.
25 Vol. 5, pp. 307–23.
26 *Diary*, p. 182.
27 There is a full account transcribed by J. G. Nichols in *Manners and Expences* . . ., 1797.
28 B.M. MS. Add. 35324, ff. 18–21v.
29 Op. cit., pp. 71–4. Unfortunately the formulary relating to earls is incomplete.
30 L. Stone, *Crisis of the Aristocracy*, 1955.
31 MSS. of the Earl of Rutland (R.H.M.C.), p. xvii.
32 B.M. MS. Harl 1354, f. 46.
33 Ibid., f. 45.
34 R. Davey, *History of Mourning*, 1889.
35 B.M. MS. Add. 35324, f. 46.

CHAPTER XV Grand Funerals II

1 MS. Add. 5408 (reproduced in *Vetusta Monumenta*, Vol. 3, p. 26).
2 MS. Add. 35324, ff. 27–37v. A third version, engraved by Badoureau, all on one block, contains many errors.
3 B.M. MS. Lands. 885, ff. 115–23v.
4 B.M. MS. Harl. 1301, f. 12.
5 R. R. Steele, *Tudor and Stuart Proclamations* . . . (1910), Vol. 1, item 1225.
6 J. Strype, *Ecclesiastial Memorials*, Vol. 2, Appendix p. 12.
7 The funeral is described in *London Gazette*, No. 465, for 2nd May 1670.
8 *Funeral of the Duke of Albemarle* . . ., 1670.
9 College of Arms MS. I 4, f. 68v.
10 *Diary*, ed. William Bray, 1907, Vol. 2, p. 215.
11 *The Journeys of Celia Fiennes*, ed. C. Morris, edn. 1947 (quoted by M. Harrison and O. Royston in *How They Lived* . . .).
12 *History of England*, Vol. 4, p. 536.
13 *Gentleman's Magazine*, Vol. 6, p. 54.
14 J. Weever, *Antient Funeral Monuments*, p. xviii (1767).
15 Wagner, op. cit., p. 116.
16 *Selected Letters*, edn. 1926, pp. 63, 64.
17 J. S. Clarke and J. MacArthur, *Life of Nelson*, Vol. 5, p. 204 seq.
18 College of Arms MS. I 4, ff. 53v–55.
19 *Gentleman's Magazine*, Vol. 87 (1817), p. 453.

CHAPTER XVI Mourning

1 J. R. Planché, *Cyclopedia of Costume* (1876), Vol. 2, pp. 114, 115.
2 *Canterbury Tales* (ed. Skeat), ll. 2882–4.
3 Ibid., l. 2977.
4 *Troilus and Cresyd* (c. 1385), ed. Skeat.
5 Transcribed by Sir W. Dugdale in *Antiquities of Warwickshire* (1656), pp. 354, 355.
6 Hall's *Chronicle*, Henry V, p. 50.
7 B.M. MS. Harl, 1776, f. 7v.
8 Ibid., f. 9v. Palsgrave (1530) defines Beck as "Peake of a ladye's mournynge heed".
9 *The Early Diary of Frances Burney 1768–1778*, ed. by Annie R. Ellis, Vol. 2, p. 323.
10 Anne Buck in *High Victorian Costume 1860–1890*, p. 33 (Costume Society, 1969), quoting from the *Ladies Treasury*, 1881.

11 *Dearest Mama—Letters between Queen Victoria and the Crown Princess of Prussia 1861–1864*, ed. R. Fulford, 1968.
12 B.M. MS. Harl. 1776, f. 9.
13 *Gentleman's Magazine*, Vol. 30, p. 488 (1760). (A frock was a loose coat with turn-down collar.)
14 *Gentleman's Magazine*, Vol. 31, p. 42.
15 Newspaper cutting in B.M. MS. Add. 6310, f. 38.
16 *Political and Social Letters of a Lady of the 18th Century* (ed. E. Osborn), 1890.
17 Natalie Rothstein, *The Silk Industry in London, 1702–1766*, 1961 (unpublished).
18 Quoted (ibid.) from House of Lords MSS., Vol. 10, 1712–14 (1953), No. 3009.
19 *Autobiography and Correspondence of Mrs. Delany*, Vol. 3, p. 606.
20 *Elizabeth Montagu—Queen of the Bluestockings*, ed. Emily J. Climenson, 1906.
21 *Diaries of Mrs. Philip Lybbe Powys 1756–1808*, ed. Emily J. Climenson, 1899.
22 *Autobiography and Correspondence of Mrs. Delany* (1861), Vol. 3, p. 475.
23 Rothstein, op. cit.

CHAPTER XVII Widows' Weeds

1 *Elizabeth of Bohemia*, 1938, p. 332.
2 *Letters of Mrs. Elizabeth Montagu*, ed. M. Montagu, 1809–13.

CHAPTER XVIII Children

1 J. Turner, *Burial Fees* . . .
2 *English Folklore* (edn. 1940), p. 53.
3 Treasurer's Accounts in *Letters to James VI* (Maitland Club), Edinburgh, 1835.
4 MS. Account Book of G. Rickword, Colchester Public Library.
5 John Stow, *Annals* (1592), p. 1162–63.
6 *Archaeologia*, Vol. 5.
7 *The Life and Letters of Endymion Porter* (1897), p. 88.
8 *The Jerningham Letters,* Vol. 1, Illustration VI.
9 *Life of Mrs. Sherwood*, p. 328.
10 Ibid., pp. 350, 351.
11 Mrs Sherwood (*née* M. M. Butt), *History of the Fairchild Family* (1818), p. 156.
12 Mrs John Sherwood, *Manners and Social Usages*, 1884.
13 Illustration (1882) reproduced in de Vries, *Victorian Advertisements*, 1968.

SELECT BIBLIOGRAPHY

Publication is in London unless otherwise stated.

Abbreviations B.M. British Museum
                ed. edited by
                Edn edition
                E.E.T.S. Early English Text Society
                R.H.M.E. Royal Historical Manuscripts Commission

Aitken, James (ed.), *English Diaries of the XVI, XVII and XVIII Centuries*, 1941.

Andrews, William (ed.), *Curious Church Customs*, 2nd Edn, 1898.

Anthony, Pegaret, and Arnold, Janet, *Costume, A General Bibliography*, V & A, 1968.

Antiquarian Repertory, see Grose.

Ashmole, Elias, *A complete Account of the Ceremonies observed in the Coronations of the Kings and Queens of England*, 2nd Edn, 1727.
    Institution, Laws and Ceremonies of the most noble Order of the Garter, fol. 1672. Engravings W. Hollar.

Ashton, John, *The Fleet, Its River, Prison and Marriages*, 1888.
    Social Life in the Reign of Queen Anne, 1882.

Austen, Jane, The Letters of, (1775–1817), ed. R. Brimley Johnson, 1926.

Babies and how to take care of them (Preface signed J.C.) [1879].

Bendann, E., *Death Customs . . .*, 1930.

Benenden Letters, London Country and Abroad, 1753–1821, ed. Charles F. Hardy, 1901.

Benson, E. F., *Queen Victoria*, 1935.

Bentley, Samuel (ed.), *Excerpta Historica*, 1831.

Besant, Sir Walter, *London in the Time of the Stuarts*, 1903.

Bingley (ed.), see Hartford.

Blomefield, Francis, *The History of the Ancient City and Burgh of Thetford . . .*, Fersfield, 1739.

Blundell, Nicholas, *Blundell's Diary and Letter Book, 1702–1728*, ed. Margaret Blundell, Liverpool, 1952.

Bond, Francis, *Fonts and Font Covers*, 1908.

Bonser, W., *Bibliography of Folklore: 80 years of the Folklore Society*, 1958.

Booke of Precedence: the Ordering of a funerall etc., ed. F. J. Furnivall in E.E.T.S. extra ser. 8 (1869).

Booth, Charles (ed.), *Life and Labour of the People in London*, 3rd Series (Revised Edn), 1902.

Bradford, Charles A., *Heart Burial*, 1933.

Brand, John, *Observations on the Popular Antiquities of Great Britain*, 1854, Vol. 2.

Briggs, Asa (compiled) *How They Lived: an Anthology of Original Documents, written between 1700 and 1815*, Oxford, 1969.

Buchan, Dr William, *Advice to Mothers*, 1803
Domestic Medicine Edinburgh 1769 and edns 1803, 1812.

Bull, Dr Thomas, *Hints to Mothers . . . during the Period of Pregnancy and in the Lying-in-Room . . .*, 15th Edn, 1864.

Burney, "Fanny", *The Early Diary of Frances Burney 1768–1778*, ed. Anne R. Ellis, 1913.

Cadogan, Dr William, *Essay upon Nursing and the Management of Children from their Birth to Three Years of Age* (in a letter to a Governor of the Foundling Hospital), 1748.

Calverley, see Yorkshire Diaries.

Chamberlain, John, *Letters written by John Chamberlain*, ed. Sarah Williams (Camden Soc.), 1861.

Chambers, Robert (ed.), *Chambers' Book of Days, a miscellany of Popular Antiquities . . .* 1863/4.

Chapman, George, *The Funerals of the High and Mighty Prince Henry Prince of Wales . . .*, 1613.

Chaucer, Geoffrey, *The Complete Works* of, ed. Walter Skeat, Oxford, 1912.
The Canterbury Tales, translated into modern English by Nevill Coghill, 1965.

Chavasse, Pye H., *The Young Wife's and Mother's Book. Advice to Mothers . . .*, 2nd Edn, 1842. (Other edns entitled *Advice to Mothers . . .*)
Advice to a Wife . . . during the periods of . . . Pregnancy, Labour and Suckling, 3rd Edn, Birmingham, 1854.

Clark, E. C., "English Academical Costume (medieval)" in *Archaeol. Jour.*, Vol. 1 (1893); also "College Caps and Doctors Hats", ibid., Vol. 2 (1894).

Clarke, J. S., and McArthur, John, *The Life of Admiral Lord Nelson*, 1809. The Guildhall Library copy has contemporary newspaper cuttings pasted in.

Cleland, James, *A Monument of Mortalitie . . .* (1624), containing "Pompous Funerals of the gracious Prince Lodovick".

Clifford, *The Diary of the Lady Anne Clifford*, ed. V. Sackville-West, 1923.

Coke, *Letters and Journals of Lady Mary Coke* (1756–99, ed. the Hon. J. A. Home), 1889–96.

Coleman, D. C., *Courtaulds: An Economic and Social History*, Oxford, 1969, Vol. 1.

Costume Society, *High Victorian: Costume 1860–1890*, V & A Museum, 1969.

Cote, W. N., *The Archaeology of Baptism*, 1876.

Courtaulds, see Coleman.

Cox, J. Charles, *The Parish Registers of England*, 1910.

Creston, Dormer, *The Youthful Queen Victoria*, 1952.

Crossley, Frederick, *English Church Monuments 1150–1550*, 1921.

Culpeper, Nicholas, *A Directory for Midwives* (1651), "corrected edn", 1693.

Cunnington, C. W. and P. Five *Handbooks of English Costume* in historical series, pubd. Faber. Edns 1969–71.

Davey, Richard, *A History of Mourning*, 1889.

Davies, Henry, *Young Wife's Guide during Pregnancy and Childbirth*, 2nd Edn, 1854.

Dearmer, Rev. Percy, *The Story of the Prayer Book*, 1940.

Delany, *Autobiography and Correspondence of Mary Grenville, Mrs. Delany*, ed. Lady Llanover, 1st Series (3 vols), 1861; 2nd Series (3 vols), 1862.

Deloney, Thomas, *Pleasant History of* . . . *"Jack of Newbury"*, 1597.
The Gentle Craft (1597–1600).

Dewees, Dr William P., *A Treatise on the Physical and Medical Treatment of Children*, 1826.

Diaries of XVI, XVII and XVIII centuries, see Aitken.

Dickens, Charles, *Sketches by Boz*, 1836; and novels of.

Dillon, see Warwick.

Doran, John, *A Lady of the Last Century* (*Mrs. Elizabeth Montagu*) *illustrated in her unpublished letters, with a biographical sketch* . . ., 1873.

Elwin, Malcolm, see Noels.

Encyclopaedia of Superstition, see Radford.

Encyclopedia of Religion and Ethics, see Hastings.

England, *A Complete History of England* . . ., Vols. I and II ed. J. Hughes, Vol. III ed. W. Kennet, 1706.

Evans, Joan, *English Art 1307–1461*, Oxford, 1949.

Evelyn, John, *The Diary of* . . . ed. Wm. Bray, Edn 1907.

Fanshawe, *The Memoirs of Ann Lady Fanshawe* [b. 1625, d. 1680], 1907.

Ferrier, Susan E., *The Inheritance*, a novel (1824), edn 1894.

Fiennes, *The Journeys of Celia Fiennes*, ed. C. Morris, edn 1949.

Florio, John, *A Worlde of Wordes* (Italian English Dictionary), 1598.

Fuller, Thomas, *The Church History of Britain from the birth of Jesus Christ until 1648* (1655), ed. James Nichols, edn, 1868.

Gay, John, *Trivia or The Art of Walking the Streets of London* [1716], ed. W. H. Williams, 1922.

Godfrey, Elizabeth, *Home Life under the Stuarts 1603–1649*, 1903.

Goldsmith, Oliver, *The Citizen of the World* (1762), edn 1799.
The Good-natured Man (1768), ed. A. S. Collins, 1936.

[Gough, Richard], *Sepulchral Monuments in Great Britain* . . ., 1786.

Graham, see Oliphant.

Gray, Mrs Edwin, *Papers and Diaries of a York Family, 1764–1839*, 1927.

Greene, Robert, *The Honourable Historie of Friar Bacon and Friar Bungay* (1594), ed. G. B. Harrison, 1927.

Greig, see Northumberland.

Grose, Francis (ed.), *Antiquarian Repertory*, edn 1807–9 (4 vols).

Haines, Herbert, *A Manual of Monumental Brasses . . . British Isles*, 1861, Vol. I.

Hall[e], Edward, *Chronicle: containing the History of England . . .* (1548–50), edn 1809.

  Henry VIII, ed. Charles Whibley, 1904; a re-issue of the chapter on Henry VIII's reign in the *Chronicle*.

Halliwell, James, *A Dictionary of Archaic and Provincial Words*, edn 1904.

Ham, Elizabeth, *Elizabeth Ham, by Herself. 1783–1820*, ed. Eric Gillett, 1945.

Hanbury, Mrs, *The Good Nurse . . .*, 2nd Edn, 1828.

Hargreaves-Mawdsley, W. N., *A History of Academical Dress in Europe until the end of the Eighteenth Century*, Oxford, 1963.

  Legal Dress in Europe until the end of the Eighteenth Century, Oxford, 1963.

Harrison, Molly, and Royston, O., *How They Lived II, 1485–1700*, 1962.

Hartford, Countess of, *Correspondence between Frances Countess of Hartford (afterwards Duchess of Somerset) and Henrietta Louisa Countess of Pomfret between the years 1738 and 1741*, ed. W. Bingley, 1806.

Hastings, James (ed.), *Encyclopaedia of Religion and Ethics*, Edinburgh, 1911.

Heanley, R. M., "The Vikings: Traces of their Folk-Lore in Marshland" in *Saga Book of the Viking Club*, 1902.

Heath, James, *Chronicle of the Late Intestine War . . .*, 2nd Edn, 1676.

Heber, Mary, *Dear Miss Heber . . .* [Letters to Mary Heber 1765–1806], ed. Francis Bamford, 1936.

Herbert, Sidney C., Baron, *Henry, Elizabeth and George, 1734–80* (Pembroke Papers . . .), ed. Lord Herbert, 1950.

Herrick, Robert, "Hesperides" in *Poetical Works of Robert Herrick*, ed. G. Saintsbury, 1893.

Hertz, Robert, *Death and the Right Hand*, trans. by R. and C. Needham, Aberdeen, 1960.

Hewer, Mrs Langton, *Our Baby: for Mothers and Nurses*, 1897.

Hind, Arthur *et al.*, *Engraving in England in the 16th & 17th Centuries*, Cambridge, 1952–7. Part I, *The Tudor Period*, 1952. Part II, *The Reign of James I*, 1955. Part III, *The Reign of Charles I*, comp. from notes of A. Hind by Margery Corbett and M. Norton, 1964.

Hoby, *The Diary of Lady Margaret Hoby 1599–1605*, 1930.

Hole, Christina, *English Folklore*, 2nd Edn, 1945.

  English Home Life 1500–1800, 1947.

Houblon, Lady Alice Frances Archer, *The Houblon Family . . .*, 1907.

Howard, Lord William [of Naworth Castle], *The Household Books of* . . . [seventeenth century], Surtees Society, 1877.

Hunter, Joseph, *Hallamshire—The History & Topography of Sheffield*, ed. A. Gatty, Sheffield, 1869.

Hutchinson, *Memoirs of the Life of Colonel Hutchinson* by his widow Lucy (1806), edn 1880.

Hutton, *The Life of William Hutton* . . . written by himself, ed. C. Hutton (1816), edn 1841.

James VI, *Letters to King James VI (with Appendix): Extracts from the Accounts of the Lords High Treasurers of Scotland* (Maitland Club), Edinburgh, 1885.

Jeaffreson, John C., *Brides and Bridals*, 1872.

Jerningham, *The Jerningham Letters 1780–1843*, ed. Egerton Castle, 1896.

Jones, William, *Finger-Ring Lore: Historical, Legendary, Anecdotal*, 1877.

Kellaway, William, "Burial in Woollen" in *Trans. of the London & Middlesex Archaeol. Soc.*, Vol. 18.

Kennet, see England.

Kilvert's Diary, 1870–1879, ed. William Plomer, 1944.

Leland, John, *J. Lelandi . . . Collectanea* [ed. T. Hearne], edn 1770, 6 vols.

Loggan, David, *Cantabrigia Illustrata . . .*, Cambridge, 1690.
   Oxonia Illustrata, Oxford, 1675.

Lyly, John, *Euphues* (1579), ed. Morris Croll and Harry Clemons, 1916.

Lyme Letters 1660–1760, by Lady Newton, 1925.

Lyttelton, Lady, *The Correspondence of Sarah Spencer 1787–1870*, ed. The Hon. Mrs Hugh Wyndham, 1912.

Machyn, *The Diary of Henry Machyn, Citizen and Merchant Taylor of London from A.D. 1550–A.D. 1563*, ed. John G. Nichols (Camden Soc.), 1848.

Marlborough, Sarah Duchess of, *Letters of a Grandmother (1732–1735)*, ed. Gladys Scott Thomson, 1943.

May, Arthur, *Marriage à la Mode. A Surrogate's Tales of Strange Wedding Dramas*, 1925.

Milbanke, see Noel.

Misson, *M. Misson's Memoirs and Observations in his Travels over England* . . . (1698), trans. John Ozell, 1719.

Monro, I. S., and Cook, D. E., *Costume Index: a subject index*, New York, 1937; supplement 1957.

Montagu, *Elizabeth Montagu, the Queen of the Blue-Stockings: her correspondence from 1720–1761*, ed. Emily Climenson, 1906.
   The Letters of Mrs. E. Montagu, with some of the letters of her correspondents, 4 vols, 1809–13. See also Doran.

Morse, H. K., *Elizabethan Pageantry*, 1934.

Moryson, *An Itinerary by Fynes Moryson Gent.* (1617), complete edn, 4 vols, Glasgow, 1907–8.

Newbury, Jack, see Deloney, Thomas.

Newton, Lady, see Lyme.

Nichols, John (ed.), *Illustrations of the Manners & Expences of Antient Times in the 15th, 16th and 17th centuries*, 1797.

   The Progresses and Public Processions of Queen Elizabeth . . ., edn 1823.

Nichols, John G. (ed.), *A Selection from the Wills of Eminent Persons proved in the Prerogative Court of Canterbury, 1495–1695* (Camden Soc.), 1863.

Nicolas, Sir Nicholas, *Testamenta Vetusta: Wills from the reign of Henry II to the Accension of Q. Elizabeth*, 1826.

Noble Collection of press cuttings and MSS. referring to Old London. (Box C.22 ·8 and ·9 on funerals, etc.), Guildhall Library.

Noel, *Some Letters and Records of the Noel Family*, comp. Emilia F. Noel, 1910.

Noels, *The Noels and the Milbankes, their Letters 1767–1792*, presented as a narrative by Malcolm Elwin, 1967.

Nollekens, see Smith.

Northumberland, Duchess of, *The Diaries of a Duchess* . . . [Elizabeth Percy] . . . *the first duchess of Northumberland, 1716–1776*, ed. James Greig, 1926.

Oliphant, Margaret E. Blair, *The Beautiful Mrs. Graham* . . . *and the Cathcart Circle*, 1927.

Oman, Carola, *Elizabeth of Bohemia*, edn 1964.

Osborn, Emily (ed.), *Political and Social Letters of a Lady of the Eighteenth Century (the Hon Mrs. McDonnel) 1721–1771* [1890].

Oxinden, *The Oxinden and Peyton Letters 1642–1670*, ed. Dorothy Gardiner, 1937.

Palsgrave, Jean, *L'Eclaircissement de la Langue Française* (1530), edn 1835.

Papendiek, Charlotte Louisa H., *Court and Private Life in the Time of Queen Charlotte* . . ., ed. Mrs V. D. Broughton, 1887.

Paston Letters (1422–1509), ed. James Gairdner, 1904 (6 vols).

Peck, Francis (ed.), *Desiderata Curiosa*, 2 vols, folio, 1732–5.

Pennant, Thomas, *Account of London*, 1790.

Pepys, Samuel, *The Diary of Samuel Pepys 1659–1669*, ed. Henry B. Wheatley, 8 vols, edn 1926.

Picart, Bernard (ed.), *Cerémonies et Coutumes religieuses* . . . [Figures by Picart et al. Text by the Abbés Banier and Mascrier], ed. Jean Bernard *et. al.*, 1st ed. (8 vols) Amsterdam, 1723–43, edn Paris 1741–1747, trans. by John Ozell as *Ceremonies and Religious Customs* . . . (7 vols), 1733–9.

Plumpton, *The Plumpton Correspondence* . . ., ed. Thomas Stapleton (Camden Soc.), 1839.

Porter, see Townshend.

Powys, *Passages from the Diary of Mrs. Philip Lybbe Powys of Hardwick House, Oxon. A.D. 1756–1808*, ed. Emily J. Climenson, 1899.

Puckle, Bertram S., *Funeral Customs*, 1926.

Pugin, A. Welby, *Glossary of Ecclesiastical Ornament and Costume*, 3rd Edn, 1868.

Radford, E. & M.A. *Encyclopaedia of Superstitions*, ed. and revised Christina Hole, 1961.

Richardson, Samuel, *Pamela*, 1740.

Robinson, Robert, *The History of Baptism*, 1790.

Rochefoucauld, François de La, *A Frenchman in England, Being the Mélanges sur L'Angleterre* [1784], trans. S. C. Roberts, Cambridge, 1933.

Rothstein, Natalie K. A., *The Silk Industry in London, 1702–66*, unpub. London Univ. Thesis (History M.A.), 1961.

Routh, C. R. N., *They Saw it Happen: an Anthology of Eye-Witnesses' Accounts of Events in British History . . . 1485–1688*, Oxford, 1956.

Rowsell, Mary C., *The Life-Story of Charlotte de la Trémoille Countess of Derby*, 1905.

Roxburghe Ballads, The, ed. Charles Hindley, 1873.

Russell, W. H., *The Wedding at Windsor: a memorial of the Marriage of H.R.H. Albert Edward Prince of Wales . . .* [in 1863], 1863.

Rutland, *MSS. of the Duke of Rutland, K.G.* (Roy. Hist. MSS. Commission), 1905.

Ryder, Dudley, *The Diary of, 1715–1716*, ed. William Matthews, 1939.

Sandford, Francis, *Genealogical History of the Kings of England . . . 1066 to the year 1677*, 1677.

 A History of the Coronation of . . . James II . . ., 1687.

 The Order of Ceremonies Used for and at the Solemn Interment of George Duke of Albemarle 1670, collected by F. Sandford [*c*. 1670], engravings after Francis Barlow *et. al.*

Sewell, Rev. W. H., *Practical Papers on Funeral Reform, Mourning Dress and Obituary Memorials*, reprinted from the *Literary Churchman*, 1883.

Shakespeare's England, various authors, Oxford, edn 1950.

Sharp, Jane, *The Midwives' Book*, 1671.

Sherwood, Mrs John, *Manners and Social Usages*, New York, 1884.

Sherwood, Mrs John (*née* M. M. Butt), *The Life of Mrs. Sherwood, Chiefly autobiographical*, ed. Sophia Kelly, 1854.

 A History of the Fairchild Family, 1818.

Sibbald, *The Memoirs of Susan Sibbald (1783–1812)*, ed. Francis P. Hett, 1926.

Sidney, *Funeral Procession of Sir Phillip Sidney*, engravings by Theodor de Bry after T. Lant, 1588.

Sim[e]on, *Historical Works of Simeon of Durham*, trans. and ed. Rev. J. Stevenson, 1855.

Skelton, John, "Elynour Rummyng" (*c.* 1490–1500) in *Poetical Works of John Skelton*, edn Boston 1856.

Smellie, Dr William, *Smellie's Treatise on the Theory and Practice of Midwifery* Edn (3 vols) 1876–8.

Smith, John Thomas, *Nollekens and his Times*, edn 1949.

Smollett, Tobias, *The Adventures of Sir Launcelot Greaves* (1762), edn 1895.
  The Adventures of Roderick Random (1748).
  Humphrey Clinker (1771).
  Peregrine Pickle (1751).

Spencer-Stanhope, Lady Elizabeth, *The Letter-Bag of Lady Elizabeth Spencer-Stanhope*, compiled from the Cannon Hall Papers (1806–73) by A. M. W. Stirling, 1913.

Stanley, *The Early Married Life of Maria Josepha Lady Stanley*, ed. Jane H. Adeane, 1899.

Steele, Sir Richard, *The Funeral, or Grief à la Mode* (Drury Lane, *c.* 1701), edn 1723.

Stevenson, Rev. Joseph (ed.), *The Church Historians of England*. Vol. I contains the *Historical Works of the Venerable Bede and the Historical Works of Simeon of Durham*, 1853.

Stone, Lawrence, *The Crisis of the Aristocracy 1558–1641*, Oxford, 1965.
  Sculpture in Britain in the Middle Ages, 1955.

Stothard, Charles A., *The Monumental Effigies of Great Britain*, edn 1876.

Stow, John, *Annales or A Generall Chronicle of England . . . augmented . . . unto the end of . . . 1631, by Edmund Howes*, 1631.

Strong, Roy, *National Portrait Gallery Tudor & Jacobean Portraits*, 1969.

Strutt, Joseph, *. . . Dress and Habits of the People of England* (1796). Planché's 1842 edn reprinted 1970.

Strype, John, *Ecclesiastical Memorials . . .*, 1721.

Thiselton-Dyer, T. F., *Old English Social Life as told by the Parish Registers*, 1898.

Thompson, C. J. S., *Love, Marriage and Romance in Old London*, 1936.

Thoresby, Ralph, *The Diary of Ralph Thoresby, F.R.S. author of the topography of Leeds (1677–1724)*, ed. Joseph Hunter, 1830.

Titman, George (ed.), *Dress and Insignia worn at Court*, 1937.

Townshend, Dorothea, *The Life & Letters of Mr. Endymion Porter sometime Gentleman of the Bedchamber to King Charles I*, 1897.

Tricks of the Town, being reprints of three 18th century Tracts, ed. Ralph Straus, 1927 (includes Trip through the Town, 1735).

Trip through the Town, see *Tricks*.

Troubridge, Jacqueline Hope-Nicholson, *Life Amongst the Troubridges* (*Journal of Laura T.*), 1966.

Turner, J., *Burial Fees . . . and all necessary information for Undertakers* [1838].

Tyack, George, *Historic Dress of the Clergy* [c. 1898].

Vaux, J. E., *Church Folklore, a record of some post Reformation Usages*, 1894.

Verney, *Memoirs of the Verney Family 1642–96* ed. Lady F. P. & Lady M. M. Verney (4 vols), 1892–99; 2 vols, 1904 (rev. & abridged).

Victoria, Queen, *Dearest Mama. Letters between Queen Victoria and the Crown Princess of Prussia 1861–1864*, ed. Roger Fulford, 1968.

de Vries, Leonard, *Victorian Advertisements*, text by James Laver, 1968.

Wagner, Sir Anthony, *Heralds of England*, 1967.

Walpole, Horace, *Horace Walpole and his World*, ed. L. B. Seeley. *Selected Letters of*, edn. 1926.

Ward, Ned, *The London Spy* (1709), ed. Arthur Hayward, 1927.

Warwick, *Pageant . . . of Richard Beauchamp Earl of Warwick* (facsimile), ed. Viscount Dillon and Sir W. St J. Hope, 1914.

Weever, John, *Antient Funeral Monuments* "with brief notes extracted out of . . . old MSS" (1631), edn 1767.

Wharncliffe, *The First Lady Wharncliffe and her Family (1779–1856)*, by Caroline Grosvenor and Charles Beilby, 1927.

Whitaker, T. D., *History and Antiquities of the Deanery of Craven*, 3rd Edn, ed. A. Morant, 1878.

Williamson Letters 1748–1765, ed. F. J. Manning, Streatley near Luton, 1954 (Beds. Historical Record Soc.).

Willoughby, Accounts in *Report on the MSS. of Lord Middleton preserved at Wollaton Hall, Notts.*, by W. H. Stevenson (R.H.M.C.), 1911.

Woodforde, *The Diary of a Country Parson, the Rev. James Woodforde* [1758–1781], ed. John Beresford (5 vols), 1924–31.

Wynne Diaries, The, 1789–1820, ed. Anne Freemantle (3 vols), 1935–40.

York Family, see Gray.

Yorkshire Diaries and Autobiographies of the 17th and 18th Centuries. Vol. 2, contains *Memorandum of Sir Walter Calverley*, ed. S. Margerison, Surtees Soc. pubs. 75 & 77, Durham, 1886.

(Where only occasional issues are relevant the dates of these are in brackets)

Archaeologia (Society of Antiquaries of London), 1777–.
Baby: the Mother's Magazine (1887–91).
Babyhood, a Magazine for Mothers (1891).
Belle Assemblée, see *Maids Wives, etc.*
British Apollo 1708–11; 3rd edn 1726.
Cassell's Family Magazine (1879).
The Daily Graphic, 1890–.
The Englishwoman's Domestic Magazine, 1852–77.
The Gentleman's Magazine, 1731, etc.
The Gentleman's Magazine of Fashion, 1829, etc.
The Graphic, 1869–.
The Guardian, (1713); 5th Edn 1729.
The Illustrated London News, 1843–.
The Ipswich Journal.
The Ladies' Magazine, 1749–53.
The Ladies' Treasury, 1858–95.
The Lady's Magazine: or, entertaining companion for the fair sex, 1770–1832.
The Lady's Magazine and Museum of Belles Lettres, 1832–7.
The Lady's Magazine: or, polite Companion for the Fair Sex, 1859–63.
The Lady's Newspaper (1847–51).
Leisure Hour, a Family Journal . . ., 1852, etc.
The London Gazette, 1665–.
The London Magazine: or, Gentleman's Monthly Intelligencer, 1732–85.
The London Saturday Journal, 1839–42.
Maids Wives and Widows Magazine, 1832, 1833; continued as
    The Weekly Belle Assemblée, 1833, 1834; and as
    The New Monthly Belle Assemblée, 1835–70.
The Monthly Record of Births, Deaths and Marriages, 1861.
The Morning Herald (1780, etc.).
The Morning Post, 1772–.
Notes and Queries, 1849–.
Nursing Notes (1893).
The Old Whig, 1735–8.
The Oracle. Monthly Journal of . . . Philosophy etc., 1861.
The People's Magazine (1868).

The Queen, 1861–.
Read's Weekly Journal (1736).
The Sunday at Home, 1854–.
Sylvia's Home Journal etc., 1878–91.
The Tailor and Cutter, 1868–.
The Times, 1788–.
Vetusta Monumenta (Soc. of Antiquaries of London), Vols. 1–7, 1747–1893.
Woman's World (new series), 1868, etc.
The Woman's World (formerly *The Lady's World*) (1889).
The Young Englishwoman etc., 1878–91 (continued as *Sylvia's Home Journal*).

The Plates

1. Virgin nursing Child. Nursing dress of *c.* 1250. The Child is
suckled through a slit in the bodice portion of her surcoat and of
the underlying kirtle. Kneeling at their feet is a nun in the blue
and green habit of the "Order of Fontevrault". Note her wimple.

Amesbury Psalter f. 4. *Oxford, All Souls College MS. 6. Reproduced
by kind permission of the Warden and Fellows.*

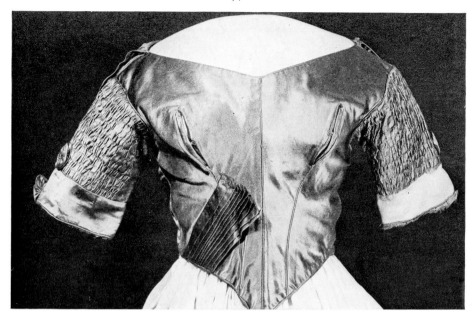

2. (*a*) Nursing dress of 1840–43. Second bodice to one skirt. It has a small opening at top of each front dart, closed by hook and eye.

(*b*) and (*c*) Layette pincushions. (*b*) dated, on back, 1798. Mottoes pricked out in pins.

Original specimens, Gallery of English Costume, Manchester.

(b)   (c)

3 (*a*) Birth of Samuel. The midwife with towel and basin wears a
loose mantle over her kirtle and the barbette and fillet head-
dress. The nurse known as the "rocker" is in a kirtle only
and bare-headed being a young girl. *c.* 1320.

Queen Mary's Psalter *B.M. MS. Roy. 2 B VII f. 48.*

(*b*) Baby wearing two biggins. 1665.

Effigy, St Giles Church, Ickenham, Middx.

4. Baby with arms free but robe fitting tightly round the body. (See p. 31). 1631.

The Savage tomb, St. Mary's Church, Elmley Castle, Worcs.

5. Mother and baby *c.* 1597. Baby's mantle crimson, lined and edged with white; he wears two biggins on his head.

Detail from the scenes in the life of Sir Henry Unton, surrounding his portrait in the National Portrait Gallery. Artist unknown.

6. Mother and baby 1600–1610. Baby's mantle is red, edged with gold embroidery. It is carried right over the head. The robe beneath matches the embroidery on the mother's stomacher.

"The Cholmondeley sisters" (detail) British School *17th century. T. 69 Tate Gallery.*

7. Mother in bed wearing a lace-trimmed coif. The lady friend
(? gossip) holds the baby wearing an embroidered mantle. Note
wedding ring on her thumb. 1635–40.

*Detail from the Saltonstall family portrait "The Visit to the Bedside" by
David des Granges. By courtesy of Sir Kenneth Clark.*

8. Mother and baby in "The Last New Fashion" indulging in the "display of finery". (See p. 37). Baby in heavily laced cap and a robe in style conventional for babies, having V-shaped yoke and panel. 1842.

Lithograph by W. Clark after painting by J. C. Wilson.

9. Priests, wearing albs, baptize naked
   infants. Godparents wear the ordinary
   costume of their day, c. 1330.
   (a) Priest about to immerse the child.

(b) In the traditional manner, both godfather and godmother hold the child.

B.M. MS. Roy. E VI ff. 171 and 317v.

10. Early 16th century carvings on a font. (*a*) Confirmation of infants (following baptism). Infants in long robes, each carried by godfather or godmother. The figure on extreme left is a man in a short gown. The bishop's mitre has been destroyed. For other costumes see (*b*).

(*b*) Marriage. Importance of the occasion suggested by the trains of the bride and (?) her mother. Otherwise ordinary costumes. Men in gowns with hanging sleeves, women with "English-hood" headdresses. Priest in cope.

All Saints Church, Gresham, Norfolk.

11. Christening in the home. Infant's white robe, gold-em-
broidered. One godmother (?) wearing the black hood then in
vogue and a pendant gold watch. The other has a white and
red dress and decorative apron. Parson in gown and professional type of wig. Mother languishing in negligée. Child
(upsetting water) in fashionable blue cap with streamers and
feathers. *c.* 1731.

Hogarth "The Christening" (detail). Private Collection.

12. (a) 18th century christening robe with characteristically shaped yoke; embroidery by French nuns; length 4 ft.

Property of Miss Cecile Hummel, to be seen at Castle Howard Costume Galleries. Photograph by Massers', Malton, Yorks.

(b) Detail of the same.

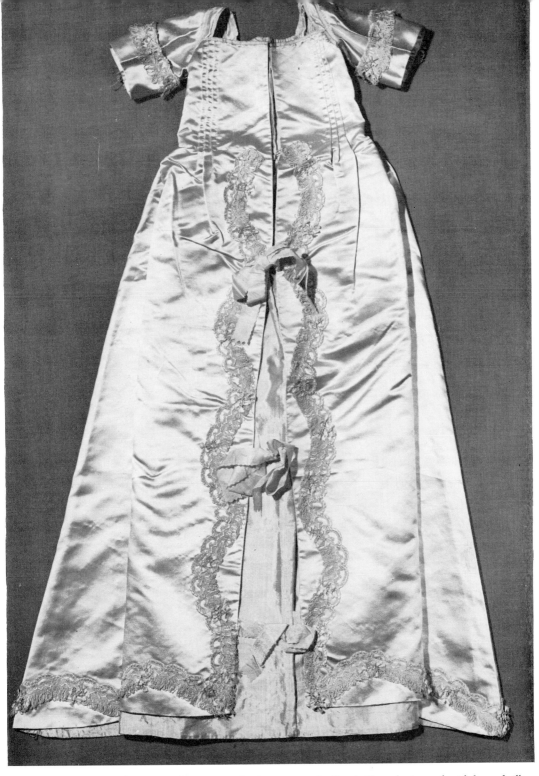

13. 18th century christening robe in cream satin, lined silk and trimmed with looped silk braid. Open at the top behind and tied at neck. Length 34 in.

Specimen, Gallery of English Costume, Manchester. Photograph by courtesy of City Art Gallery, Manchester.

14. (a) "Sack-back" wedding dress in blue and white figured silk, worn at the wedding of Ann Whittle of Hollingworth Hall, Mottram-in-Longdendale in 1766.

Gallery of English Costume, Manchester.

(b) Wedding dress, 1870; blue silk, trimmed with Torchon lace.

London Museum.

15. "Signing the Register", *c.* 1855. Bride and groom in evening dress style. Bride with long veil and roses on hair and bosom. Bridegroom in cut-away tailcoat and white waistcoat. See text pp. 62 and 110.

Hand coloured lithograph.

16. "Signing the Marriage Register", 1890. Bride with long veil over an orange blossom wreath. The sailor bridegroom, and the father in a smock, wear white button-hole rosettes. See text p. 70.

After a painting by James Charles.

17. "Taking the Benefit of the Act", *c.* 1829. See p. 76. Bride in low-necked evening dress; bridegroom in evening dress suit, black tailcoat, white trousers and waistcoat.

Contemporary lithograph.

18. (*a*) Parable of the wedding feast, depicted in the 12th century. Guests with and without wedding garments. See p. 77.

Bury St. Edmunds Gospels, Pembroke College, Cambridge, MS. 120 f. 2v (detail). Reproduced by kind permission of the Master and Fellows of the College.

(*b*) Marriage, depicted in the 13th century. See text pp. 77-8. The Archbishop wears Mass vestments "canonical" in the broad, not the restricted, sense; cf. pp.165-6.

Hereford Cathedral Library MS. O.7 VII. Photograph by courtesy of F. C. Morgan. Reproduced by kind permission of the Dean and Chapter.

19. "The Marriage", 1735. The bride's head-dress is a "pinner" with lappets hanging behind. The bridegroom wears a "campaign wig", a travelling wig. See text p. 82.

Engraving after painting by Hogarth (detail). Soane Museum.

20. "Pamela is married", 1740. See text p. 82. Priest in surplice assisted by a clerk in gown and bands.

Detail of illustration to Fielding's Pamela, *by J. Highmore, Tate Gallery.*

21. (*a*) "A Marriage Procession to Church", *c.* 1765. See text p. 85.

Engraving by J. Taylor.

(*b*) "The Wedding", 1832. Bride in white wears a large hat trimmed with feathers. Bridegroom in frock coat carries a top hat.

From a painting by Miss L. Sharpe in a tale by the Hon. Charles Phipps published in the Keepsake, 1832.

22. (*a*) Marriage of King of Portugal to Duke of Lancaster's daughter. See text p. 98.

B.M. MS. Roy. 14 E IV f. 284 (detail).

(*b*) Marriage of Edward II to Isabella, daughter of Philip IV of France. See text pp. 98–9.

B.M. MS. Roy. 15 E IV f. 295 (detail).
(*a*) & (*b*) Both MSS. illuminated in Flanders for Edward IV, c 1470–80.

Maried May A⁰ 1662

23. Marriage of Charles II to Catherine of Braganza. See text p. 99.

Engraving in James Heath A Chronicle of the late Intestine War *1676.*

24. Princess Charlotte's wedding dress, 1816. White silk net with silver embroidery and silver tissue; long train.

London Museum.

25. Queen Victoria's wedding, 1840. See text p. 103. Personalities L. to R:- bridesmaid holding up train, Prince Albert, Queen Victoria, Viscount Melbourne with sword, Duke of Sussex, Bishop, Duchess of Kent.

Engr. C. E. Wagstaff after painting by Sir George Hayter.

26. Marriage of Princess Royal ("Vicky") to Frederick, Crown Prince (later Emperor) of Germany, in 1858. With Queen Victoria are the Prince of Wales and his brothers in Highland dress; Bishop in rochet with exaggerated sleeves.

Reproduction of the painting by J. Phillips (Royal Collection) in The Graphic Vol. 37, p. 659.

27. Marriage of Princess Maud and Charles, Crown Prince of Denmark, later King Haakon of Norway. Note the bride's train. See text pp. 106-7.

Illustrated London News, *Vol. 99, pt. 2.*
Royal Wedding number, 25 July, 1896.

28. Wedding group outside Devizes Castle in 1867. (*Author's family portrait*). The bride is dressed in white silk with a veil of white tulle. "Her bridesmaids were eight of her sisters, all of whom were dressed in white muslin with either blue or pink trimming".

(*Report of a local newspaper.*)

29. Wedding procession, 1885. The bride's train is carried by pages wearing dark blue plush suits lined with gold satin. Bridesmaids, in white veiling, blue sashes, white collars and blue silk stockings, carry gilt baskets full of flowers.

Reproduced in Our Mothers *ed. Alan Bott, text by Irene Clephane 1932.*

30. (a) Martha Cranfield wearing wedding ring on her thumb, in the fashion of her day. 1620.

Painting by Mytens (detail). Knole, Kent.

(b) Henrietta Maria, wife of Charles I as widow in 1649–50. Note wedding ring on thumb. Whole attire in black and white except for one red bow. Neckwear and head-dress slightly old-fashioned. (cf. p. 264).

Artist unknown. Private Collection.

31. Funeral of a guardsman of dragoons, his boots and cuirass hanging from saddle of his riderless horse, his helmet on coffin. Pall-bearers in parade uniform; widow in black hood; little boy in cloak and top hat with weeper. *c.* 1840s.

Engr. J. H. Robinson after E. Corbould.

32. Gown of the Lord High Chancellor of Scotland borne at his funeral. 1681.

MS. Adv. 31.4.22 by courtesy of the Trustees of the National Library of Scotland.

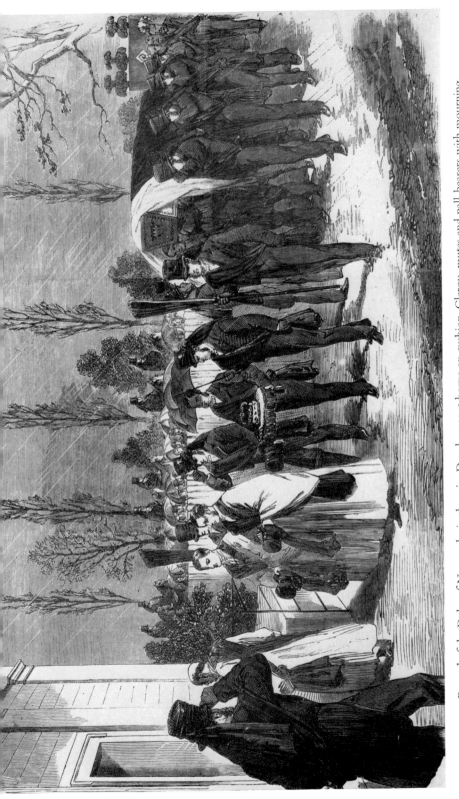

33. Funeral of the Duke of Newcastle, in the rain. Ducal coronet borne on cushion. Clergy, mutes and pall-bearers with mourning shoulder-scarves and weepers in their hats. 1864.

Illustrated London News (*1864*) *p. 469.*

34. Anglican funeral in 1736. Three pairs of pall-bearers holding pall by tassels. Two clergy in pudding-sleeved gowns; other men in coats and shoulder-scarves. All have weepers in hats. Mute with draped wand and lads with "branches".

Illustration by J. V. Scheley in B. Picart Histoire . . . des cérémonies . . . religeuses. *Vol. 4 (1736).*

35. Bishop at burial, wearing black cope, mitre and holding crook. Mourners with hoods covering their faces, *c.* 1440–50.

Bodleian Library MS. Add. A 185, a French Book of Hours, *f. 106v. (The Bodleian Library has published a 35mm. coloured film strip of this MS.)*

36. A piece of Courtauld's mourning crape made in the 1890s, showing the "figure", "crimp" and "spot" effects. See Appendix 9.

Photograph by courtesy of Courtaulds Ltd.

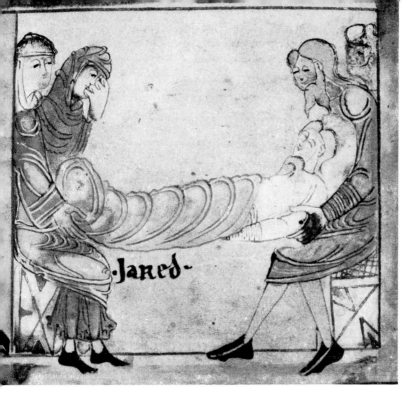

37. (a) Corpse with face exposed, pending burial. White tunic with red ornament at cuffs and waist, mauve winding sheet.

(b) Corpse ready for burial. Shroud (blue), folded rather than wound spirally. Both 11th century.

B.M. MS. Claudius B IV ff. 11v and 10v

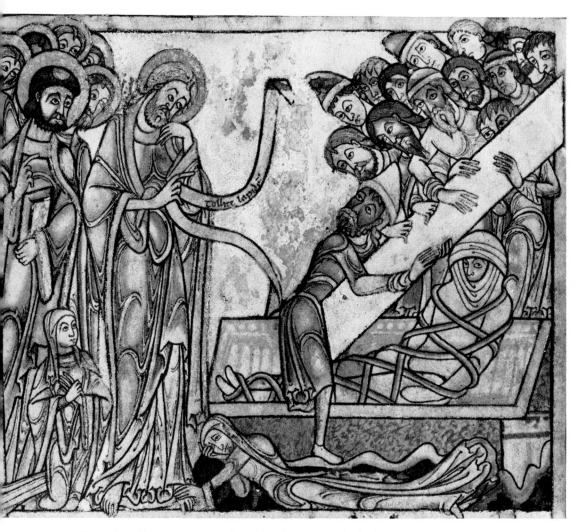

38. Corpse in a clinging investment (cerecloth ?) wrapping the limbs and head individually.
Swaddling bands.
(Raising of Lazarus, depicted in 1150–1160).

B.M. MS. Nero C. IV f. 19.

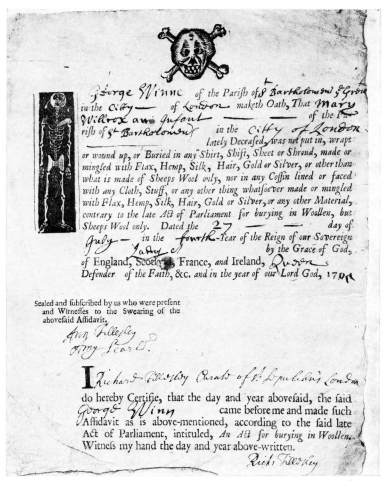

George Winne of the Parish of *St Bartholomew ye Great*
in the City — of *London* maketh Oath, That *Mary*
Willcox an Infant — of the Pa-
rish of *St Bartholomew* in the City of *London*
lately Deceased, was not put in, wrapt
or wound up, or Buried in any Shirt, Shift, Sheet or Shroud, made or
mingled with Flax, Hemp, Silk, Hair, Gold or Silver, or other than
what is made of Sheeps Wool only, nor in any Coffin lined or faced
with any Cloth, Stuff, or any other thing whatsoever made or mingled
with Flax, Hemp, Silk, Hair, Gold or Silver, or any other Material,
contrary to the late Act of Parliament for burying in Woollen, but
Sheeps Wool only. Dated the *27* — day of
July — in the *fourth* Year of the Reign of our Sovereign
Lady by the Grace of God,
of England, Scotland, France, and Ireland, *Queen*
Defender of the Faith, &c. and in the year of our Lord God, *1705*

Sealed and subscribed by us who were present
and Witnesses to the Swearing of the
abovesaid Affidavit.

Ann Tillesley
Amy Pearle

I *Richard Tillesley Curate of St Dunstans London*
do hereby Certifie, that the day and year abovesaid, the said
George Winn came before me and made such
Affidavit as is above-mentioned, according to the said late
Act of Parliament, intituled, *An Act for burying in Woollen.*
Witness my hand the day and year above-written.

Richᵈ Tillesley

39. (*a*) Certificate that one George Winne was "buried in wool" according to Act of Parliament. (See p. 159). 1705.

Guildhall Library, Noble Collection, C 22.83 T. 1705.

(*b*) Life size funeral effigy on the coffin of Anne of Denmark, queen to James I, in her
robes of estate: purplish-crimson, ermined mantle, red cap and stockings; yellow shoes
with blue roses; crown and sceptre; loose hair, as at coronation. Black pall with
embroidered escutcheons. 1618.

College of Arms MS. I 4 f. 5.

40. Funeral effigy of General Monk, Duke of Albemarle, on his coffin, wearing his own ducal robe and coronet, a complete suit of armour, the garter and collar of his Order and a periwig. Bearers of pall, canopy and banners wear the nearly extinct mourning gown and tippetted hood. Pall with escutcheons. 1670.

Engr. after Francis Barlow in Francis Sandford Order of the . . . Interment of George Duke of Albemarle . . . *1670.*

41. The Harlot's funeral. Ladies in black hoods try on gloves (white, as the deceased was a woman). Child in mourning cloak with weeper in hat; parson in gown holding hat with weeper. Rosemary. 1731.

Engr. G. King after Hogarth's Harlot's Progress Series.

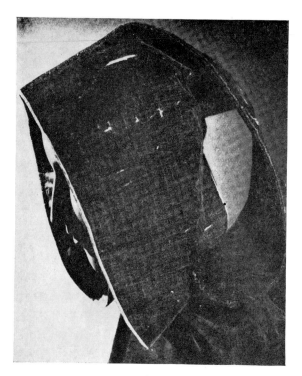

42. (a) 16th century black velvet mourning hood for funerals, its prolonged apex, the "tippet", hanging behind. Photo. of a surviving specimen.

Connoisseur Vol. 93 (1934).

(b) Mute with crape draperies of maximal size over hat, shoulder and wand; all white, for a child's or girl's funeral. Mid 19th century.

"A Funeral Bearer", Oil painting by Rev. Septimus Buss.

43. Almsfolk's funeral at Jesus Hospital, Rothwell, Northants. Poverty precludes mourning. 1888.

The Graphic, *Vol. 38, p.689*

44. Funeral of Anne of Cleves. Two mourners in the chariot with coffin, henchmen riding chariot-horses and herald banner-bearers, all have hoods on the head. Yeomen torch-bearers "in black coats". The queen's "fayre white palfrey with a syde saddle". *c.* 1557.

B.M. MS. Add. 35324 f. 8v (detail).

Children of the Chappell.

Gentlemen of the Chappell.

45. Choirboys and clergy of Queen Elizabeth's chapel at her funeral, wearing black cassocks and white surplices; the clergy in copes of different colours embroidered with gold, and black hats. *c.* 1603.

B.M. MS. Add. 35324 f. 31v (detail).

46. Chief mourner (at a knight's funeral) with characteristic long train to his gown; hood over the face. Train-bearer in more modest mourning—black cloak, bare head. *c.* 1580.

B.M. MS. 35324 f. 2v (detail).

47. At Queen Elizabeth's funeral:
(a) French ambassador with th[e]
ambassadorial long train to h[is]
black mantle. Train-bearer i[n]
typical mourning cloak. c. 160[3]

(b) Trumpeters in mourning cloaks. An officer-at-arms in black gown and hood; being a
pursuivant (junior to a herald) he wears his royal tabard sideways on, so that its short
"sleeves" are fore and aft.

Both from B.M. MS. Add. 35324 (ff. 36 and 27v, details).

foure Trumpetors

Phillip Hollande
Rose Pursuyuant
of Armes

48. Funeral of Princess Charlotte, 1817. Heralds with black scarves over tabards; old-fashioned bag-wigs for dignity.

Colour aquatint by Thos. Sutherland after R. B. Davis.

The Countesse of Surrey chiefe
Mourner.

n Schynoer Knight &c

stead of 2 Barons

Sr Thomas Browne Knight

Mrs Coote the Queenes
woman.

49. Chief mourner with two men escorts. She wears an open hood edged with white; mantle
with long train, surcoat with front train folded over girdle. Pleated bib-like garment
replaces barbe, on both women. Train-bearer in humble attire—Paris head-dress, no
mourning hood. 1578.

B.M. MS. Add. 35324 f. 21 (detail).

50. Yeoman "conductors" leading Lady Lumley's funeral, 1578. Black coats and black staves, fashionable cross-gartering. Almswomen in black gowns and wired out veils.

B.M. MS. Add. 35324 f. 19.

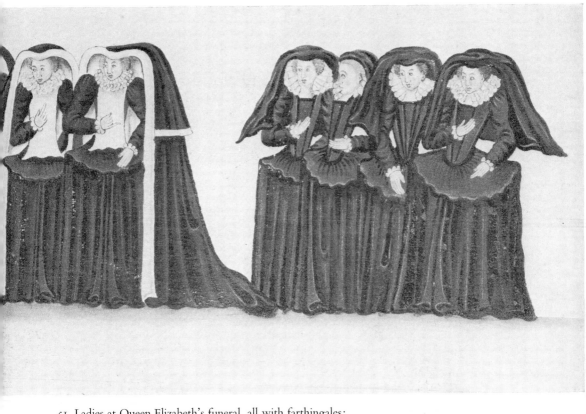

51. Ladies at Queen Elizabeth's funeral, all with farthingales;

(*a*) two of the 15 principal mourners; arched hoods combined with their mantles, and wired out perhaps to protect the ruffs. Barbes replaced by white fronts.

(*b*) Maids of honour, of less importance; they lack hoods and barbes but their veils are wired.

B.M. MS. Add. 35324 f. 38 (detail).

52. Funeral of Mr. Gladstone, 1898. Pall-bearers now without scarves and weepers. (Lord Rosebery behind the bearded Mr. Armistead). Duke of Norfolk with Earl Marshal's jewelled rod.

Illustrated London News *Vol. 113, p. 802/3 (detail).*

53. Gilded metal ("latten") weepers on tomb of Richard Beauchamp, Earl of Warwick, at Warwick, showing early style of mourning. 1453.

(*a*) Lord, in peer's robes with hood over the eyes.

(*b*) Lady with head-dress over the eyes, holding rosary.

C. A. Stothard Monumental Effigies . . . Great Britain, *Edn. 1876.*

54. Lady, who has died in childbed, mourned by her husband, Sir Thomas Aston, and their small son. Both entirely in black and white. Cradle draped in black. 1635. See text p. 243.

Painting by John Souch (detail). Manchester City Art Gallery.

55. Girls (? orphans) in deep mourning with arum lily, other white flowers and purple pansies.

After painting by Miss E. Osborn exhibited R.A., 1864. Reproduced in Illustrated London News
11 June, 1864.

56. Fashionable mourning, with accessories, 1888. Bustled dress heavily craped. Bonnet with crape trimming and veil. Parasol, gloves and handkerchief all in mourning.

Messrs. Jay's advert. (detail) in The Graphic, *Vol. 38, p. 99.*

57. Monumental effigies showing widows' head-dresses.

    (a) Pleated barbe and the cheeks covered; goffered coverchief over an inner pleated head-dress dipping in front like a bec.

    (b) Very finely pleated barbe just over the chin: the hair completely covered. Fashionable head-dress over all.

    (cf. wimple in Pl. 1)

(a) *Philippa Duchess of York (d. 1431) Westminster Abbey.*

(b) *Margaret Beaufort, Countess of Richmond and Derby. National Portrait Gallery, painter unknown. ? Based on a portrait made just after her death in 1509. (Other versions show the frill of the barbe in black.)*

58. Vigil for Anne of Brittany (twice queen of France) 1514. Lady mourners in black hoods with the point over the forehead. (See p. 262) Male mourners and heralds in typical mourning garb. Tabards and two escutcheons show arms of France and Brittany. The Queen's crown and two sceptres lie on the pall.

B.M. MS. Vesp. B III f. 17v.

59. (a) Widow in already old-fashioned
arched head-dress, the exaggerated dip in front is suggestive of
a "widow's peak". Typical ruff.
(Widows' barbes no longer worn
in any form). Dress, etc. black.

*Sculpture of Lady Roper (beside effigy of her
dead husband), erected between his death in
1622 and hers in 1625. Lynsted church, Kent.*

    (b) Lady Bagot, 3 years widowed.
Widow's peak worn under a
long black veil. Black dress with
the decolletage unfashionably
filled in (with white). Black
ribbon for tear-drop pearl pendant, 1676.

*Portrait of Lady Mary Bagot and grand-
child, by J. Michael Wright (detail).
Reproduced by kind permission of Mrs.
J. M. Wallace, Lochryan, Stranraer.*

60. Widow in deepest mourning: white indoor cap with long veil, and weeper cuffs, but dress in the latest fashion with "kick-up" sleeves. Little girl in white with black sash (not the full black of earlier Victorian days). 1890.

Messrs. Jay's advert. The Queen *Vol. 88 (2nd Aug. 1890).*

61. Political satire on repeal of Stamp Act, 1766. Funeral of an infant—therefore mourners' scarves are white. Chief mourner has weeper in his hat. Parson in gown with "pudding" sleeves. Bishops' rochets have the extreme form of "bishop" sleeves in vogue at the time. 1766.

Engr. B. Wilson. B.M. Print (1766).

62. Young woman and little girl in black "mourning dresses" of the latest fashion, i.e. with very high waists and low necks. The child has a white cap with black ribbon. 1809.

Ackermann's Repository of Arts, *Vol. 2.*

63. The widow and her grandchildren at Mr. Gladstone's graveside, Westminster Abbey, 1898. Boy in Eton suit. Small girl in black dress, hat, shoes and stockings. Mrs. Gladstone wears white weeper cuffs. All ladies wear black veils hanging from their bonnets.

Illustrated London News *Vol. 112, p. 799 (1898)*.

64. Little girls carrying a child's coffin by means of white bands; all wearing white dresses and caps with black ribbons. Ladies in black hoods (a late survival) *c.* 1846–1850.

Illustration to hymn "The Tolling Bell" published by S.P.C.K.

INDEX

Numerals in italics are *page* numbers showing where Figures occur; there may be text references on the same page.

A page number may denote more than one text reference.

Citing an illustration does not necessarily imply a reference in its caption.

Abbreviations:

n = footnote

passim = separate references on consecutive pages

Pl. = plate

q = indicates that the reference occurs in a quotation (in the smaller print).